MIMESIS
INTERNATIONAL

SOCIOLOGY
n. 15

FRANCESCO NICOLA MARIA PETRICONE

WOMAN TODAY

Comparative Sociological-Juridical Research on Gender Inequality

MIMESIS
INTERNATIONAL

© 2022 – Mimesis International
www.mimesisinternational.com
e-mail: info@mimesisinternational.com

Book series: *Sociology*, n. 15

Isbn: 9788869774058

© MIM Edizioni Srl
P.I. C.F. 0241937030

Image cover: Paola Casalino

TABLE OF CONTENTS

To the women of Ukraine,
To each and every one of them…

INTRODUCTION

1. Social and legal presuppositions of the research: premises

During 2021, between January and June, the qualitative sociological research "The Importance of being woman today (IWT)" was conducted to investigate the role and importance of women in contemporary society, in different social, political and economic contexts. 2021 was chosen because it marked the tenth anniversary of the Istanbul Convention with which the Council of Europe decided to implement an international legal instrument to combat violence against women, a violence that in that context was recognized and understood for the first time as a violation of human rights. The primary purpose of the Istanbul Convention is identified in the creation of a Europe free from violence against women, placing formal and substantial equality between men and women as a prerequisite for the realization of this goal.

We cannot ignore the fact that by the time this book goes to print, the Western world plunges into the abyss of Putin's attack on Ukraine. And once again, the weakest people, Ukrainian women and children, displaced by the millions from their land, are at the expense.

What do women have in common today then? The speed with which information moves online determines the possibility of comparing different situations and social contexts. This is what we have done with a group of scholars, academics and researchers from fourteen countries: Cuba, Haiti, India, Iraq, Iran, Italy, Ivory Coast, Mexico, Pakistan, Peru, Poland, Tunisia, United States and Venezuela to try to answer a question, basically: what is the importance of being a woman today? The analysis of the content, in a socio-political perspective, has been carried out in a hybrid way using both computer-based content analysis and, for the qualitatively more sophisticated areas of representation, entrusted directly to the evaluation, and to the interpretation of expert researchers (human content analysis). The multidisciplinary composition of the research group has guaranteed the coexistence of sociological, political, juridical and mass-media skills in the construction of the tools and categories of analysis of the results.

The social impact of the project has been achieved through the restitution and dissemination of the results to the social, institutional and professional subjects involved in the study. It aims to investigate the stereotypes and prejudices that permeate the narrative and social representation of gender inequality and to build innovative practices and methodologies for its contrast even among young and very young generations. We believe that this type of activity favours the dissemination of research results beyond and the restricted academic context and disciplinary scientific sector, prefiguring a strong social impact.

It has been investigated, on the one hand, the legal context, including international, and the legal measures of contrast. On the other hand, the cultural and symbolic aspects underlying gender inequality: starting from socialization to the unequal relationships between genders that represent the premise, to then continue with the analysis of the social representation of gender inequality in the social network and mass media, up to research on attempts at deconstruction. The general objective of the lines of research carried out by our reasechers has been to identify and describe the presence of bias in the public representation of gender inequality.

As a methodological approach, the research units of the project IWT, albeit in their own specificity, refer to the theoretical, cultural and legal framework of the Istanbul Convention and CEDAW (the Convention for the Elimination of All Forms of Discrimination Against Women) making their own both the definition of violence against women and the objectives, in particular as regards the identification, production and promotion of a culture that respects equality between men and women, to be conveyed and disseminated through training processes to young on the one hand and to legal and journalistic professionals on the other.

About 2500 people, men and women, aged 18 and over, belonging to all social groups were interviewed - in Italian, English, French, Spanish, Urdu, Polish, Persian, Arabic, Haitian Creole and Malayalam.

As a percentage, mainly women answered the questionnaire with an average of 78.2 percent.

Below are the response rates based on gender, for each of the countries considered:

Figure 1. Gender - Source: IWT Research

Cuba

Haiti

India

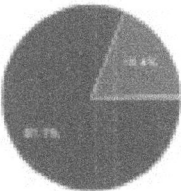

Iran

18) What is your gender

188 responses

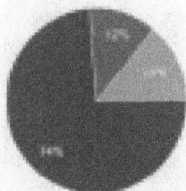

- Female
- Male
- Female

Iraq

18) What is your gender

158 responses

- Female
- Male
- Other
- Prefer not to answer
- Prefer not to answer
- Males

Italy

18) What is your gender

215 responses

- Female
- Male
- Other
- Prefer not to answer

Ivory Coast

18) Quel est votre sexe
141 réponses

- Femme
- Mâle
- Autre
- Préfère ne pas répondre

Mexico

18) Cuál es tu genero
288 respuestas

- Femenino
- Masculino
- Otro
- Prefiero no responder

Pakistan

18) What is your gender
198 respuestas

- Female
- Male
- Other
- Prefer not to answer

Peru

18) Cuál es tu genero
125 respuesta

- Femenino
- Masculino
- Otro
- Prefiero no responder

Poland

18) What is your gender
116 responses

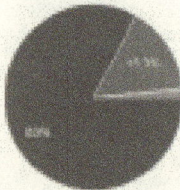

- Female
- Male
- Other
- Prefer not to answer

Tunisia

18) Quel est votre sexe? 18) الجنس
152 responses

- Femme انثى
- Male ذكر
- Autre غير ذلك
- Préfère ne pas répondre لا أرغب بالإجابة

United States

18) What is your gender
(69 responses)

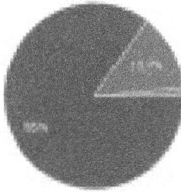

- Female
- Male
- Other
- Prefer not to answer

Venezuela

18) Cuál es tu genero
(10 responses)

- Femenino
- Masculino
- Otro
- Prefiero no responder

In all the countries considered, an average of almost one in two respondents - exactly 49.5 percent - say they are between 18 and 30 years of age; about 40 per cent (39.9) between 31 and 56 years old; the remaining 10 per cent of respondents (exactly 10.5 per cent) over 56 years old.

Below are the graphs of how the interviewees responded, for each of the fourteen countries, based on age:

Figure 2. Age - Source: IWT Research

Cuba

Haiti

India

3) Which is your age?
193 respondents

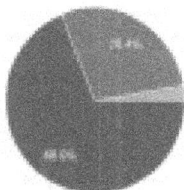

- 18-30
- 31-55
- Over 56

Iran

3) Which is your age? - من شما چقدر است؟
100 responses

- 18-30
- 31-55
- Over 56 سال

Iraq

3) Which is your age? - كم هو عمرك؟
193 respondents

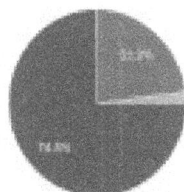

- 18-30
- 31-55
- Over 56 سنة

Italy

3) Which is your age?
214 responses

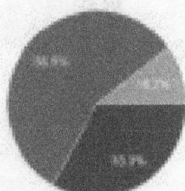

Ivory Coast

3) Quel est votre âge?
141 responses

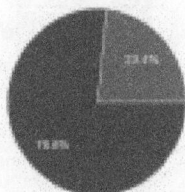

Mexico

3) Cuál es tu edad?
388 responses

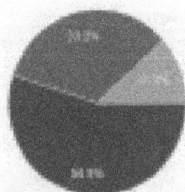

Pakistan

3) Which is your age?
194 responses

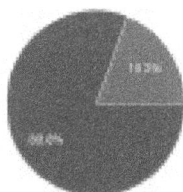

- 18-30
- 31-55
- Over 56

Peru

3) Cuál es tu edad?
229 responses

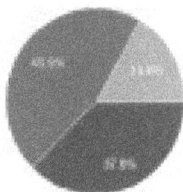

- 18-30
- 31-55
- Mas de 56

Poland

3) Which is your age?
178 responses

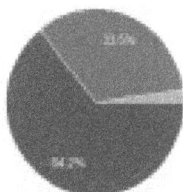

- 18-30
- 31-55
- Over 56

Tunisia

3) Quel est votre âge? ما هو عمرك؟
132 responses

- 16-30
- 31-56
- Plus de 56 من أكثر

United States

3) Which is your age?
165 responses

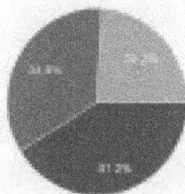

- 16-30
- 31-56
- Over 56

Venezuela

2) Cuál es tu edad?
152 responses

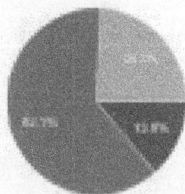

- 16-30
- 31-56
- Más de 56

These are people who, on the average of all the countries considered, declare that they work mainly: 54.3 per cent of the interviewees answer that they carry out a profession, while 43.7 per cent of them declare themselves students. More generally, 22.7 per cent of respondents claim that they carry out activities in the family, while 4.7 per cent say they are unemployed, on average in the fourteen countries. Finally, 4.3 per cent of respondents claim to be retired.

Below, country by country, the percentages relating to the activity declared by those who participated in the interviews.

Figure 3. Which is your main activity? - Source: IWT Research

Cuba

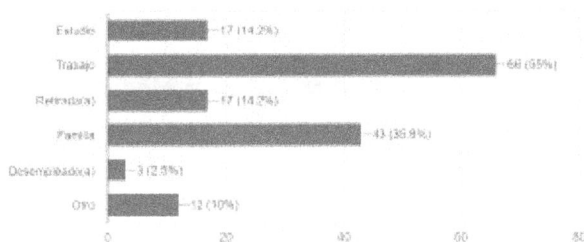

Haiti

India

4) Which is your main activity? You can answer one or more of the following options
190 responses

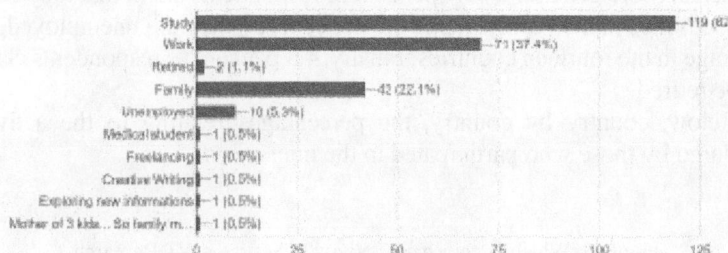

- Study — 119 (62%)
- Work — 71 (37.4%)
- Retired — 2 (1.1%)
- Family — 42 (22.1%)
- Unemployed — 10 (5.3%)
- Medical student — 1 (0.5%)
- Freelancing — 1 (0.5%)
- Creative Writing — 1 (0.5%)
- Exploring new informations — 1 (0.5%)
- Mother of 3 kids... So family m... — 1 (0.5%)

Iran

4) Which is your main activity? You can answer one or more of the following options - فعالیت اصلی شما
کدام است؟ می توانید به یک یا چند گزینه زیر پاسخ دهید
100 responses

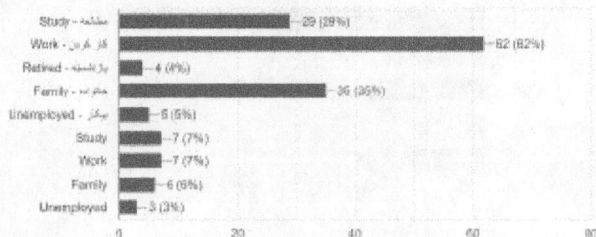

- Study - مطالعه — 29 (29%)
- Work - کار کردن — 82 (82%)
- Retired - بازنشسته — 4 (4%)
- Family - خانواده — 36 (36%)
- Unemployed - بیکار — 5 (5%)
- Study — 7 (7%)
- Work — 7 (7%)
- Family — 6 (6%)
- Unemployed — 3 (3%)

Iraq

4) Which is your main activity? You can answer one or more of the following options ما هو نشاطك
الرئيسي، يمكن ان تختار واحد او أكثر من النقاط الآتية
155 responses

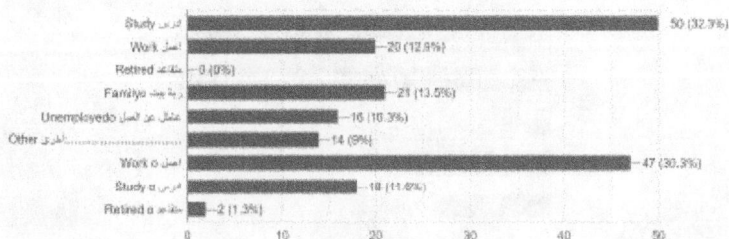

- Study درس — 50 (32.3%)
- Work اعمل — 20 (12.9%)
- Retired متقاعد — 0 (0%)
- Familya ربة بيت — 21 (13.5%)
- Unemployedo عاطل عن العمل — 16 (10.3%)
- Other اخرى — 14 (9%)
- Work o اعمل — 47 (30.3%)
- Study o درس — 18 (11.6%)
- Retired o متقاعد — 2 (1.3%)

Italy

4) Which is your main activity? You can answer one or more of the following options

216 responses

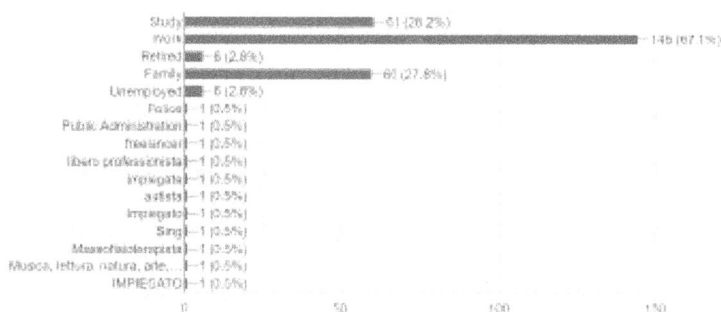

Activity	Value
Study	61 (28.2%)
Work	145 (67.1%)
Retired	6 (2.8%)
Family	60 (27.8%)
Unemployed	6 (2.8%)
Police	1 (0.5%)
Public Administration	1 (0.5%)
freelancer	1 (0.5%)
libero professionista	1 (0.5%)
impiegata	1 (0.5%)
artista	1 (0.5%)
impiegato	1 (0.5%)
Sing	1 (0.5%)
Massofisioterapista	1 (0.5%)
Musica, lettura, natura, arte,...	1 (0.5%)
IMPIEGATO	1 (0.5%)

Ivory Coast

4) Quelle est votre activité principale? Vous pouvez répondre à une ou plusieurs des options suivantes

141 responses

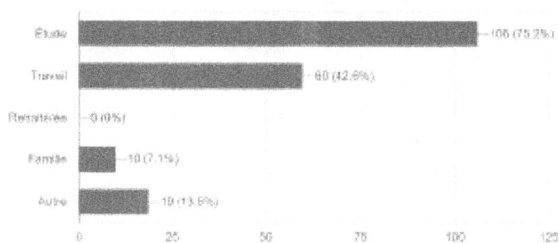

Activité	Value
Étude	106 (75.2%)
Travail	60 (42.6%)
Retraitée	0 (0%)
Famille	10 (7.1%)
Autre	19 (13.5%)

Mexico

4) ¿Cuál es tu actividad ? Puedes responder una o mas de las siguientes opciones

358 responses

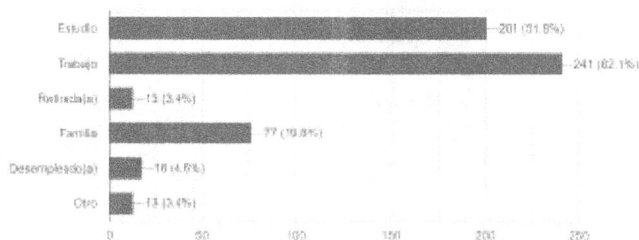

Actividad	Value
Estudio	201 (51.6%)
Trabajo	241 (62.1%)
Retirada(o)	13 (3.4%)
Familia	77 (19.8%)
Desempleado(a)	18 (4.6%)
Otro	13 (3.4%)

Pakistan

4) Which is your main activity? You can answer one or more of the following options
198 responses

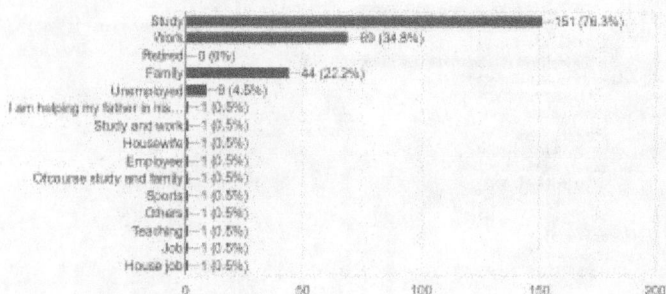

Study — 151 (76.3%)
Work — 69 (34.8%)
Retired — 0 (0%)
Family — 44 (22.2%)
Unemployed — 9 (4.5%)
I am helping my father in his... — 1 (0.5%)
Study and work — 1 (0.5%)
Housewife — 1 (0.5%)
Employee — 1 (0.5%)
Ofcourse study and family — 1 (0.5%)
Sports — 1 (0.5%)
Others — 1 (0.5%)
Teaching — 1 (0.5%)
Job — 1 (0.5%)
House job — 1 (0.5%)

Peru

4) ¿Cuál es tu actividad ? Puedes responder una o más de las siguientes opciones
229 responses

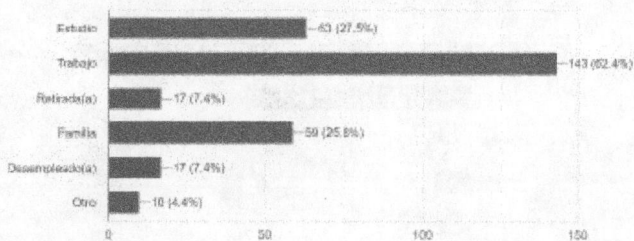

Estudio — 63 (27.5%)
Trabajo — 143 (62.4%)
Retirada(a) — 17 (7.4%)
Familia — 59 (25.8%)
Desempleado(a) — 17 (7.4%)
Otro — 10 (4.4%)

Poland

4) Which is your main activity? You can answer one or more of the following options
176 responses

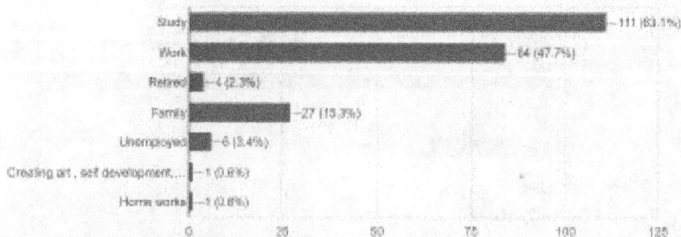

Study — 111 (63.1%)
Work — 84 (47.7%)
Retired — 4 (2.3%)
Family — 27 (15.3%)
Unemployed — 6 (3.4%)
Creating art, self development,... — 1 (0.6%)
Home works — 1 (0.6%)

Tunisia

4) Quelle est votre activité principale? Vous pouvez répondre à une ou plusieurs des options suivantes
ما هو نشاطك الرئيسي، يمكن ان تختار واحد او أكثر من الأنشطة الأتية
132 responses

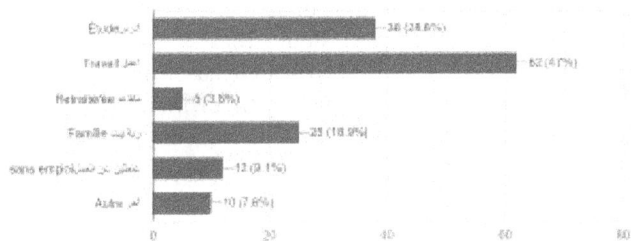

United States

4) Which is your main activity? You can answer one or more of the following options
153 responses

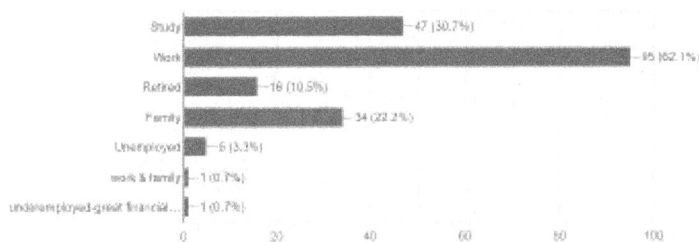

Venezuela

4) ¿Cuál es tu actividad? Puedes responder una o más de las siguientes opciones
132 responses

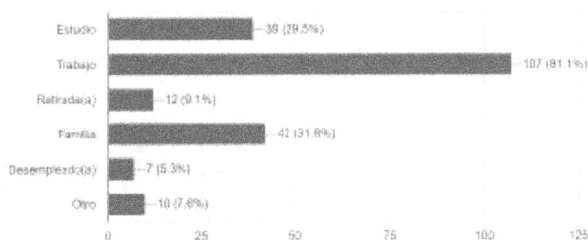

The survey sought to know how women are seen and see themselves in the society in which they live, comparing the historical and cultural situations of seven different continents from the West to the East of the world: North, Central and South America; Europe, Africa and Asia.

What is the woman missing and what are her expectations, aspirations, frustrations, sufferings, ambitions, both from a social, political and economic point of view? The IWT research has tried to answer these questions. Many profiles were examined starting with the perception of the *difficulty* of being a woman today in one's own society, as indicated in the following chapter.

CHAPTER I
STEREOTYPE AND PREJUDICE

1. Legal roots and social representations of gender discrimination

In the analysis of the phenomenon of gender inequality, the causes, its different social representations, stereotypes, prejudices and the ways in which it is reproduced, particular importance is assumed by the theory of the social control of sexuality, which underlines the role of the socio-economic context and socialization, through which individuals learn values and behavioural models related to gender (Saccà 2001, 2003, 2016, 2021). The studies conducted so far have the merit of bringing out how socialization translates into the reproduction of those stereotypes and prejudices in daily practices and in power relations between men and women making them appear as inevitable but which are, instead, subject to historical and cultural change (Davis 1983; Saccà 2003, 2016; Pitch 2002; Camino 2011; Meo 2012; Ercolani 2016). The Convention of Istanbul represents a very important instrument, both from a legal and a cultural point of view, because it attacks and reveals the key elements of the underlying substratum of discrimination, together with the structural ones that produce it. The Convention it defines mainly violence as "... a violation of human rights and a form of discrimination against women and shall mean all acts of gender-based violence that result in, or are likely to result in, physical, sexual, psychological or economic harm or suffering to women, including threats of such acts, coercion or arbitrary deprivation of liberty, whether occurring in public or in private life".

By framing violence against women as an instrument of power and control right from the preamble, it immediately clarifies how it is necessary to address the structural conditions of the relations between the sexes in order to achieve "1: .1 *de jure* and *de facto* gender equality" which it is "a key element in preventing violence against women". In fact, we must not forget that the path towards female emancipation which has led, among other things, to the conquest of seeing women recognized as "human", as bearers of rights as much as men, it was long, tortuous and certainly not without accidents. The difference, the crucial point of development today is that the awareness of this disparity, of these power relations, of this domination over women has been sanctioned, at an international juridical level.

As it emerges in the varied panorama of the countries considered in the investigation IWT, it's an awareness not isolated, not episodic and no longer and not only at the level of slogans, movements, posters, films and books, of a cultural avant-garde in short, which a breath of wind can sweep away. It permeates instead the consciences and awareness of most women in the world: from our research it emerges that on average more than one in two people - exactly 56.5 per cent - believe that, in general, it is still *difficult* to be a woman in own country today, with percentages ranging from minimum 31.2 per cent in Ivory Coast at the highest 80.4 per cent in Mexico.

More specifically, 76 percent of respondents in Iran, 74.2 percent in Haiti, 67.1 percent in Iraq, 66.5 percent in Poland and 62.1 percent in India are convinced of this. Similar percentages are recorded in the United States, Peru and Pakistan, where 58.8 percent, 57.2 and 54 percent respectively find it difficult to be a woman in their own country. Less than one in two respondents believe that it is difficult to be a woman in Italy (37.5 per cent), Cuba (39.2 per cent), Venezuela (42.4 per cent) and Tunisia (44.7 per cent).

Below in Figure 4, a comparison between all countries of the affirmative answers to the question: is it difficult to be a woman today in your country?

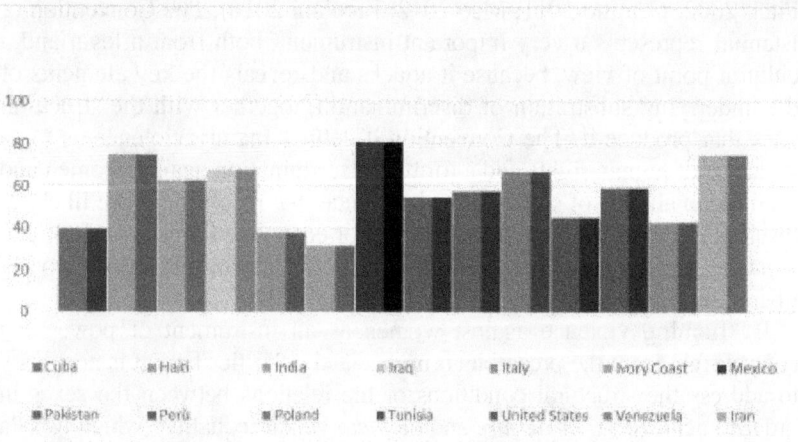

Figure 4. Affirmative answers to the question: is it difficult to be a a woman in your country, nowadays? Source: IWT Research

The complete diagrams, country by country, of those who answered affirmatively and negatively to the same question are shown below.

Figure 5. Is it difficult being woman in your country?Y/N - Source: IWT Research

Cuba

1) ¿Es dificil ser mujer hoy en tu país?
120 responses

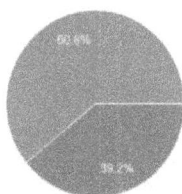

● Si
● No

Haiti

1) Est-ce difficile d'être une femme aujourd'hui dans votre pays?
120 responses

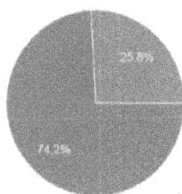

● Oui
● Non

India

1) Is it difficult being woman today in your country?
190 responses

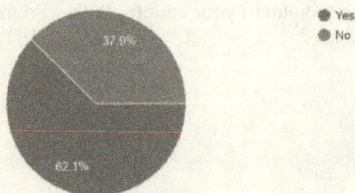

- Yes
- No

37.9%

62.1%

Iran

1) Is it difficult being woman today in your country? - آیا امروز زن بودن در کشور شما دشوار است؟
100 responses

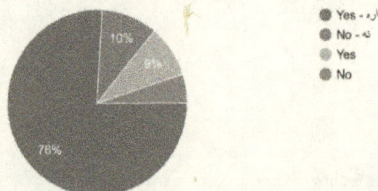

- اره - Yes
- نه - No
- Yes
- No

10%
9%
76%

Iraq

1) Is it difficult being woman today in your country? هل هناك صعوبة بان تكوني امرأة في بلدك اليوم؟
155 responses

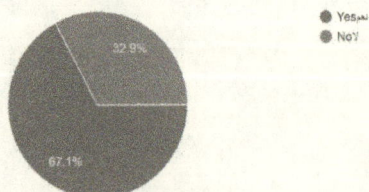

- نعم Yes
- لا No

32.9%

67.1%

Italy

1) Is it difficult being woman today in your country?
216 responses

- Yes
- No

82.5%

37.5%

Ivory Coast

1) Est-ce difficile d'être une femme aujourd'hui dans votre pays?
141 responses

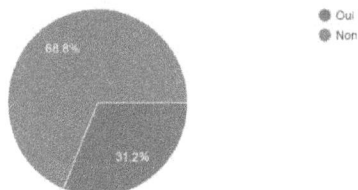

- Oui
- Non

68.8%

31.2%

Mexico

1) ¿Es difícil ser mujer hoy en tu país?
388 responses

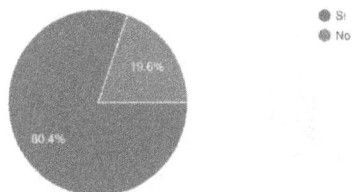

- Sí
- No

19.6%

80.4%

Pakistan

1) Is it difficult being woman today in your country?
198 responses

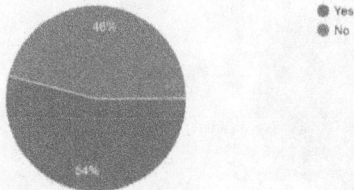

● Yes
● No

46%

54%

Peru

1) ¿Es difícil ser mujer hoy en tu país?
229 responses

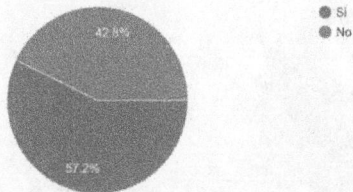

● Sí
● No

42.8%

57.2%

Poland

1) Is it difficult being woman today in your country?
176 responses

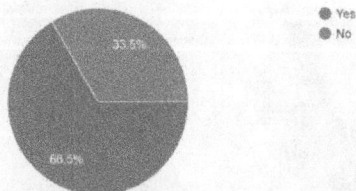

● Yes
● No

33.5%

66.5%

Tunisia

1) Est-ce difficile d'être une femme aujourd'hui dans votre pays? هل هناك صعوبة بأن تكوني امرأة في بلدك اليوم؟

132 responses

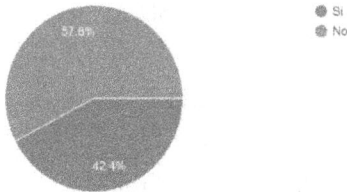

- Oui نعم
- Non لا

55.3%
44.7%

United States

1) Is it difficult being woman today in your country?

153 responses

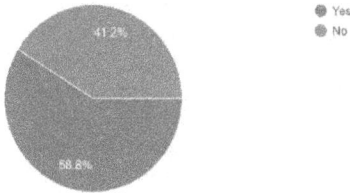

- Yes
- No

41.2%
58.8%

Venezuela

1) ¿Es difícil ser mujer hoy en tu país?

132 responses

- Si
- No

57.8%
42.4%

When asked to explain the reasons of the answer, the considerations are varied, reflecting the choices and percentages of each country. The arguments, sometimes very widespread, appear surely once again of extraordinary interest. Here are just some of these answers, country by country:

Can you explain the reasons of your answer?

CUBA: La dificultad que tenemos para todos los aspectos tanto laborales como sociales; Debido a la situación sociocultural y política; El comunismo; Por la situación social, política y económica; Considero que aunque no exista igualdad al 100/100 con el hombre, las mujeres tenemos nuestros derechos, entre ellos el acceso a la cultura que es la que hace libre al hombre y a la mujer; Vivir en un régimen comunista es complicado para todos, mujeres y hombres; No hay discriminación, y respetan todos los derechos de la mujer; Porqur hay MAS posibilidad de trabajo; No existe discriminación; No hay igualdad; tenemos los mismos derechos; Por la falta de Libertad y la imposición machista por eso que causa para música lista de contacto de vivir; Somos uguale a Los hombres en derecho; Tenemos iguales derechos constitucionales; Por el doble trabajo que por lo genetal hacemos; La sociedad cubana sigue siendo machista; Porque se tienen los mismos derechos civiles; Porque no contamos nada; No encontré ninguna dificultad cuando vivía ahí; Es un orgullo ser mujer en Cuba; Brecha salarial, opiniones vejatorias, violaciones con casi impunidad legal; Por qué las mujeres no tienen los mismos derechos; Porque somos luchadoras; Seguimos teniendo brecha laboral, mayor carga familiar, y menos oportunidades; Existe discriminación a pesar de las políticas del gobierno, además hay violencia doméstica e institucional; Las políticas del gobierno son inclusivas para las mujeres; No hay aseos, si eres madre de familia es un problema la comida,comprarla ,no hay diversión ni para la mujer , ni para niños; Estamos en igualdad de condiciones; La mujer tiene menos posibilidades que los hombres en todos los sentidos Esta poco considerada y respetada Y muchas veces obligada para hacer trabajos indignos; Ser mujer hoy en día es un privilegio y en nuestro país se nos trata como las reinas que somos; Tenemos prácticamente las mismas oportunidades y derechos que los hombres; No es que sea difícil pero no tienes las mismas oportunidades que un hombre; No es difícil ser mujer en mi país ahora en estos momentos, ya que la revolución, nos ha dado muchos oportunidades que antes la mujer no tenía, realizamos las mismas tareas y funciones al igual que los hombres.

HAITI - Les hommes se croient supérieurs aux femmes et ces dernières le pensent aussi, parce que ce sont eux, les hommes qui occupent les meilleurs postent de travail. Pour se faire accepter dans un travail, il y en a qui sont obligées de se soumettre aux avances de leur patron. Au niveau du salaire aussi, les femmes, si elles occupent le même poste que leurs collègues hommes sont pays moins que ceux-ci. Les femmes haitiennes sont constamment victimes de viol,d'harcèlement et de toutes sortes de violences; Les femmes n'ont pas accès dans le pays; Être femme en Haiti,demande beaucoup de courage et de retenu,elles sont victimes de toutes sortes de violences,conjugales,domestique s etc.; Le genre féminin est considéré en quelques sorte comme un handicap. Une femme avec les compétences requises pour un job peut trouver des difficultés pour être recruter contrairement à un homme; certaines zones sont non accessibles aux femmes car elles sont sujets à beaucoup de menaces et de contraintes; Parce-que les femmes ont une rôle très importante dans la société Haitienne; Parce-que la femme n'est pas consideree comme un individu a part entiere. Pour moi etre femme n'a rien de difficile Ca peut arriver la structure de mon pays peut parfois pousser des femmes a s'humilier, mendier meme se prostitué mais nous sommes fortes, gentilles, suaves, independantes et tres determinées; 1- l'accès à l'éducation est toujours jugée non essentiel pour les filles. 2- Dans le secteur de l'emploi, la priorité est toujours accordé aux hommes malgré la mention candidature feminine vivement souhaitée. 3- des fillettes sont toujours mariées de force dans certaines régions sans oublier la pratique du ' taté'. Le harcelement sexuel est présent dans tous les secteurs de notre vie; Parce-que être femme en Haiti, c'est se faire harceler constamment, c'est être considéré comme une proie tout simplement parce qu'on est femme; Parce que nombreuses de femmes vivent dans une vie très compliqué il y a des femmes violée, désespérées, que vivent comme esclaves qu'ont peur.

INDIA. Knowingly and unknowingly, there are many girls got abused still; People in my country generally expect women to be engaged in households' activities; Because of the atrocities against woman and inequalities; She is unique; We can't travel alone; India is a country where the family system is very powerful; I am from an urban south Indian Society so in my opinion It's not difficult to be women; Safety issues mostly. Rather than blaming and punishing a violator, society seems to point out the 'faults' of the victim and an equally supportive and fertile judiciary for the offenders; Sometimes it was very difficult. A men can't live women's role in society; Patriarchy runs deep. We don't have the basic right to choose our own partners and have to listen to people complain about everything we do, from the way we talk to the way we dress; Except in certain regions of my country, women are educated and a big percentage of women are employed also; Women are dead restricted and oppressed by various social institutions like family, religion, marriage and so on The pressure to marry young and bear children; Sexual abuse; It is very difficult; I am proud to be a women because I am independent; Given equal importance; Because women not safe to night travel; It's because of women denied of basic human rights at some time.so it is harder to being a women; Security problems;

IRAN – We are some limitations- the rights are not our support; because we have no rights, everything is compulsory; compulsory Hijab, limits for women; We have specific day as woman day in Iran; because it's important being a woman either in family or in society; there's no freedom; Not having the right for choosing my own clothes Not having equal rights in divorce Not having equal rights in child custody Not having equal right in family heritage Not having equal right in courts' testimony; Lots of social equality; Now the living conditions in my country are difficult for men and women. Economic pressure. Lack of mental security as a woman and lack of freedom and a view of sexism ......; gender discrimination Social constraints Legal privileges for men; because all women's rights are meant after men's rights, for example to get out of our country, your husband must agree and also thousands more ugly and bigger problems, such as having more than one wife, mandatory Hijab , do not rely on women □ Diya (Islamic law); Compulsory hijab, harassment of women on the street, the patriarchy system in marriage, limits for sporting activity; in my opinion there is freedom, but maybe on some topics there are limits for example hijab and ... but in general it is not difficult and it depends on your point of view; thousands of reasons, for example the low salary of a woman who does not meet the expenses of a family □ the lack of freedom, the difference between women and men in every sense; Compulsory hijab, mandatory Hijab, not having freedom of expression and ....; they look at you as a commodity, they don't see your ability and your power, they don't even think for a second that you eventually become desperate, fed up, it's worse that sometimes they see you as a prostitute. it is very difficult to be the woman in the world that her bosses are men, gender discrimination laws.

IRAQ - For activists and who ever raise opposition against corruptions Iraq is very dangerous, for a woman in ME society it's even worse! They don't attack her physically but they attack her reputation, her family and her friends! ; Tribalism sizing the role of the women., beside unstable region is a big challenge to achieve the targets of all the plan to empower the woman; Women are often seen as just being a body Because of the customs and traditions of society, the difficulty of granting women full freedom, as well as the lack of awareness in society; Society, customs, traditions and many other reasons restrict women's freedom I completed my university education as an employee, There is no reason; Because of the distinction between men and women I don't think it's hard to be a woman in my country Customs, traditions, and the wrong religious character of people and restricting freedom in all things; I AM FORBIDDEN TO DO A LOT OF NORMAL ACTIVITIES AND BEHAVIOURS JUST BECAUSE I'M A WOMAN. IRAQI WOMEN ARE RESTRICTED IN ALL RESPECTS; Tribalism sizing the role of the women. Arab women in general and Iraqi women in particular are subject to persecution due to customs and traditions established by men and used against them under the pretext of religion and Sharia to justify his actions Because of criticism and bullying .... I am a Muslim woman and I walk within the framework of Sharia, and I believe and cherish the position that my religion has given me.

ITALY – Parità; bisogna conciliare lavoro fuori e dentro casa, figli e famiglia tutta; I don't feel to much difference. Except for the fear for a woman to walk alone in the dark; essere donna significa dover accettare molti compromessi: Is it no difficult being woman today because gender equality has been achieved; Ormai nei paesi sviluppati non c'è più questa distinzione tra sessi; We must catch every day to survival in a men- society; It seems to me that the woman is respected; penso che ormai ci sia la piena parità di diritti e di possibilità; Is the same to being man; pink tax and gender prejudice. Questions like "do you plan to have kids?" during job interviews and hygiene products not being priced as necessary basic products. Not to mention the cat calling each of us face and the abuse that more than 90% of us got through before our 20s; because our work is underestimated; perché lo stato non ti tutela e non ti da i servizi sufficienti x poter inserirti nel mondo del lavoro; presenti pari opportunità; rispetto a prima la situazione della donna si è evoluta; it is difficult to be a woman because, despite the equality, the woman finds obstacles in the working and social world; sure there is yet a lot of work to be done about gender equality; violenza sulle donne; perché non si è liberi di amare, di vivere e di far ciò che si vuole; c'è parità tra i sessi; uomini e donne abbiamo gli stessi diritti; non ho riscontrato mai difficoltà; le donne guadagnano meno degli uomini. Devono lasciare il lavoro all'arrivo di un figlio. Aumentano i casi di femminicidio; non ci sono limitazioni evidenti; avere una famiglia e mantenere un lavoro con orari conciliabili con la famiglia è molto difficile. Occorre avere nonni o babysitter altrimenti non si può. Molte donne sono costrette a rinunciare al lavoro professionale e il loro lavoro in famiglia non è stimato né valorizzato; troppa discriminazione di genere, c'è ancora tanto maschilismo;

IVORY COAST - Parce que les femmes vulnérable dans ce pays elle sont utilisées comme les objets sexuel; parce que les femmes sont libre et on le même droit que les hommes, je dirais même qu'elle sont favorisé; pour ma part être une femme est difficile du fait qu'elle ne puisse prendre de décision sans l'accord d'un homme,; tout simplement parce que la femme est vue plus comme objet de satisfaction qu'être humain; parce que dans ma société les femmes sont mises en avant et sont privilégiées; les femmes ont autant de droit que nous les hommes en tout cas a Abidjan la ville où je vis; parce que les conditions sont entrain d'être améliorées; 1-le travail : les employeurs préfèrent embaucher des hommes que des femmes (les congés de maternité, les permission pour les enfants malades...) 2-la pression sociale en termes de statut matrimonial, les enfants; parce-que parmis les ministres du gouvernement il y'a des femmes; elles sont confrontées à des harcèlement sexuel; les femmes sont traités plus ou moins de la même manière que les hommes; Je suis indépendante et mes droits sont respectés; elles sont beaucoup influencées par les tars de la société; car ici les femmes sont libres et peuvent faire ce qu'elles veulent; le gouvernement décrète des lois permettant aux femmes d'occuper pleinement des rôles au même titre que les hommes.(Ex:quota des femmes à la députation imposé aux partis politiques); les femmes ne sont pas respectées comme il le doit; elles continuent d'être défavorisées dans les milieux de la société. Nombreuses sont celles qui meurent en donnant la vie. Elles subissent des violences sexuelles. les mutilations génitales féminines, les viols et violences; Elle est beaucoup respectée surtout cher les Akans; c'est difficile car la mentalité africaine n'a pas encore réellement accepté l'égalité homme femme, fait absurde selon beaucoup; la femme joue un rôle important dans notre société. Elle est irremplaçable. La famille repose sur la femme.

MEXICO - Es inseguro; machismo; por la falta de oportunidades; en mi caso no sido un problema ser muje; por inseguridad; violencia; violencia; por la falta de igualdad y reconocimiento de la mujer por la mujer misma. Machismo; siempre nos tenemos que estar cuidando de lo que decimos, lo que hacemos, lo que nos ponemos. Cuando eres mamá trabajadora, es complicado acceder a un puesto de alto nivel o alta responsabilidad y además sufrimos discriminación por lo mismo; es q no es difícil ser mujer en México; en muchos ámbitos simplemente por ser mujer o no te atienden o quieren sacar ventaja o venderte mas caro sin pueden, o hay diferencias salariales respecto a los hombres o no se considera a la mujer para ciertas posiciones la laborales, entre otras cosas; porque México es un país machista y las mujeres son menospreciadas hasta un punto dónde la violencia mata a la mujer; feminicidios, maltrato, exclusión, patriarcado, injusticia social y política; violencia, abuso, cero credibilidad, cero acción por parte del gobierno; hay libertad de superarse, hay educación al alcance de todas, es aceptado ser madre soltera, hay libertad de credo; no soy mujer no podría compartir la experiencia; en mi país las mujeres no tienen la oportunidad de salir vestidas como quieran y no pueden salir de noche sin sufrir alguna forma de asedio; Nos matan, violan y desaparecen todos los días y si no lo hacen, tenemos miedo de que lo hagan; la mayoría de las mujeres sufren de acoso en la calle, violencia verbal como física; mucha violencia en contra de la mujer, mujeres desaparecidas y miedo a lo que actualmente está sucediendo; creo que a pesar de que ya tenemos igualdad de género en muchos aspectos, aún hay miles de cosas que nos siguen queriendo hacer menos, sin mencionar la inseguridad que vivimos día con día; existe machismo y exclusión hacia la mujer; porque abusan de ti por el simple hecho de ser mujer; país machista donde la mujer está en desventaja y es agredida fácilmente sin tener consecuencias; porque si somos víctimas de una violación, acoso sexual, muchas personas creen que la culpa es nuestra por el hecho de ser mujer; por la inseguridad tenemos muchos feminicidios, existe mucha violencia contra las mujeres; hay 10 feminicidios al día y muchas mujeres violentadas; Ya no puedes salir con seguridad, siempre existe el temor de que te pueda pasar algo, o que te priven de tu liberta o en el peor de los casos no regresar a tu casa; soy independiente y generadora; mucha inequidad de género; acoso sexual, mucha discriminación y feminicidios; todavía existe la desigualdad en muchos aspecto como laborales o de actividades básicas; por los estereotipos, el abuso y acoso.

PAKISTAN - First reason is my society is very conservative. Secondly is mostly families not allow education; Because she can stand 4 her rights without any fear; women aren't safe in streets, homes they are being forced to bear difficulties; she has freedom; male dominated society; we have equal rights; Due to lack of safety and security; because our country still has humanity; because now women have all rights; because our country provides all the freedom and rights to the women that they deserve; Bcz of rape cases, harassment cases, blackmailing and kidnaping of females; The male gender is very dominant in our society. That is why women's rights are being ignored. If a woman speaks in her favour. And if a woman stands up for her rights, problems arise in her way, she is called bad. Even her family members try to silence her. A woman even trained her son in this way. It is a pity that society does not try to understand or comprehend it. So, I think if you are a Pakistani woman, it is very difficult for you to live your life according to your own, the mentality of our country's people sucks. Islam give rights to women as well as man but our society doesn't; poverty /unemployment; there is more respect of women in Pakistan; women in our country face discrimination .some of the problem faced by women in our country are domestic violence, honour killing, rapes and abduction, forced marriages; most of the population is living under the line of poverty that automatically restricts pathways to avail all the opportunities given to males who are supposed to hypothetically support their families and on the other hand at every stage of life males are preferred to be chosen for any job; no; social pressure; we are in a Islamic Country, and it's not difficult for being a women in our Country; females are targeted and harassed; yes it is so difficult for women today's in our country; Alhumdulilah Allah has bestowed his blessings upon me by giving me parents that understand me and trying their level best to keep me away from the Grinding of social efforts for being alive. Furthermore, I haven't faced any tragedy in the public or in-person so I will not say alike that living in the current commonwealth as a woman or my survival is difficult; because still there are many areas where women are not allow to get their education and fulfil their dreams; just because of upcoming rape system; no support from husband, Pakistan is an Islamic country so that Islam gave the importance to women; recently I joined insurance company for job but I have to face many problems regarding so called "honour"; not only women infact children nowadays are not safe in our country.

PERU – Machismo; machismo más que nada; yo creo que ya no es tanto como antes que maltrataban a la mujeres y no había derechos para la mujer; hay opciones de trabajo,estudio y emprendimiento; muchas mujeres aún en los lugares alejados del país viven marginadas y agredidas por sus parejas y no reciben apoyo del estado hasta terminan asesinadas; porque tenemos muchas oportunidades en todos los campos, laboral, profesional, entre otros; hay oportunidades para mejorar la calidad de vida siendo un país que respeta la igualdad de genero; por qué tanto hombre como mujer tienen los mismos derechos; no hay oportunidad para todos; por que hay hombres machistas; somos importantes en todo momento consejeras, madre, amiga; en lo laboral creo que se tiene las mismas oportunidades que los hombres, pero en temas de seguridad pues si es difícil Perú es el país con más taza de feminicidios en Latinoamérica; no es fácil conseguir un empleo y las personas piensan que por ser mujer no es apto para aquel trabajo; Tenemos participación en el congreso y en el legislativo; No. Porque tenemos los mismos derechos como los hombres; una de ellas son los feminicidios; la sociedad está llena de machismo, feminicidio etc. Nos matan por ser mujer; aunque más disimulado hay mucho machismo latente en la sociedad peruana actual; no hay igualdad de oportunidades; machismo y desigualdades; no es difícil porque una mujer se respeta no seria difícil ser mujer en el Perú; discriminación; el rol de la mujer en el País es dificil ya que muy pocas pueden llegar a acceder debido hasta hoy a una educación básica completa (primaria y secundaria) y por ende a una educación superior sobre toda en partes de nuestra sierra y selva amazónica además existe una alta tasa de analfabetismo en mujeres; hay tantas maltrados hacia una mujer, estamos en peligro constante. Ya que los hombre son machistas; hay muchos machistas en Perú; Existe mucho machismo; en muchas ocasiones nos niegan el trabajo porque no es para nuestra talla como mujer; no es difícil porque en nuestro estado las mujeres ya han conseguido tener derechos tan iguales a los hombres, solo falta lograr los niveles salariales que hace la diferencia; en el Perú existe mucho el machismo un ejemplo durante muchos años es el cargo de presidente; la gente las sexualiza y son machistas; hoy en día ya no paramos seguro de nada hay mucha violencia y machismo contra las mujeres los ven con un objetivo; puedes realizar lo que deseas,es tu decisión; hay igualdad; mucha violencia a la mujer; por el machismo; no siempre valoran tu trabajo; por que algunas personas hacen difícil que ellas sean tratadas por igual, piensan ser superiores a ellas y no aceptan que todos somos iguales (hombres y mujeres); los estereotipos, el acoso y todo lo que hoy en dia sucede a la mayoria de mujeres; existen muchos casos de maltrato fisico y psicológico contra las mujeres.

POLAND – women have the same rights as men and can have the same job as them; no; the average salary for a woman is lower than for men. Strong influence of the catholic church on society, church oppose the equality of women. there are many problems that women must deal with; these are different times and I think that a woman now plays an increasingly important role in social life; it is easy to see that women are treated worse. it's harder for them to find jobs and their opinion is almost irrelevant; it is because of abortion thing, bad government and patriarchy; because i think that women rights are really limited in Poland; I think that women are not treated equal with man; because of I'm afraid of going out at night, people thinking that women are weak and less intelligent than men; women have the same rights as men. They are very respected in polish culture; women have a lack of representation in both government and business, making it hard to be represented at any level of the country's laws or corporate engulfment; Discrimination in many fields, also intersectional (e.g., women +50), stereotypes related to the "Polish mother"; I didn't feel on myself that I am ignoring because of my sex. I can study on university include on technical unit, I can work, and I can make the same money as male; recently, the government in our country has started to take away women's rights. It's about a situation with a ban on abortion; women have better in Poland than in many countries around the world, but they are often victims of stereotypes and new anti-abortion law in Poland is bad; The state makes access to abortion practically impossible. no more difficult than in any other country in Europe; women in my country must prove herself each day, we are multitasking but either way we don't get as high salary as men's, I never encountered different treatment for being a woman; nowadays our country doesn't really care about women and their problems or needs. As a woman, I am treated worse than men. Often, I could not find a job because most of the offers are intended for men; I think so, because women are generally considered to be the weaker sex than men; Women have a better social status than 10 years ago; We have election rights, but we still have problems at work. Men earn more money and have bigger salary than women, even they have the same duties. Nowadays we have less right than the rest of women in Europe. I choose yes because in our country are slowly receiving some important rights; we are treating worse than men, we are just sexual object for them; chauvinism; stereotypes, take away basic rights; because woman can work at the same positions as man and they don't discriminated against by gender; An example is the ban on abortion, most of us, of course, oppose it a bad thing, but truth is that we should be entitled to it; our rights are limited, especially when we want to decide about our body (abortion); Lack of major laws (illegal abortion); in Poland we have equal rights.

TUNISIA - Le fait que les femmes sont exposés à des mutilations et tentent de la neutraliser; la seule difficulté est celle économique; (société masculin); Il n'y a pas de respect; du manque de protection et le fait de considérer la femme comme un être imparfait; le mot de la fin revient toujours à la femme chez nous; Dans un pays où l'être humain se décline au masculin les femmes ont du mal à se frayer un chemin; En Tunisie la femme est libre et protégée par la loi); Inégalité et injustice sont les principaux arguments de ma réponse; pour ce que nous entend concernant le harcèlement et la violence je peux confirmer et c'est développer, la femme tunisienne est devenue libre plus que le nécessaire); à mon pays il y a des lois sévères pour la femme); la Tunisie est un pays moderne où la femme est respectée non uniquement par le peuple mais aussi protégée par la loi et les droits des femmes; la femme n'a pas le droit d'être libre ni de penser ni de faire ce qu'elle veut; harcèlement continu; l'homme considéré la femme un être faible qu'en peut s'en abuser, l'homme peut violer la femme pour la condamner après car il la considère une honte et sorcellerie et elle mérite tous ce qui lui arrive; le problème de harcèlement dans les rues, la femme obtient un salaire plus bas que celui d'un homme en Tunisie; on est arrivé au même niveau que l'homme; car on a tant de problème en Tunisie talque la corruption, le harcèlement partout dans les rues même au lieu du travail; la femme à sa place dans son pays mieux que d'autres parts; la femme n'a pas les mêmes droits que l'homme); notre société est une société patriarcale, donc la position de l'homme est plus fort que la femme qu'elle doivent toujours combattre pour avoir ses droits; car la femme n'a pas les mémés droits que l'homme ; parmi les plus importantes raisons est le harcèlement continuel et l'injustice ; raisons culturelles, religion, politique.

UNITED STATES– Discrimination; no; there are still gender norms and stereotypes that make it more difficult for women to be successful in the workplace, and puts pressure of them to take parental/family roles that are not equitable; no protection; a lot to do; I haven't found any difficulty; no help; it that difficult, but there are areas in which gender inequality can improve; hard for this as a yes or no question but I have experienced the ability to chase what I want to chase and freely make choices here in the Us. Much to do with the fact that I'm white and have an education; bias and undervaluation; four years of the Trump administration. Supreme Court heavily weighed now conservative and against women's rights; very hard to be a women; biases, lower pay for equal job, discrimination; a woman usually works more, especially when she has a family and a job; it is not difficult because in the metropolitan area in which I live women have a better lifestyle and parity than in many other areas; But what this really means is that women should make themselves "like men" by shutting down their reproductive system with birth control, by advancing in their career, by putting off marriage and/or children, and by finding child care and continuing their career after children. The "option" for woman to pursue a feminine desire of caring for home, family, and neighbour does not exist, and women are belittled for making such a choice; Additionally, toxic masculinity and rape culture pose a serious danger to women. Women are conditioned by society to take countless precautions to avoid being attacked by men — and if they are attacked, all too frequently, the perpetrator is given a lenient sentence or not held accountable; it's not as difficult as it was for women living in decades/ centuries of the past, but sexism/misogyny is still prevalent in society today and holds many women back; as a woman, I don't find it difficult; women are given opportunities to grow and succeed; same rights men and women; agism, hard to be single in America, and economic mobility; women are in power and control everything; often have to prove that we are just as qualified as men; Equal rights prevail; social stigma, predefined gender roles; unfair laws; in my personal experience, when I was a young woman and started my career, I did face some age discrimination. Otherwise, being female has not been difficult. I feel as if I have the same opportunities as men; no laws to protect; work and home; sometimes not feeling safe doing things alone; equal rights; there is pressure to excel in the workplace and be the perfect involved mother. There is much more pressure placed on working mothers in this respect than on working fathers;; at the professional environment, women still have less opportunities, with excuses such as, if you get pregnant, you won't be at your 100% committed in your job dues; in my opinion they still tend to have more office management type jobs such as secretary or administrative assistants; better laws against discriminating women; I think it can be difficult sometimes for a Christian/ Catholic woman in regards to the pressure for their bodies--abortion, birth control, etc; Women do face more challenges but overall I do not think it is exceptionally difficult in the US to be a woman; while women still experience wage discrimination and sexism, we are free to choose the career we would like and enjoy living in a beautiful country with many advantages in life. Always looking over my shoulder to make sure I'm not being followed. I was taught to carry a knife or mace in my pocket or, at the very least, sharp keys between my fingers. The number of female acquaintances I have who were assaulted or suffered violence is enormous; In my case, my husband helps sometimes carries these out, but I am the mastermind behind groceries, dinner, kids' needs (social, school, clothes, food, health, etc.) household finances, family social calendar, etc. On the other hand, being a woman gives me the opportunity to experience family and career to the fullest; we are discriminated; I'm retired so I don't have workplace issues. When working I was fine; difficult is a strong word, and for the most part--being a woman in the US is simply being; I have many privileges that allow me to live freely with all the rights of any other person. If anything, I think women have an additional right which I think is immoral, the right to abort a child. I have never felt discriminated in a way that held me back, but I have felt the effects of sexism and paternalism particularly with older men and family members, some rights.

VENEZUELA - No es dificil porqué en Venezuela hay igualdad de género; tenemos acceso al área laboral y de educación; porque ni siquiera toallas sanitarias y productos de aseo personal; depende de cada quien!; la delincuencia, violencia de género, etc.; me siento feliz siendo mujer en mi pais; muchas responsabilidades... oportunidades de trabajo mal remuneradas; existe un poco más de equidad en lo laboral, y en lo educativo la mayor población estudiantil es femenina; por la dificil situación que se vive, las condiciones inhumanas, el miedo a no saber si se puede seguir adelante y sobre todo a ser victima de una tragedia contra nuestra propia vida por la inseguridad, la falta de apoyo de parte de las instituciones, algunas veces ese miedo vive dentro de nuestra propias casas El terror de no saber si esta situación cambiara algun día, sobrevivir dia a dia; soy luchadora; con el confinamiento se han elevado los casos de abuso a la mujer; esto se debe a la forma de pensar de las personas; por que la mujer hoy en dia a superado muchos obtáculos de los cuales era privada antes ...somos mas independientes, con diferentes profesiones las cuales ejercemos sin ningun temor; existen muchos puestos de trabajo que no quieren incluir como su fuerza capital a las mujeres; hay los mismos derechos; discriminación; la mujer actualmente estámos empoderadas en nuestros roles; hay más empleo, para mujeres que para hombres; lo que es difícil es ser respetado. La dignidad del ser humano en general día a día se vulnera con un sin fin de necesidades no resueltas; la verdad es que nunca he sentido dificultades en ser mujer. He encontrado obstáculos puntuales con personas puntuales; no considero que en mi país exista un machismo significativo. En tal caso, en el único aspecto que considero que es difícil es el no poder salir a la calle sola por miedo a que me pase algo. Pero a nivel laboral, familiar, económico, no es difícil; violación de sus derechos, violencia intrafamiliar, como por ejemplo maltrato físico, verbal, moral por parte del cónyuge. El mismo Gobierno no respeta los derechos que tienen la mujer como madre, como cónyuge; las condiciones laborales no son iguales para las mujeres que para los hombres; en esta época las mujeres han desmostado que pueden ejercer todo lo que se proponga; tengo libertad de elección, decisión.. Puedo ejercer mi profesión y opinión; aquí la mujer venezolana tenemos que ser muy echada pa'lante si no no puedes enfrentar el día a día. hoy día es mas difícil sí pero no imposible; actualmente la mujer ha asumido rol importante, es independiente, trabaja en la calle, no depende de un hombre para salir adelante; Venezuela es un país machista; si, ya que tenemos cada día más responsabilidades, los hombres nos agreden cada día más, incluyendo los jefes, o sino sufrimos de acoso por parte de ellos, sino le hacemos caso nos agreden. También cada día hay menos oportunidades en el campo laboral, ya que los pocos empleos son ofrecidos más a hombres que a nosotras, eso debido a que la mayoría somos madres solteras y tenemos que buscar horarios más flexibles para ate ser a nuestros hijos; en mi experiencia no he visto ni he sentido discriminación por ser mujer; la dificultad de vivir en Vzla es para ambos sexos; las mujeres se sienten desplazadas y con poca importancia; Xq hay mujeres que son padre y madres y tenemos que salí a la calle temprano a laborar y aveces es díficil ver con quién dejamos a nuestros hijos; no podemos salir solas sin un hombre estando completamente seguras; para mi no es difícil siempre que uno tenga un propósito de vida; si es dificil porque aún hoy en dia en Venezuela existen diferencias de género en el trabajo. Ademas de existir muchas personas que afectan la seguridad de la mujer en la sociedad y no existe un sistema que te garantice justicia.

At the same time, nearly 73 percent of respondents (exactly 72.98 percent) - an average of all countries considered - believes that being a woman in their own country is generally different from being a man. More specifically, 91.7 percent of Haitians are convinced of this; 87 percent of Iraqis; 85 percent of Iranians and the same percentage of Americans ; 82.7 percent of Mexicans and 81 percent of Indians who answered the question. On the contrary, only about one in two people in Italy - exactly 57.4 percent - and in Cuba - 50.8 percent - and less than one in two people in Venezuela, that is 49.2 percent, are convinced of this. Poland is around the overall average of 73 percent, with 75 percent of respondents considering being a woman different from being a man in their own country; Pakistan, where 74.7 percent of respondents are convinced; Ivory Coast and Tunisia, both with 67.4 percent of respondents and Peru, where 66.8 percent of respondents are convinced.

The complete diagrams of the above data are shown below, country by country, according to the answers given to the question "Is being a woman in your country different from being a man?"

Figure 6. Being woman in your country is different from being man? Y/N -
Source: IWT Research

Cuba

5) Ser mujer en tu pais es diferente a ser hombre:
120 responses

● Sí
● No

49.2%

50.8%

Haiti

5) Être femme dans son pays est différent d'être homme
120 responses

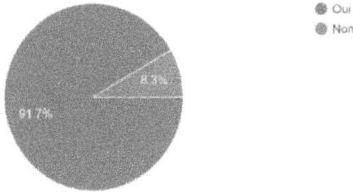

● Oui
● Non

8.3%

91.7%

India

5) Being Woman in your country is different from being man
190 responses

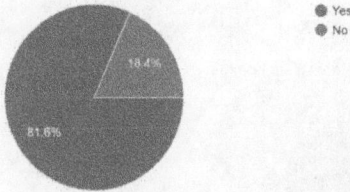

- Yes
- No

18.4%

81.6%

Iran

5) Being Woman in your country is different from being man - زن بودن در کشور شما با مرد بودن متفاوت است
100 responses

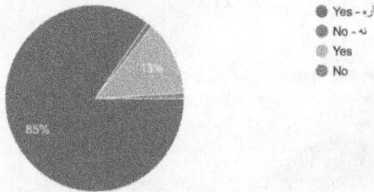

- Yes - أر
- No - نه
- Yes
- No

13%

85%

Iraq

5) Being Woman in your country is different from being man ان تكون / تكوني امرأة في بلدك هل هو مختلف عن ان تكوني رجل؟
155 responses

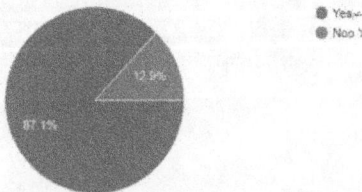

- Yes
- Noo لا

12.9%

87.1%

Italy

5) Being Woman in your country is different from being man
216 responses

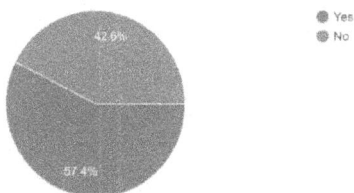

● Yes
● No

42.6%

57.4%

Ivory Coast

5) Être femme dans son pays est différent d'être homme
141 responses

● Oui
● Non

32.6%

67.4%

Mexico

5) Ser mujer en tu pais es diferente a ser hombre:
388 responses

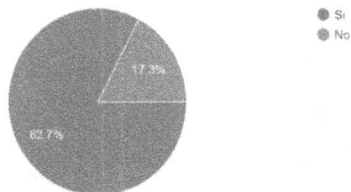

● Si
● No

17.3%

82.7%

Pakistan

5) Being Woman in your country is different from being man
198 responses

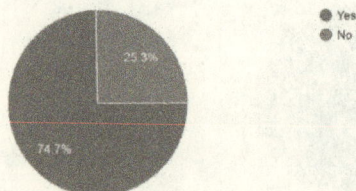

● Yes
● No

25.3%

74.7%

Peru

5) Ser mujer en tu país es diferente a ser hombre:
229 responses

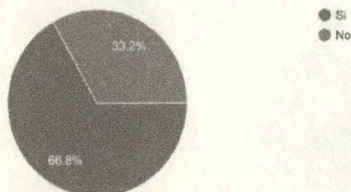

● Sí
● No

33.2%

66.8%

Poland

5) Being Woman in your country is different from being man
176 responses

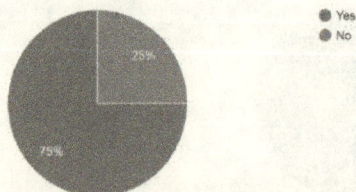

● Yes
● No

25%

75%

Tunisia

5) Être femme dans son pays est différent d'être homme? ان تكون / تكوني امرأة في بلدك. هل هو مختلف عن ان تكوني رجل؟
132 responses

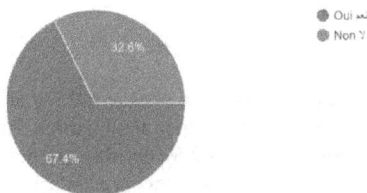

- Oui نعم
- Non لا

32.6%
67.4%

United States

5) Being Woman in your country is different from being man
153 responses

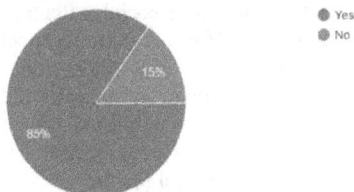

- Yes
- No

15%
85%

Venezuela

5) Ser mujer en tu pais es diferente a ser hombre:
132 responses

- Si
- No

50.8%
49.2%

Also in this case, when asked to motivate personal answer, the statements are varied and reflect the choices and percentages indicated above, making them extraordinarily interesting. That's why we report some of them literally, summarized below, country by country.

Can you explain why, on your opinion, being woman in your country is different from being man?

CUBA Desigualdades de todo tipo como por ejemplo salariales - Los hombres son considerados en todo mejor - No tienen los mismos derechos ni el mismo status social - Menos oportunidades - Los hombres tienen más posibilidades de tener un futuro mejor. La mujer es menospreciada y minusvalorada - Ser mujer es diferente porque somos diferentes biológicamente y porque con el sistema político que tenemos todo aquel que no piensa a favor del régimen es cuestionado y "perjudicado" - Porque es distinta su Fuerza fisica y su carater - Tenemos los mismos derechos hombres y mujeres - No hay diferencias genéricas en Cuba - Siento que como mujer debo demostrar más que el hombre, mi valía - El hombre siempre tiene todo el poder siempre - No veo Diferencias - Techo salarial, acceso a puestos de trabajo, conciliación familiar... .

HAITI - Différence morale. Traitement social, attentes différents, homme comme étant chef de la femme - En Haïti, la femme est celle qui s'occupe du foyer. Les hommes ont droit à tout : se faire plaisir comme ils veulent avec leurs amis, mais les femmes n'ont aucun droit que celui d'être traitées comme un objet sexuel. J'ai parlé de la discrimination au travail. C'est une réalité. Beaucoup de femmes ne trouvent encore le courage d'en parler au risque d'être mal vues par la société y compris celles qui se sont violées dès leur plus jeune âge. Et, qui continuent d'être traitées comme une chose rien que parce qu'elles sont nées femmes - Parce-que les femmes sont réduites souvent aux travaux ménagères avec le système patriarcal qui domine, les hommes ont toujours tendance que les femmes sont faites pour s'occuper d'eux et de leurs enfants, que laver les vaisselles, balayer la maison, cuisiner sont faites que pour les femmes - L'inégalité salariale, une femme peut occuper le même poste qu'un homme et même avoir plus de compétence que lui, cela n'empêche pas que dans la majeure partie des cas le salaire de l'homme soit plus élevé - Sur le plan conjugal les hommes peuvent tout faire comme pratiquer la polygamie. Il y a des métiers même si la femme a les compétences requises on vous dit que ce n'est pas pour les femmes etc....- Le rôle des Hommes est indétrônable.

INDIA - Woman has a limitation in many things – Inequality - Girls are getting abused still and lots of prostitutes and sex rackets are cheating innocent girls and force them to do sexual activities. This is Still happening in red streets of Delhi and many other Indian states. We don't want any sex workers. We want a better India and better social workers - Men are very free in all fields, whereas women must get permission from their parents or husband for many matters - Difference in opportunities both in education and in employment. Difference in wages. Women are facing more inequalities and insecurities - It's true because. They can do whatever they want at any time.... But women can't travel anywhere alone because exploitation toward women increases when is alone - Simple reason is they must pay dowry when they marry - I didn't feel any differentiate between men and women - Men have many priorities. Even today in my country men suppresses women in various things even in her dressings or behaviour. If anything is happened between a man and a woman, the whole people first accuse her not him - It's a patriarchal society no equal opportunity.

IRAN - In our country, even a woman's ransom is half that of a man - Women have different social rights than men. And this has led to the fact that almost all men, directly and indirectly, have this belief in mind, and that they themselves give women less rights in the family - Because men are valued more than women, although in our current society, both men and women work side by side, but still women have more restrictions - Freedom of expression - Wrong culture and religious rule - I cannot ride a motorcycle - I cannot cover my hair. I cannot wear comfortable clothes - Man means me. Decision maker. Everything in life and woman means obedient and submissive - It is difficult to be both a man and a woman in Iran, but men have more freedom. At least in 40 degree heat, they cannot wear coats and scarves – Hijab - Men's clothing is their choice, they have more security, they find jobs more easily, they receive higher salaries, marriage laws are in their favour, they do not need anyone's permission to leave the country, they have more fun than women due to more security - Yes, because in my country, a man has always forced a woman to marry a man who wants to lower her knees - There is patriarchy in Iran - Yes, women are not used in any position in key positions. President of the Expediency Council and the Islamic Consultative Assembly and other mandatory hijab.

IRAQ - Because today, women are equal to men, and there is no difference in everything - In my country there is a so-called patriarchal society, there are 60% or more families who prefer males over women - As a woman, I did not face the difficulties of employment like my male colleagues - You can't look for an ID or passport for any of her children - You cannot work freely or even express your opinion because you are a woman - I am a woman and I am proud of myself. There is no difference between a man and a woman, but there are customs and traditions that are imposed on women and not imposed on men - clan traditions.

ITALY - We have equal rights and duties – Discrimination - Gender equality - Because man and woman have the same rights – Equality - Men and women are treated equally - Because gender equality has been achieved - There is no distinction - The woman are in background always - I don't find any differences in the daily vote - A full equality has not been reached yet - There is no gender difference except for some employment figure that the average population sees as anomalous for women - There are the same rights - Because I think the differences are really minimal - Men occupy the best work positions - Apparently not. But in essence, yes. All-round completeness is required of us women. Man can only work, and he is complete - Equal opportunities are guaranteed in Italy - Because now woman is considered equal such as man.

IVORY COAST - Women have more opportunity than men - We have the same rights as men, especially the right to education. Even if sometimes the company does not give us the same chances in the field of employment. Women are not accepted by some recruiters - Exposure to risks of rape or prostitution for an adventurer, difficulty of integration etc ...- Because men don't have the same rights as women - Most women are underestimated in most areas - Inequality and prejudice - The culture - We do the same studies but do not have the same chances the same opportunities - Men are favoured even though there are many laws in favour of women.

MEXICO - Por qué no nos dan los mismos derechos - Los hombres tienen mejor acceso a puestos de trabajo altos - Tenemos los mismos derechos - Los hombres en mi profesión tienen más oportunidad -Dan preferencia a los hombres, incluso mejores salarios - Soy Directora de una empresa familiar y no veo diferencia - Una de las razones principales es el machismo mal entendido de nuestro país y de los países latinos en general - Las mujeres en México son el único grupo discriminado que no es minoría. Eso obviamente afirma de como los hombres suelen tener más privilegios que las mujeres, porque la mayoría de las mujeres somos discriminadas por ser mujeres. Entonces, si la vida como mujer en Mexico puede ser más difícil que los hombres - La falta de oportunidades.

PAKISTAN - It is an Islamic country and Islam gives us an equal right - Women have more responsibilities and work to do - Males can go outward without any fear, while female cannot. Mans are dominant, females were used and abused also. Males have all opportunities of job, but females have only some. Generation to generation male name is passed. Male can go outside any time but female cannot – I want to do job in PAK ARMY but whenever I do search the vacancy I just found nothing for women except the psychologist On the other hand there are plenty of jobs for men women are doing great with their fields but they are not supported if a women is supported from her job then her family not support her and if family support then she is facing vacancy issues - Yes in an Islamic state where the religion give more rights to men and not the women there is a BIG difference - I want to do work in the police station but when I try l find out no more jobs - Misogynistic social values.. Male dominant society - Our society is based on patriarchal system - Women are different due to patriarchal system. The head of a family is a man, and he is the decision maker.

PERU - Tenemos las mismas oportunidades - Hoy en dia tienen las mismas oportunidades de trabajo - Les pagan más a los hombres - Normalmente el hombre suele tener más privilegios que la mujer, ser mujer en país significa ser inferior y ser restringida en diversas actividades - Los tratos en puestos laborales son diferentes según el género, a pesar de predicarse lo contrario - Si bien estamos avanzando poco a poco como sociedad, aún nos falta mucho romper esas barreras de genero tan marcadas y naturalizadas que existen. Se ve en el trabajo, en la politica, en la escuela, en la familia, en todos los nucleos. Hay una relación muy fuerte de poder y superioridad por parte del hombre, que hace que tenga mayores ventajas y accesos que la mujer. Lamentablemente, nos educan así, los medios de comunicación venden esa imagen del hombre y mujer - Porque aún hay machismo en nuestra sociedad - En muchas ocasiones en algunos trabajos los requerimientos son que exclusivamente sus trabajadores tienen que ser hombre - No, porque la igualdad de genero esta muy fuerte hoy en dia.

POLAND - Man can do more on many levels - Men get paid more than I do - even though we do the same job - employers treat women less seriously - It is different because we're being treated differently - In our country it is not a problem - There are still stereotypes where the woman takes care of the home. There is also a tendency for women to be directed towards less prestigious professions, for example, teachers in lower secondary schools - I can do everything that man can do - men earn more than women, and their functioning in working environment is immensely easier - Being a woman in our country is hard. Women are often discriminated against at work because they have children. Many employers, especially in private companies, ask too personal questions about their private lives during job interviews because of their families - I think that women these days are independent and very successful - Women are not treated as equal to men - I think that being women is good as much as like be man - Women have no reproductive rights, have more difficult situation on labour market, are less present in media and politics - we are the same.

TUNISIA - L'homme est libre de faire ce qu'il veut, mais la femme est limitée par les coutumes et les traditions - Une société injuste envers les femmes -Exiger que vous travailliez en même temps, que vous vous occupiez de votre maison, de vos enfants, de la mère et du père de votre mari, et éventuellement de votre mère et de votre père. Bien sûr, vous devez être belle pour ne pas être remplacée - Une femme doit suivre et respecter un homme - Nous avons les mêmes droits et devoirs - Il n›y a pas de différence -Les hommes sont supérieurs aux femmes - Certes la loi impose l›égalité entre Homme et Femme en Tunisie, mais la réalité prouve généralement le contraire. L›homme exerce plus de pouvoir que la femme en Tunisie et parfois ces pouvoirs condamnent la femme et la prive de ses droits basiques - L›homme est le corps sur la femme et il est le décideur - Les femmes sont différentes parce qu›elles n›osent pas contredire l›opinion d›un homme – La religion surtout.

UNITED STATES - Men get better jobs - Women must work harder to overcome pay gaps and conscious and unconscious bias, as well as disadvantageous double standards and policies that perpetuate the problem – Discrimination - Income gap for men women - Men are paid more for same job - generally they have the same rights but in some states for example the right of abortion is at stake - No difference - Men dominate many fields, corporate boards, and leadership roles still. We still do not have a female President though at least we have a VP. It's disappointing that worldwide woman still cannot lead in the Catholic Church. Progress is good but slow - While I personally don't believe there is a difference, there are definitely disparities in salary, outdated role expectations, inequities in gender diversity at the workplace, etc - I believe we have the same opportunities so it's not difficult - It's still a man's world at the top of most companies, women experience pay gaps, and continue to burden the bulk of childcare and household duties - We have equal opportunities - No laws for us - I think there are still implicit biases that favour men in terms of pay and promotions at work, etc.

VENEZUELA - No, porqué la mujer puede hacer muchas actividades al igual que el hombre - tenemos diferencias en aspectos, pero tenemos los mismo derechos - Nunca lo ha sido - hoy en día son muchas las leyes que protegen a la mujeres y la igualdad esta en todos los ámbitos - Puedo ejercer mi carrera con las mismas oportunidades que los hombres - Para dar un ejemplo, los choferes de autobus Son casi todas mujeres - la mujer esta hecha para situaciones delicadas, y el hombre es más para la fuerza - Las mujeres venezolanas cumplen prácticamente las mismas funciones que los hombres - Por que tanto el hombre, como la mujer, estamos padeciendo las mismas penurias, dolores, impotencia ante todo lo que vivimos - Hay iguales derechos - Los hombres tienen más oportunidades - La mujer en Venezuela es apreciada. La madre, la abuela, la hermana es querida. La familia es matriarcal - En teoría existen los mismos deberes y derechos, mas no son aplicados a la práctica - Además de lo evidentemente sexual, las diferencias en los puestos de trabajo, las responsabilidades e incluso, las discriminaciones, n las sufre el hombre - impera el dominio del hombre sobre la mujer - No hay igualdad.

What are the reasons for these difficulties considered? And how much of this difficulty is considered due today to the choices of the political decision-makers of one's own country? Can we still say that the situation has improved compared to the past, taking for example a medium-long term of ten years? And is it possible for women, finally, to make their voices heard in public life, meaning this not only as participation in political activities, but also in the mass media and social networks? This is the theme that is addressed in the following chapter.

CHAPTER II
LAW, POLITICS AND PUBLIC LIFE

1. The judgment on the role of the law in gender equality

How to recover this difference then and what is the judgment on the policies adopted by the respective governments for women?

Laws are crucial to get out of the context of the accidents of history. They make them less changeable, less capricious, less sporadic and fragile. But by themselves they are not enough to solidly incardinate rights in the present and even less in the future. The Convention for the elimination of all forms of discrimination against women (CEDAW) launched by the General Assembly of the United Nations on 18 December 1979, entered into force on September 3rd, 1981, and the Council of Europe Convention on preventing and combating violence against women and domestic violence - the so-called Istanbul Convention - opened for signature on May 11th, 2011, focused on the need of more equality between woman and man. In terms of legal study, the need to investigate the quality of the ratification, application and implementation processes - within the national legal system - of the prescriptive and programmatic provisions contained in the framework of conventional sources, allows the carrying out of a comparative analysis of the legal experiences internal more susceptible to comparison (due to the recurrence of appreciable profiles of homogeneity and resonance). But the construction of the domestic and the international legal warps is innervated by the concomitant stratification of cultural and social factors capable of supporting the dynamics of affirmation, where the formal structuring of the normative protections represents the outcome of complex constructive paths, thematized in a sociological and legal key, as well as cultural.

The analysis of the social and normative matrices of the legal system for the protection of women from exposure to the phenomena of gender inequality begins from the analysis, training models respectful of gender equality aimed at girls and school children. The Recommendation no. 33 of 2015 of the CEDAW committee affirms, in the legal field, "stereotypes distort perception and lead to decisions based on preconceived beliefs and myths rather than on relevant facts. Judges often adopt rigid standards regarding what they consider an appropriate behaviour for women and penalize those who do not conform to these stereotypes. The use of stereotypes affects the credibility of women's voices, their arguments and their statements as offended persons or witnesses. These stereotypes can also lead judges to incorrect interpretations or applications of the law ".

Starting from these assumptions, from the IWT investigation it emerges that on average only 35.7 percent of respondents believe that policies on women in their country are right. They are correct for 6 percent of respondents in Iran, 8.4 percent for Iraq, 8.5 percent for Poland, 10.3 percent for Mexicans, 11.8 percent of Peruvians and 13.3 percent of Haiti. On the other hand, government policies on women are valid for 51.7 percent of the interviewees in Cuba, and for the 46.2 percent in Tunisia. The remaining countries move around the overall average: India 24.7 percent; Italy, 31 percent; Ivory Coast, 31.2 percent, Pakistan 36.9 percent; United States 32.7 percent; Venezuela, 27.3 percent.

Differently, the national policies on women, on average in the countries considered, are clearly wrong for 17.8 percent of the interviewees. Almost one in two respondents in Poland – exactly 45.5 percent -, Iran - 43 percent - and Iraq - 40.7 percent - are convinced of it. Believe it about two out of ten respondents in Tunisia (25.8 percent), while in the other countries the percentages drop considerably: Cuba, 15.8 percent; Haiti 9.2 percent; India 5.3 percent; Italy, 9.7 percent; Ivory Coast, 3.5 percent; Mexico, 11.3 percent; Pakistan 8.1 percent; Peru 15.7 percent; United States, 6.5 percent; Venezuela 9.8 percent.

Moreover, the judgment changes when it is asked whether policies for women are sufficient: on average in the fourteen countries considered, almost 37 percent - exactly 36.7 percent - believe that these policies are insufficient or not enough. Even this is the opinion of 65.5 percent of respondents in Mexico, 59.4 percent in Peru, 52.3 percent in the United States of America, 50.8 percent in Haiti, 49.2 percent in Venezuela, 47.4 percent in India and 43.3 percent in the Ivory Coast. National policies and government choices in favour of women are also insufficient for 21.7 percent of the interviewees in Cuba; 18 percent of respondents in Iran and 8.4 percent in Iraq. They are also insufficient for the 37.5 percent in Italy, according to 28.3 percent in Pakistan, 23.3 percent in Poland and 11.4 percent in Tunisia.

It is also interesting to consider that, even if minimal, there is a percentage of respondents who believe that the policies for women implemented by the governments of their respective countries do not exist at all. On average among all the countries considered, it is the opinion of the 6.6 percent of respondents, but the percentage is over two out of ten respondents in Iraq (25.1 percent) and Iran (21 percent). The following are the specific percentages for each country, among which Cuba certainly hits with 0 percent: Haiti, 10 percent; India, 2.6 percent; Italy, 7.4 percent; Ivory Coast, 2.1 percent; Mexico, 2.6 percent; Pakistan, 6.6 percent; Peru, 1.7 percent; Poland, 5.7 percent; Tunisia, 2.3 percent; United States, 1.3 percent and Venezuela 4.5 percent.

In short, in the countries considered on average over six out of ten respondents - exactly 61.1 percent - express a negative opinion on the policies for women adopted by their respective governments, believing that they do not exist, are wrong or in any case insufficient. Even 82 percent of respondents in Iran are convinced of this; in Mexico, 79.4 percent; in Peru, 76.8 percent; in Poland 74.5 percent; in Iraq, 74.2 percent; in Haiti, 70 percent. The percentages for the remaining countries are as follows: Cuba, 37.5 percent; India, 55.3 percent; Italy, 54.6 percent; Ivory Coast, 48.9 percent; Pakistan, 43 percent; Tunisia, 39.5 percent; United States of America, 60.1 percent; finally, Venezuela, 63.5 percent.

Below, Figure 7, shows the responses for each country referring to policies to protect women adopted by the respective governments considered non-existent, wrong or insufficient:

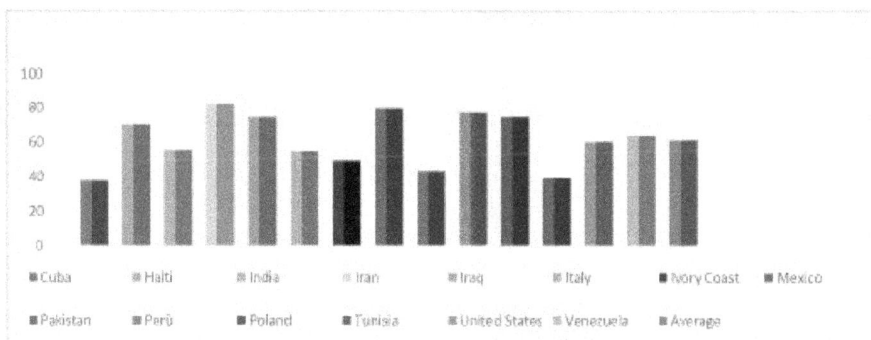

Figure 7. Government's policies do not exist, are wrong or insufficient.
Source: IWT Research

On the other hand, the data relating to those who merely answer "I don't know" to the question of how they consider the policies in favour of women implemented by their respective governments cannot be ignored. On average, they are almost 15 percent (14.9) with very different percentages for each country, as shown below: Cuba, 10.8 percent; Haiti, 16.7 percent; India and Iran, 20 percent; Iraq, 17.4 percent; Italy, 14.4 percent; Ivory Coast, 19.9 percent; Mexico, 10.3 percent; Pakistan, 20.2 percent; Peru, 11.4 percent; Poland, 17 percent; Tunisia, 14.4 percent; United States of America, 7.2 percent; Venezuela, 9.1 percent.

Below, therefore, a comparison of the data country by country, also complete with the different percentages to the answers indicated above:

Figure 8. According to you, the policies of your country about women are - Source: IWT Research

Cuba

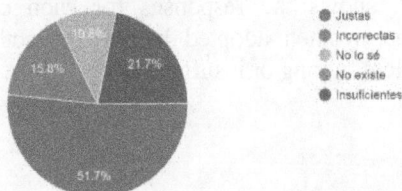

7) En general, según tu, las políticas de tu país sobre la mujer son:
120 responses

- Justas
- Incorrectas
- No lo sé
- No existe
- Insuficientes

Haiti

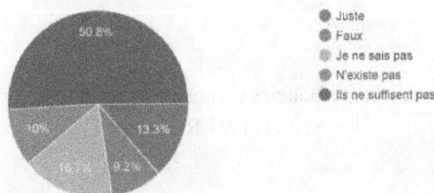

7) De manière générale, selon vous, les politiques de votre pays concernant les femmes sont:
120 responses

- Juste
- Faux
- Je ne sais pas
- N'existe pas
- Ils ne suffisent pas

India

7) Generally speaking, according to you, the policies of your country about women are:
190 responses

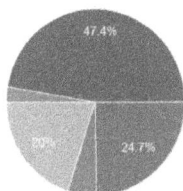

- Fair
- Wrong
- I don't know
- Do not exist
- Not enough

47.4%
24.7%
20%

Iran

7) Generally speaking, according to you, the policies of your country about women are: به طور کلی ،
یطلق گفته شما ، سیاست های کشور شما در مورد زنان عبارتند از
100 responses

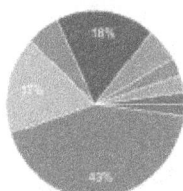

- Fair - نمایشگاه
- Wrong - اشتباه
- I don't know - من نمی دانم
- Do not exist وجود ندارد
- Not enough - کافی نیست
- Wrong
- I don't know
- Not enough
- Do not exist

18%
43%

Iraq

7) Generally speaking, according to you, the policies of your country about women are: 7) بشكل عام
بحسب رأيك / أن كيف تجد سياسة بلدك تجاه المرأة؟
155 responses

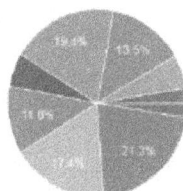

- Fair عادلة
- Wrong خاطئة
- I don't knowo لا اعرف
- Do not exist لا وجود لها
- Not enough لا شيء
- Wrongo خاطئة
- Do not existo لا وجود لها
- Fairo عادلة
- Not enougho لا شيء

19.4%
13.5%
11.0%
17.4%
21.3%

Italy

7) Generally speaking, according to you, the policies of your country about women are:
216 responses

- Fair
- Wrong
- I don't know
- Do not exist
- Not enough

Ivory Coast

7) De manière générale, selon vous, les politiques de votre pays concernant les femmes sont:
141 responses

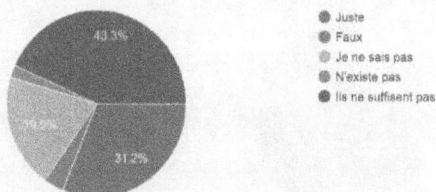

- Juste
- Faux
- Je ne sais pas
- N'existe pas
- Ils ne suffisent pas

Mexico

7) En general, según tu, las políticas de tu país sobre la mujer son:
388 responses

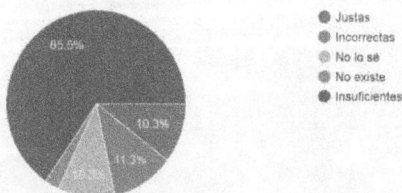

- Justas
- Incorrectas
- No lo sé
- No existe
- Insuficientes

Pakistan

7) Generally speaking, according to you, the policies of your country about women are:
198 responses

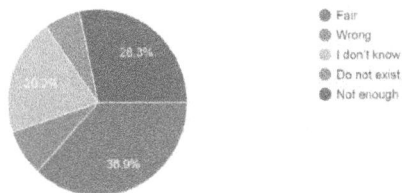

- Fair
- Wrong
- I don't know
- Do not exist
- Not enough

Peru

7) En general, según tu, las políticas de tu país sobre la mujer son:
229 responses

- Justas
- Incorrectas
- No lo sé
- No existe
- Insuficientes

Poland

7) Generally speaking, according to you, the policies of your country about women are:
176 responses

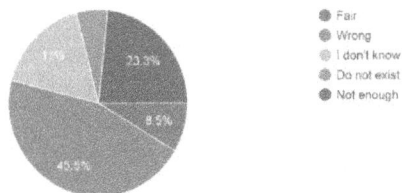

- Fair
- Wrong
- I don't know
- Do not exist
- Not enough

Tunisia

7) De manière générale, selon vous, les politiques de votre pays concernant les femmes sont: 7)
بشكل عام، بحسب رأيك / كِ كيف تجد سياسة بلدك تجاه المرأة؟
132 responses

- Juste عادلة
- Faux خاطئة
- Je ne sais pas لا أعرف
- N'existe pas لا وجود لها
- Ils ne suffisent pas لا شيء

14.2% · 11.4% · 46.2% · 25.8%

United States

7) Generally speaking, according to you, the policies of your country about women are:
153 responses

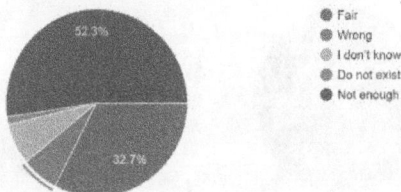

- Fair
- Wrong
- I don't know
- Do not exist
- Not enough

52.3% · 32.7%

Venezuela

7) En general, según tu, las políticas de tu país sobre la mujer son:
132 responses

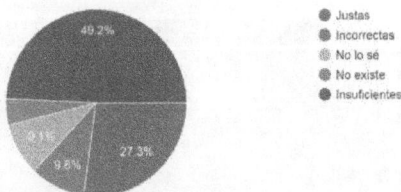

- Justas
- Incorrectas
- No lo sé
- No existe
- Insuficientes

49.2% · 27.3% · 9.8% · 9.1%

2. *Socio-juridical changes in women's policies*

The IWT project sought to understand also whether in the opinion of the interviewees, the conditions of women in their own country have changed - and if so, how much - compared to ten years earlier.

To allow for differentiating the answers, a scale from 1 to 5 has been indicated, corresponding to the judgment 1 = not at all and 5 = a lot, passing by 2 = a little, 3 = enough 4 = more than enough.

As can be seen from the graphs below, most of the answers are concentrated between enough and a lot, in the typical pyramid trend, on average with a relative majority for answer 3, i.e., "enough". In Cuba and Venezuela only, the "much" rating exceeds 30 percent of preferences - 32.5 and 32.6 percent respectively - and is higher than all the others. On the contrary, only in one country, Tunisia, is there a relative percentage preference, equal to 28.8 percent, referring to answer 1, i.e., "not at all", higher than the other options.

Moreover, if we cumulatively analyse the answer options from 3 to 5 - and therefore "enough", "more than enough", "a lot" -, we see that on average in all countries there is a very large majority of respondents who believes that in their own country the status of women has in any case changed for the better today than ten years ago: this is - on average, *repetita iuvant*, in the fourteen countries considered by the research - almost four interviewees out of five, exactly 77.1 percent. Slightly above the average is the percentage of Cuban respondents, 79.2 percent and close to the same average is that of respondents in Iraq (71 percent). On the other hand, there are eight of the countries considered in which more than four out of five of those who respond are convinced that in the last ten years the conditions of women have changed for the better. It is Venezuela, with 90.2 percent, Ivory Coast, for 87.2 percent; Peru, 86.9 percent; India, 86.3 percent; 84.2 percent of respondents in Mexico; Poland, for 82.4 percent; Italy, with 81 percent of respondents and Pakistan, with 80.8 percent.

The only countries where the majority is more contained are Iran, with 68 percent; the United States for 67.3 percent and Haiti and Tunisia, where in any case almost six out of ten respondents are convinced, respectively 59.1 and 56.8 percent. Below are the analytical trends for each of the fourteen countries considered with reference to the responses on changes in the conditions of women in their respective countries over the last ten years.

Figure 9. Changes in women's conditions in the last 10 years - Source: IWT Research

Cuba

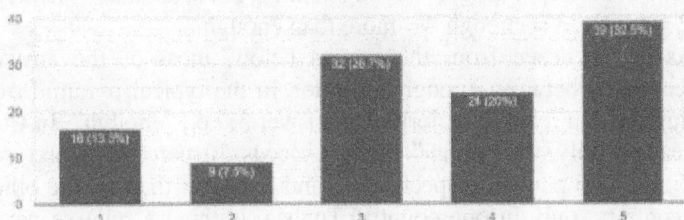

Haiti

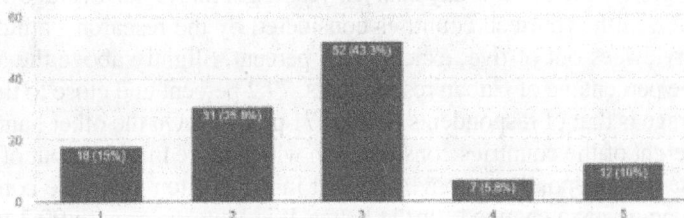

India

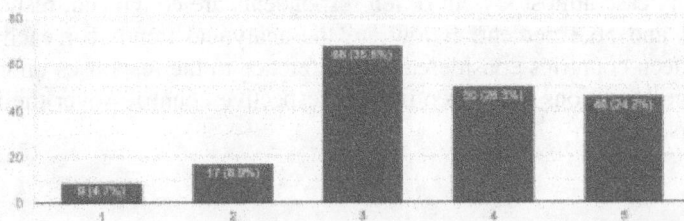

Iran

8) From 1=nothing to 5=a lot, according to you, compared to 10 years ago, women's conditions in your country have changed, not only within the worforce... در کشور شما تغییر کرده است ، نه تنها در چار چوب نگر انی؟
100 responses

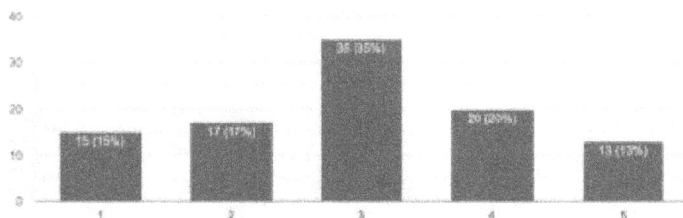

Iraq

8) From 1=nothing to 5=a lot, according to you, compared to 10 years ago, women's conditions in your country have changed, not only within the worforce?... تغیرت اوضاع المرأة في بلدك، ليس فقط داخل القوى العاملة؟
155 responses

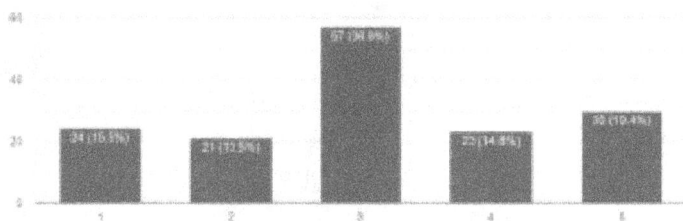

Italy

8) From 1=nothing to 5=a lot, according to you, compared to 10 years ago, women's conditions in your country have changed, not only within the worforce?
216 responses

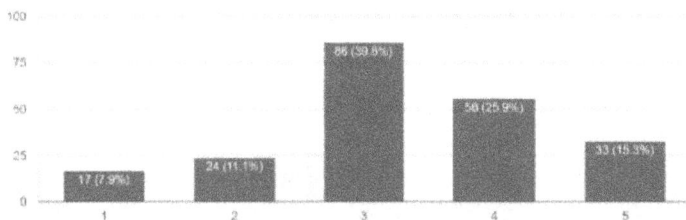

Ivory Coast

8) De 1 = rien à 5 = beaucoup, selon vous, par rapport à il y a 10 ans, les conditions des femmes dans votre pays ont changé, pas seulement au sein de la main-d'œuvre?
141 responses

Mexico

8) Considerando que 1 = nada a 5 = mucho, en comparación con hace 10 años, ¿consideras que las condiciones de las mujeres en tu país han cambiado, no solo dentro de la fuerza laboral?
108 responses

Pakistan

8) From 1=nothing to 5=a lot, according to you, compared to 10 years ago, women's conditions in your country have changed, not only within the worforce?
198 responses

Peru

8) Considerando que 1 = nada a 5 = mucho, en comparación con hace 10 años, ¿consideras que las condiciones de las mujeres en tu país han cambiado, no solo dentro de la fuerza laboral?
229 respuestas

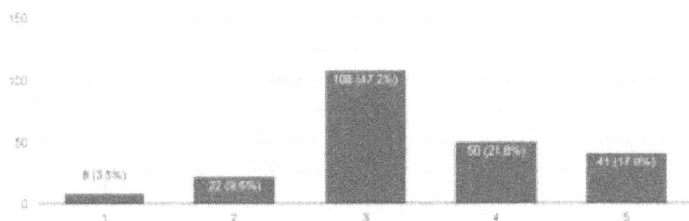

Poland

8) From 1=nothing to 5=a lot, according to you, compared to 10 years ago, women's conditions in your country have changed, not only within the worforce?
176 responses

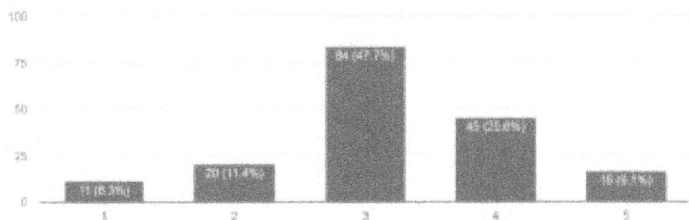

Tunisia

8) De 1 = rien à 5 = beaucoup, selon vous, par rapport à il y a 10 ans, les conditions des femmes dans votre pays ont changé, pas seulement au sein de la ... تغيرت أوضاع المرأة في بلدك- ليس فقط داخل القوى العاملة؟
132 responses

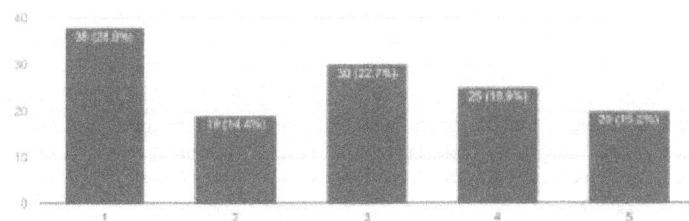

United States

8) From 1=nothing to 5=a lot, according to you, compared to 10 years ago, women's conditions in your country have changed, not only within the worforce?
158 responses

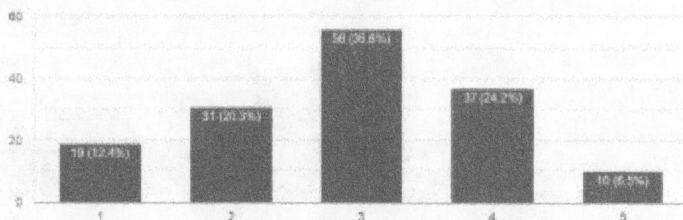

Venezuela

8) Considerando que 1 = nada a 5 = mucho, en comparación con hace 10 años, ¿consideras que las condiciones de las mujeres en tu país han cambiado, no solo dentro de la fuerza laboral?
132 responses

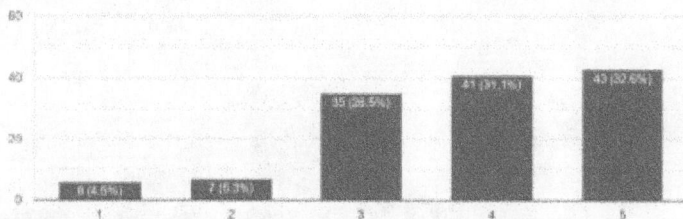

Even in this case, when asked to justify own answer, the expressed considerations are various and appear relevant. Here are some of them, country by country.

Reasons why it is/is not changed woman's conditions in own country respect 10 years ago

CUBA Desigualdad salarial - Es un país gobernado por hombres - Hemos evolucionado social, racional y políticamente - Ha cambiado bastante la situación pero a peor - Se ha avanzado mucho en materia de igualdad sobre la cuestión de la maternidad y la ayuda a la mujer trabajadora. Aunque aún hay cosas que mejorar. Hay más trabajo para los hombres que para las mujeres - Pocas políticas en sectores femeninos pobres - Aunque las leyes puedan establecer lo contrario, la realidad es que no tenemos las mismas oportunidades - Considero que 10 años atrás y ahora se mantiene los mismos derecho. Igualmente no hay cambios ni peor ni mejor. Justo - Con El Triunfo de la Revolución se mejoro la situacion de la mujer - Porque Cuba ampara a la mujer - Porque El sistema es El mismos hace 62 anos - No se ha conseguido un cambio total. Se ha avanzado, pero queda mucho camino - Sí, en estos años la Mujer ha jugado un rol protagónico en la sociedad, no solo como fuerza laboral sino que estamos en todos los frentes de batallas, en todas las organizaciones de masas como son, FMC, CDR, CTC, UJC, PCC, teniendo una destacada y activa participación, demostrando cada día de nuestra capacidad - Porque considero que antes era diferente había más y se vivía con menos - No hay ningun avance en el tiempo - Hace 10 años teníamos los mismos derechos y posibilidades que ahora - Sí la situación de la mujer en comparación de hace 10 años ha cambiado mucho, se le ha dado más participación a la mujer en la vida social , política y Laboral, además contamoscon una organización de masas fundada por Vilma Espín, que defiende los intereses, no solo de la mujer trabajadora, sino también de la ama de casa que es la FMC - En sentido general los avances son notables.

HAITI Les conditions ne changent jamais - Petite amélioration du cote des femmes a plus intégrer dans la société timidement - En fait, avec l'existence du ministère des conditions féminines, le ministère des affaires sociales et les médias qui en parlent de plus en plus, beaucoup de femmes commencent a réclamer leur droit d'être traitées avec plus de dignité. On prend plus au sérieux les abus faits aux femmes haïtiennes. Mais il reste encore beaucoup à faire pour arriver à un vraiment changement de mentalité à l'égard des femmes haïtiennes. Les femmes comprennent mieux maintenant qu'elles peuvent être médecins, avocats et pas seulement infirmières et monitrices à l'école - Je peux dire que ça a évolué un peu, qu' on retrouve beaucoup plus de femmes qui s'engage, qui essaie de remettre en question le patriarcat surtout avec les organisations féministes qui s'engagent à encadrer les femmes et les filles - Au sein de la main d'œuvre on dirait que les conditions ont changé. Mais dans les autres catégories on dirait que non. Dans les familles par exemple, pour la plupart les femmes demeurent femmes au foyer, malgré leurs connaissances et compétences - Les femmes ont plus de pouvoirs pour faire entendre leurs voix - Eh bien 10 ans de cela, des rares femmes avaient cette impacte en Haïti... maintenant elles sont beaucoup plus présente que ce soit politiquement et socialement. J'avoue aussi qu'il reste beaucoup à faire - La situation n'a pas changé - Beaucoup plus de femme dans les universités dans des bureaux occupent des places importante c'est tout un début - Les agressions, les injustices battent leur plein comme avant - Bon ça fait tantôt 5 ans si je m'abuse pas qu'un gouvernement a exigé un quota de 30% minimum de femmes aux sein des institutions étatiques que ce soit dans les conseils d'administrations des mairies, les cabinets ministériels et j'en passe. Puis ces dernières années les femmes se construisent, se forment beaucoup plus aussi, on retrouve plus de femmes dans les parti politiques, elles luttent aussi dans le secteur des droits humains...- On parle aujourd'hui d'un quota d'au moins 30 pour cent de participation des femmes à la vie politique, elles s'affichent beaucoup plus qu'avant. No.

IRAN - for work it is better, even in the family - the condition has changed but not so much - we can wear coloured clothes - there is more freedom - it has changed a bit on finding work and education - women have demonstrated her skills and left the house, becoming an active woman in society but it is not enough - before women did not participate in social activities as a saleswoman, a clerk, a secretary and ... but now they participate more (in my opinion 60%) - it has not changed - we see a little more freedom - there is no equality between women and men and only of a traditional position in the family which, having so many limits, entered society and they have participated in social activities and also work outside the - home - in my country, the situation of women has changed a lot since before. Before they had no social rights and ... but now they have entered society - the more open thoughts of Hijab than 10 years ago - still many religious laws do not allow women to be present freely in many places - expansion of social networks - job opportunities are better - not much has changed but only women have become self-sufficient - women they have been able to change the situation in their favour - everything has worsened but not improved but only we women have to defend ourselves - the social conditions of women have improved a lot - no change is seen in fact every day worse than the day before - in my opinion mandatory Hijab is a torture - it has not changed - because of Islam, women have been humiliated - only the stiffness to wear a little has decreased - it has not progressed, indeed it has worsened compared to before - the limits for the choice, for social activities, the wrong beliefs for compulsory Hijab for example wearing Chador (veil used by Iranian women) or dark clothes and ... - in recent years the situation has improved a lot - we still follow the laws from 1400 years ago - the conditions of women have worsened but not improved - in the sense of women's awareness of their rights, women feel they are important and stronger and have self-confidence - compared to 10 years ago the limits have decreased, like going in bike, although these arguments are not yet accepted by everyone.

IRAQ – Because we did not see any significant and radical change in society I had no knowledge of the law or the constitution No Development - There is no law that does justice to a woman Society has not done justice to the woman, and her reality has not changed, and they view her as a tool nothing has changed, where it occupies a place in society and enjoys freedom but not restricted Opinion because it got worse - The new generations and being open to other cultures improved relatively the security situations for women's safety. 10 years ago women been killed for not covering their hair! Thank God it's not happening now! I mean they still kill her for objecting injustice and corruption and then they attack her style of life! - There have been developments and advancements in women's work and their entry into the world of politics on the same footing as men I do not know. The woman had a great place and rights

Yes, almost a change Perhaps for the worse in many aspects of life - Now it is the woman who is trying to prove her existence in society Women entered the military and parliament, and this was not the case before Previously, despite the situation of the country and wars, as well as the lack of progress of society in terms of technology, except if there was respect for women and the woman was respected and there was no harassment. - True, they promise freedom for the cliché, but very few.

ITALY – Cultural evolution - Something is moving -Legislative evolution - Cultural and social evolution - Fortunately, patriarchal families no longer exist, to date, in most cases, the will of a woman is also taken into consideration in the family - Global mindset change – Discrimination - Gender equality - Generally yes, the conditions of the woman have improved - Gender equality is always more central and important in the society - Nobody wants to grant true equality - Women's condition have changed it has improved - It has changed more in the last 50 years - The new women generation have more knowledge about their role - There is more consideration for women - I don't see any changes - The woman is freer as regards her rights, her life, her work - Because Italy is a male-dominated people - Not a true change - Several; for example: generally - peaking, a higher sensitivity to discrimination issues; laws for 'pink quotas'; laws against revenge porn - Something is being done - Women are still discriminated on the job especially if they have a family - Because women are committed to doing many things despite men opposing them, starting with their husbands - In my opinion the whole world is changing and Italy is part of it - There are no female development plans - They got worse, thanks also to Covid - In Italy there is talk of equal opportunities, equal pay, but the situations do not change, men are always favoured in top positions, in politics and for the same job, women receive a lower wage of at least 20% - In Italy it is very advanced in terms of respect for women - Parity was not achieved - I was not an adult 10 years ago but now I don't have more problems than a boy - There have been more development in LGBT rights than in woman condition in general! - Because there Is no difference

IVORY COAST - Les femmes peuvent occuper certaines postes de travail alors que avant c'était impossible - Sauf dans les village et encore certaine tradition , toute les femmes épouse celui qu'elle veut et peut faire tout ce qu'elle aspire devenir - Les femmes sont de plus en plus scolarisées et accèdent des études supérieures - Quelques prises de décisions en faveur des femmes mais insuffisantes et non encore totalement effectives - Les femmes étaient marginalisées - Avant, la femme n'avait même pas accès à certains domaines d'activités, maintenant si - la condition de la femme en civ est un gros problème majeur... juste pour des raisons de se voir lutter un travail ou un place avec femme.... car nous les hommes voyons en les femmes une personne pour le ménage sans intérêt pour la société et sa ma fait mal de voir ça - Il est toujours difficile pour la plupart des hommes d'accepter d'être dirigé par une femme - Les femmes sont en marge de la société - Maintenant on respecte le droit des Femmes - Les femmes sont autorisés à d'autres travaux maintenant - Aujourd'hui dans mon pays, les femmes peuvent occuper de grands postes dans les entreprises, ce qui n'était pas le cas il y 10 ans - Les femmes occupent les mêmes postes que les hommes - Vu mon âge je sais pas trop ce qui se passait avant -Les femmes ont l'opportunité de travailler partout et d'être où les hommes sont - Les femmes dépriment mieux mais sont toujours sujettes à des violences physiques, morales et psychologiques - La place de la femme a changé mais il reste beaucoup à faire - Pas de véritable changement.

MEXICO - Por qué nos falta mucho por recorrer - Ahora las mujeres desempeñan cargos que antes eran impensables pero aún el trato no es igual al de un hombre - Por lo menos se nos permite participar un poco más en algunos sectores - Hoy en día tienen más voz en el país a diferencia de hace 10 años pero siguen faltando mas oportunidades para ellas - Hay más mujeres en el ámbito laboral y se han tenido que hacer adaptaciones en las estructuras familiares y de las empresas - Porque más mujeres son asesinadas actualmente que hace 10 años -Se ha mejorado, pero aún falta mucho más para que una mujer pueda sentirse segura - Ha habido algunos ajustes pero no suficientes - Es un cambio que apenas avanza, pero hace falta mucho todavía - Todavía falta mucho camino por recorrer para alcanzar la igualdad - Gracias a las redes sociales es más fácil para ellas en ser escuchadas - Antes habia mucho mas machismo - Hay leyes que protegen a la mujer en caso de abuso pero el machismo continúa siendo extremadamente fuerte y normalizado - Si han cambiado, pero no estoy segura de que sea para bien. Hemos adquirido derechos, pero que nos traen más obligaciones a nivel desproporcionado. Además la violencia es cada vez más agresiva y simbólica. No les basta con la violacion o asesinato, violentan los cadáveres y los desaparecen - Sigue siendo insuficiente la legislación.

PAKISTAN-- It's as same as 10 years ago not much is changed. Women's weren't much more than a slave and now due to education some people are recognising the worth of a women/girl -More pro women legislation, more educated and working women - Yes as compared to the last 10 years ,women in our country are more independent and free to pursue their lives on their own terms - There have been huge changes for women in terms of employment in the past decades, with women moving into paid employment - Yes it has been changed a lot - Condition of women is changed a lot because men are more free to do anything now - Over right are same - Both women and men get equal job opportunities - Man and women have equal status - Last few month u can see domestic violence incidents increased in our country - Rape and harassment cases are increasing - Before People are ignorant they cannot give importance to women now a days people are educated and gave the importance to women - Woman's are educated and independent - Due to social media, today's woman is very much aware about to her rights.

PERU - Han tomado mas fuerza - Si se a visto un cambio tanto en el aspecto laboral y domestico, pero aun sabemos que existe la discriminacion en nuestro pais - Según mi criterio, veo qué hay más oportunidad laboral para mujeres que para hombres últimamente - Poco a poco se nota el cambio - Bueno si en lo tema laboral - Porque hay mayor presencia de la mujer en el mundo laboral profesional ,hay defensorías, ministerios que apoyan a la mujer - A mejorado, pero aún persiste la desigualdad - Sí tienen más oportunidades en todos los campos - Antes el Perú es un país machista donde la mujer tenía poca - participación social - Ahora intentan realizar campañas y sanciones contra los agresores de mujeres, desde el acoso sexual callejero, violencia contra la mujer y discriminación - Porque antes había machismo y ahora cambiaron las cosas - Hay más presencia en la vida pública - Ha más oportunidad de trabajo y estudios - Si antes no había muchos trabajos para mujeres - Considero que ha cambiado de forma regular en el ámbito de conocer sus derechos. Hace 10 años no se tenia acceso de manera fácil al Internet o redes sociales hoy en día esto ha favorecido a que las mujeres puedan expresar sus derechos y lo q piensan - Pues a comparación de antes si ha cambiado un montón - Ahora sí hay discriminación se denuncia - Existe igualdad de genero - Somos más unidas, todas contra el machismo - Si bien es cierto que tenemos mas leyes para "protegernos" aun no tenemos instituciones que se den a la tarea de velar porque se cumplan - No a cambiado mucho - No hay leyes que protejan verdaderamente a la mujer, tampoco ha habido un cambio social verdaderamente fuerte que ayude a evitar el maltrato o discriminación a la mujer - Ha cambiado, pero tiene que trabajarse mas - Mas antes creo q las mujeres no eran maltratadas tanto - No ha cambiado - En los últimos 10 años la mujer a logrado acceder a importantes puestos de trabajo - las mujeres hoy en dia son fuerte e independiente.

POLAND - I think some things have changed. Women are not afraid to do jobs that were once intended only for men - It change on the wrong direction, it's much harder for women's rights now because catholic church and right wing political parti are much stronger. Last year women lost their abortion right, despite the fact that even earlier those rights were very limited -I can't see any big changes - A few years ago, women had a harder time because they were supposed to look after the children and the home. now a woman can be successful without a man - because of abortion law - tightening of the abortion law, abortion due to prenatal defects is illegal. The government also pulled back funding for fertility treatments - Woman still must stand together and fight for their rights! - I think that women's conditions surely changed for better but not that much - 10 years ago woman had less possibility to become successful than now - I think now woman are braver than they were 10 years ago, that why something had change - A woman is treated a little better, but she still doesn't have all the rights and possibilities to decide for herself - Women's salaries are lower than men's in the same positions in almost all jobs - Poland emerged from communism and the political situation has changed - 20 years ago, women were not forced to give birth to sick children - I think 10 years ago was the same situation likes now - There is equality.

Tunisia - Rien n'a changé - Parce que les femmes d'aujourd'hui s'efforcent de faire leurs preuves par elles-mêmes - La femme est un peu libérée - Notre société n'accepte pas les femmes - Des femmes meurent encore dans des camions de la mort sur le chemin du travail, des femmes sont toujours violentes et silencieuses par peur, etc. - Rien n'a changé car les femmes ont une place dans la vie de base et professionnelle - Après la révolution la femme tunisienne elle a gagné la libération d'être présente à la vie politique - Changer pour le pire. Les femmes sont absentes aux postes de direction. Il y a peu de femmes au parlement. Si une femme est harcelée ou même violée, elle est blâmée et victime de brimades. En plus des violences morales et physiques dans la rue - Il n'y a pas eu d'avancée notable - Même les professions qui étaient considérées comme masculines sont maintenant exercées par des femmes - Les nouvelles générations peuvent avoir un avenir meilleur que celui que nous avions dans le passé - Je suis devenu plus interactif dans la vie à l'intérieur et à l'extérieur de la vie conjugale - Parce que le système reste presque le même - Après la révolution, moins de sécurité et moins de liberté pour les femmes - Les femmes tunisiennes sont devenues une issue profitable pour les politiciens menteurs avec de fausses promesses - La situation des femmes a changé, mais il y a des lacunes - Rien n'est changé - je veux garder ma réponse - Harcèlement fréquent, viol, enlèvement, violence physique et sexuelle.

United States - There has been improvement, but that is still a long, long way to go - No laws to help women - There are a lot of single mothers who also have to work but are able to do all they can. There are more women in engineering, jobs that weren't considered women's jobs before - More equal rights legislation - Progress was made but has now been set back due to other priorities such as COVID and race relations. Women's issues are not a priority now - More attention to discrimination and harassment - I don't notice differences - We have significantly more women in the work force, in politics, and in leadership positions. This also means it is harder for women to balance work and family life because we are discovering women struggle to "have it all." - Women are becoming more and more vocal about wanting power and attention - Very slow changes - I have access to jobs but rising is harder. It's quite a bit of pressure to pay my own bills and still deal with inflation but no salary increases, and I'm one of the fortunate ones - I don't think things have changed much in the last 10 years - There has been more discussion of women being taken advantage of in the workplace - social media has allowed women to have a voice about being taken advantage of, overlooked or treated unfairly - Many more opportunities and equality now - Women can do anything now including being Vice-President of the United States - Laws are very scarce for women - No laws pro women - More laws protecting women - With the Pandemic I believe Father's and employers now understand a little bit more about the struggles of working mother's due to school closures. The brunt is being placed on women and many employers are taking notice and providing support - No government help - Violence, sexual abuse, cultural discrimination still exists - There have been some improvements in the last 10 years. There is more discussion of equal pay - Women becoming a greater presence in the work force and speaking up for their rights.

VENEZUELA - Ha tenido un cambio sinificativo porque puede tener libertad de expresión, de socializarce, de estudiar catreras que antes se creian que eran solo para hombres, de ejercer la política - A la hora de encontrar trabajo en mi pais prefieren contratar hombres - Por que la ley de la mujer nos proteje mas - Profesionalmente más respetadas, y en el hogar más tomadas en cuenta, incluso tomando roles de liderazgo en sectores sociales que antes "dominaban" los hombres - Hay muchos trabajos que una vez Eran solo para el genero mascolino que ahora Son ejecutados por mujeres - Antes las mujeres no trabajaban ahora es necesario - El hombre a emigrado y a abandonado a la familia y le toca a la mujer ser el sostén de la familia - Son pocos los cambios - Las condiciones son las mismas - Las condiciones sociales, económicas y políticas del país han perjudicado toda la sociedad venezolana, en espacial a las mujeres - Si se compara las condiciones hace 10 años, eran 100 por ciento mejores.

3. *Gender equality in decision-making roles*

Connected to the theme of changes in society in favour of women is certainly that of the possibility for them to participate in public life, in political activity, as men do.

On average, in the fourteen countries considered, almost 70 percent - exactly 69.3 - of the interviewees believe it is possible in their own country to participate in public life, like men. Again, the gap goes from countries like Haiti, Ivory Coast, Peru, Tunisia and Venezuela which are above or around 80 percent yes - 84.2 percent, 78.6 percent, 85.8 percent, respectively, 79.5 percent and 77.3 percent - to countries where the "yes" rate is lower, such as Iran (32 percent), Iraq (58.7 percent) and Mexico (56.4 percent). The remaining countries, on the other hand, remain mostly just above or slightly below the average, according to the percentages indicated below: Cuba, 74.2 percent; India, 71.1 percent; Italy, 73.1 percent; Pakistan, 68.2 percent; Poland, 65.3 percent; United States, 68.7 percent.

The diagrams referring to each country are shown below.

Figure 10. Do you think women can participate in public life, especially politics, in your country as men do? Y/N - Source: IWT Research

Cuba

14) ¿Crees que a las mujeres se les permite participar en la vida pública, especialmente en la política, en tu país como lo hacen los hombres?
120 responses

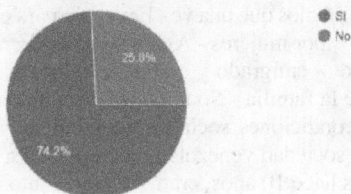

- Si
- No

25.8%

74.2%

Haiti

14) Pensez-vous que les femmes sont autorisées à participer à la vie publique, en particulier à la politique, dans votre pays comme le font les hommes?
120 responses

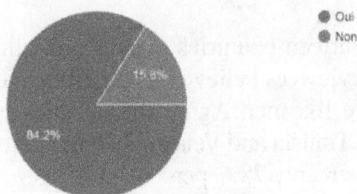

- Oui
- Non

15.8%

84.2%

India

14) Do you think women are allowed to participate in public life, especially politics, in your country as men do?
190 responses

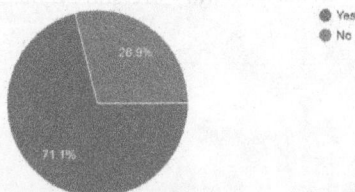

- Yes
- No

28.9%

71.1%

Iran

14) Do you think women are allowed to participate in public life, especially politics, in your country as men do? - آیا فکر می کنید زنان مانند مردان در کشور شما مجاز به شرکت در زندگی عمومی ، به ویژه سیاست هستند؟

100 responses

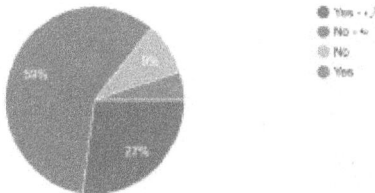

- ● Yes - ار
- ● No - ۔
- ● No
- ● Yes

Iraq

14) Do you think women are allowed to participate in public life, especially politics, in your country as men do? (14) هل تعتقد / تعتقدين، انه يُسمح للمرأة في المشاركة في الحياة العامة، وخاصة السياسية في بلدك كما للرجل؟

155 responses

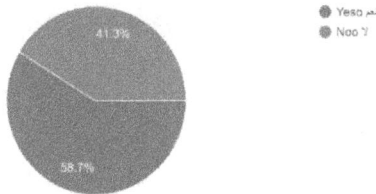

- ● Yesنعم
- ● Noلا

Italy

14) Do you think women are allowed to participate in public life, especially politics, in your country as men do?

216 responses

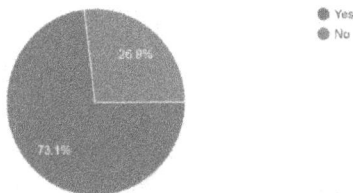

- ● Yes
- ● No

Ivory Coast

14) Pensez-vous que les femmes sont autorisées à participer à la vie publique, en particulier à la politique, dans votre pays comme le font les hommes?
141 responses

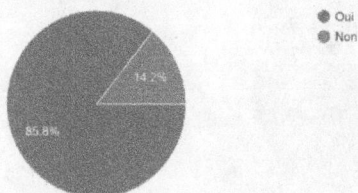

● Oui
● Non

14.2%

85.8%

Mexico

14) ¿Crees que a las mujeres se les permite participar en la vida pública, especialmente en la política, en tu país como lo hacen los hombres?
388 responses

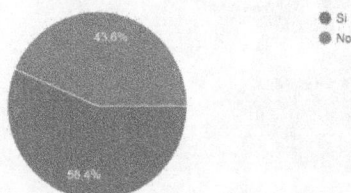

● Si
● No

43.6%

56.4%

Pakistan

14) Do you think women are allowed to participate in public life, especially politics, in your country as men do?
198 responses

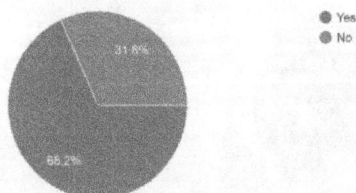

● Yes
● No

31.8%

68.2%

Peru

14) ¿Crees que a las mujeres se les permite participar en la vida pública, especialmente en la politica, en tu pais como lo hacen los hombres?

229 responses

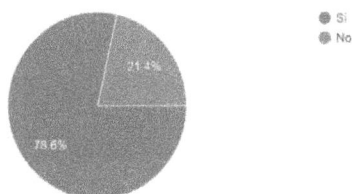

● Si
● No

21.4%

78.6%

Poland

14) Do you think women are allowed to participate in public life, especially politics, in your country as men do?

176 responses

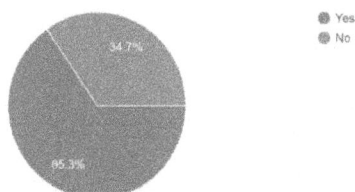

● Yes
● No

34.7%

65.3%

Tunisia

14) Pensez-vous que les femmes sont autorisées à participer à la vie publique, en particulier à la politique, dans votre pays comme le font les hommes? 14) ...؟كما لهم لها في بلدك السياسية وخاصة العامة الحياة في المشاركة

132 responses

● Oui
● Non

20.5%

79.5%

United States

14) Do you think women are allowed to participate in public life, especially politics, in your country as men do?
153 responses

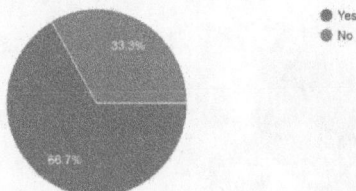

● Yes
● No

33.3%

66.7%

Venezuela

14) ¿Crees que a las mujeres se les permite participar en la vida pública, especialmente en la política, en tu país como lo hacen los hombres?
132 responses

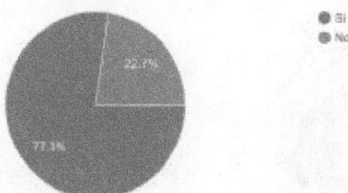

● Si
● No

22.7%

77.3%

Below are some of the considerations expressed by the interviewees, in each of the countries considered, on the possibility for women of being engaged in public life.
Opinions about women's participation in public life, especially politics, in own country

CUBA - Una mayor implicación social puede hacer que la mujer llegue más lejos - Predomina el criterio masculino - En Cuba no se participa en la vida pública - Por supuesto que las mujeres de este país hacen carreras exitosas y cada día mejores q las de muchos hombres. Aunque sean menos las q luego ocupen altos cargos. Participar en la vida pública? Pues también, a veces la imposición de la paridad puede ser aberrante. La educación, la cultura está claro q es la base para el desarrollo de la persona en cualquier ámbito si además posees habilidades que otro no tiene.... todo suma - Insisto: la educación es la llave para erradicar la desigualdad. Que muchas veces esta en nuestra cabeza. Aunque admito que ocasionalmente haya injusticias - No se les permite estar en política - Por los mismos motivos hay un porcentaje mucho menor de mujeres ocupando cargos de poder, en relación a los hombres, a pesar de que hay similares estadísticas de funcionarios del estado en cuanto a género - las mujeres participan igual que los hombres en la política aunque es verdad que de manera general todavía sigue sorprendiendo cuando una mujer está a la cabeza en un partido.

HAITI - Parce que les femmes ont le droit de participer dans tout les élections et postuler pour être un candidat - Les femmes peuvent bien participer à la vie publique et beaucoup y participent déjà - Oui toutes les femmes ont le dois de participer dans la politique même si parfois beaucoup d'entre eux sont abusés - Il est vrai que réussir une carrière en tant que femme en Haïti n'est pas facile. Mais n'empêche que certains y sont arrivés dignement tout comme un homme peut réussir. Côté politique oui et non parce-que les femmes sont si peu dans les postes politiques en Haïti, surtout dans les postes électifs mais il y'a des femmes qui font de la politique tout comme les hommes et qui sont arrivés à des postes très importantes. Pour qu'une femme puisse réussir en Haïti, se former est un atout et il faut aussi avoir quelques contacts - Il y'a depuis tantôt en Haïti une quota de 30% des femmes dans les postes politiques, - que ce soit dans les cabinets ministériels, ou les conseils d'administration des mairies - Des femmes répondant aux critères légaux sont sénateurs, ministres, directrices générales -

INDIA - Women have some hidden restrictions enforced by the society. For example, if a woman married, their priority must be changed from their career to their family according to the so-called society - Career opportunities are almost same for both men and women in our country. Except certain regions where their family status and socio-cultural view are very different - There is a prejudice that women can only grow up to a certain level. There's a glass ceiling above her. Also, a woman raising her voice or being recognized is not accepted by many - Woman are not much safe enough to participate in public life. Also, family support may not be there - Yes, there are women, and they are influential also, but when comparing to men, the number is very less - Although many of the association do support for women empowerment yet the plan is still not completely successful - Women and Men have the same opportunity as far as their families and society constraints are absent. But the constraints have a heavy role on women, creating a barrier around them, which degrades women and automatically upgrading happens to men. It's not only opportunity but also the stereotype which is why women won't get what they want - Women should get a better life.

IRAN - In our society, it is not even allowed to go to the gym, let alone do other things - The more beautiful and single women are, the easier it will be for them to find work, even if they have no skills - Women can have successful careers but have no place in politics unless they are members of high-ranking families - Because women are present in some political positions, albeit in small numbers - Women in my country are not allowed to hold positions such as the presidency and leadership, and even in order to reach the position of minister and lower officials, they must have special conditions of cover and belief - Due to religious reasons and the wrong policy of this society about women - In our country, there are very literate and intelligent women who are very successful in their jobs. But they cannot be active in politics as they should be. In this case, they cannot be active in politics like men - A woman cannot be president, a woman cannot be a judge.

IRAQ – The life of women in Iraq in general is difficult and bitter. But if we want to talk about her professional life, the matter is more difficult and complicated. It is unfair and unfair to say that women are able to have a successful professional life, as is the case for men. The man has absolute freedom to act and Live his life as he desires without fearing the customs and traditions that the society puts in place because he knows that they are by his side. Likewise, women in Iraq are often subjected to harassment by males, which narrows them to job opportunities - Women are not allowed to participate in political opinions because of the saying that she is deficient in reason and religion - Also, it does not allow a woman to participate in politics unless she is associated with a particular party that she supports.

ITALY - We live in a democratic country - Gender equality - The women have an edge - Women can have successful careers, but it doesn't mean they are offered equal opportunities. Also, the government usually is the place with biggest misogynist concentration on square meter, so a woman who got into politics had a much rougher path than a man - Equality of law - The woman still must make a choice between family and work to make a career. If you choose the job, you can have the same opportunities as a man in participation in public life. For professional development - one's own skills are certainly necessary, but the education received, and social opinion also greatly influence. In some sector, like politics sector, is very difficult to be taken seriously for roles of power.

IVORY COAST - Le genre n'est pas un handicap à ces fonctions - Oui bien sûr, on voit aujourd'hui, des femmes PDG, Fondatrices, Présidentes et bien d'autres - En Côte d'ivoire, elles sont encouragées à s'intéresser à la vie publique, à la vie politique parce qu'elles le peuvent et doivent le faire pour le bien du pays. Il a été montré à travers plusieurs exemples qu'elles le font mieux que les hommes lorsqu'elles y sont. Tout ce qui pourrait leur manquer c'est une éducation suffisante pour développer leur compétence - Les femmes sont libres mais jusqu'à un certain niveau ! Pour des responsabilités élevées on pense toujours aux hommes - Car il y a des femmes ministres juge avocate - en vérité la politique dans mon pays n'intéresse pas vraiment les femmes, ce ne sont pas vraiment leurs domaines.

MEXICO - .Las mujeres en mi país si se pueden involucrar en la política pero no se les da el mismo respeto ya que reitero que mi país tiene pensamientos bastante machistas hasta un cierto punto - Se permite todo pero son los hombres los que llevan la batuta - No hay mujeres en la politica superior y cuando si los hombres no quieren votar por ellas - No se les permitía la inclusión a lo político, y si pueden tener acceso a una carrera profesional - No, si se les a visto a mujeres en las política pero solo son reconocidas por su esposos o comentan que son fáciles de manipular como si se estuviera hablando de un niño que necesita cuidados - En la política es diferente ya que en México la mayoría de veces entran por palancas o porque pagan para obtener un lugar en la política.

PAKISTAN - Nowadays mostly women participate in politics - Male dominated society - It all depends on which family you belonged. Means status - Education are very important for themselves and they can stand for themselves and stand in politics - In urban areas women's have equal facilities join politics but people like women's work in education sector - Unwanted expectations from women to be confined to reproductive work.

PERU - Si ahora en la política peruana veo más mujeres en cargos importantes que anteriormente eran solo - Tenemos participación en la política - Las mujeres ya ocupan puestos politicos que antes solo eran para hombres, es importante una buena base como la educacion - Hasta donde puedo ver, la mujer sí tiene participación, no puedo hablar por los lugares que no alcanzo a ver, como pueblos alejados o de menor acceso a la información; sin embargo no descarto que algunas mujeres se sienten inhibidas por formación familiar - A las mujeres les es más difícil ingresar en la política - El estudio es importante para conseguir trabajo .la mujer tiene derecho a participar en la política aunque aún estamos lejos , tanto hombre como mujer tenemos las mismas capacidades para poder tener una profesión exitosa.

POLAND - There are far less women in politics - It's harder for women to achieve something but it's still possible - the key term her is "being allowed to". Indeed, Polish citizens (so far women are citizens) are allowed to become political representatives - Politics continues to be dominated by men - Women are listened to less in the political arena, they do not matter as much, and they are so much more than men - Men and Women have the same chances in Poland.

TUNISIA - Les femmes peuvent participer à la vie publique mais avec beaucoup plus de difficultés que les hommes, souvent le réseau de connaissance influe sur l'employabilité, les compétences compétentes mais ne suffisent pas

- La mentalité de ségrégation entre hommes et femmes existe toujours et il y a toujours une sous-estimation des capacités professionnelles des femmes - Aujourd'hui en Tunisie, les femmes participent à la vie politique, parlementaire et culturelle des hommes. Elle est toujours le plus capable, même qu'il est de mauvaise carrière ou bien qu'il n'y a pas un carrière, et la femme moins capable que lui - La politique sous le Président Bourguiba en faveur de la femme a encouragé les femmes à étudier et à se moderniser donc à être un sujet actif dans la société.

UNITED STATES - Women can have successful careers in the US as men, but they must work much harder for them - It may be more difficult, but it can be done - Family is not anymore, a gap for women - I do believe that women are able to be successful, but I believe that they have to work harder to prove themselves. Women in the US can participate in public life and politics, but again, they must work harder - Unfortunately, in terms of politics, women are not always able to participate at the level that men do - We now have a female vice president! But there is still a great deal of improvement across the board as far as other careers go - Although women can participate in politics, they are usually characterized as emotional and indecisive. Passion is viewed as a weakness - There are countless leaders in both politics and corporations - Many material and cultural obstacles still stand in the way of women such lack of initiatives directed to support to be mothers and also policymakers, offering solutions for wholesome child rearing.

VENEZUELA - hay límites, solo pueden participar en la política las mujeres afectas al régimen - siempre en las carreras para cargos politicos siempre buscan a los caballeros - no hay discriminación de ningún tipo, las mujeres pueden participar políticamente en cualquier contienda incluso se habla de un 50% de participación, simpre y cuando tenga el potencial, el conocimiento y la habilidad para participar libre y voluntariamente - en Venezuela aún existe cierto nivel de machismo en el ejercicio de la política - En el ámbito político, especialmente en Venezuela, la mujer necesita demasiada actitud y está sería la única área en la que me atrevería a decir que hay machismo - Son necesarias políticas de inclusión y políticas de género para terminar con la brecha entre hombres y mujeres y sus privilegios.

A part of being actresses in public life, the main challenge of gender equality is played out in the possibility of being able to find a job, to work like men do, rather than being fully integrated into society. This aspect of the investigation is evidenced in the next chapter.

CHAPTER III
THE ROLE OF THE LAW
FOR WORK AND SUCCESS

1. *The need of equality in work access*

Very different from country to country is the opinion of the interviewees on government policies to favour the work of women and in general on the possibility of finding work in their own country in the same way as men. On average, the respondents who believe that women find employment in the same way as men are just over fifty percent: exactly 51.3.

If in some countries the majority is vastly greater than the average - as in Tunisia, where 78.8 percent are convinced; in the Ivory Coast, where 70.2 percent answered in the affirmative; in Pakistan, with 64.1 percent; in India, where 63.7 percent are convinced of this or in Venezuela where 60.6 percent of the interviewees say - in other countries only a minority of respondents believe it. This is the case of Haiti, where only 25.8 percent of respondents believe that women find jobs like men; Iran, where the percentage is 30 percent; Mexico, with 32.7 per cent and Iraq, where 35.5 per cent has this opinion.

The other countries, on the other hand, are positioned around the general average: Cuba, 57.5 per cent; Italy, 51.9 per cent; Peru, 49.3 percent; Poland 52.3 percent and the United States of America 46.4 percent.

Below, in Figure 11, the country-by-country data:

Figure 11. Do you think women find a job in your country as men do? Y/N

Cuba

11) ¿Crees que las mujeres encuentran trabajo en tu país como lo hacen los hombres?
120 responses

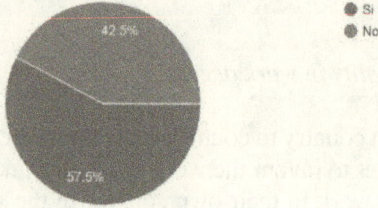

- Sí
- No

42.5%

57.5%

Haiti

11) Pensez-vous que les femmes trouvent un emploi dans votre pays comme les hommes?
120 responses

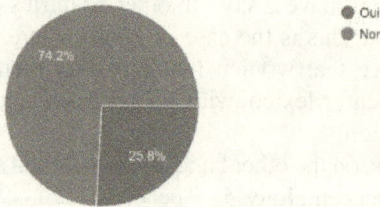

- Oui
- Non

74.2%

25.8%

India

11) Do you think women find a job in your country as men do?
190 responses

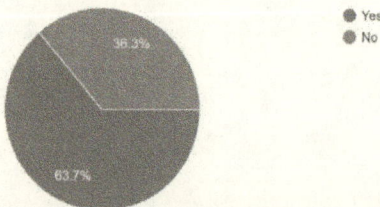

- Yes
- No

36.3%

63.7%

Iran

11) Do you think women find a job in your country as men do? - فكر می كنيد زنان مانند مردان در كشور شما شغلی پيدا می كنند؟
100 responses

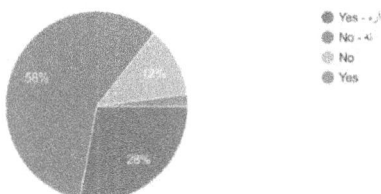

- Yes - ار
- No - نه
- No
- Yes

58% 12% 28%

Iraq

11) Do you think women find a job in your country as men do? (11 هل تعتقد / تعتقدين ان المرأة تجد العمل في بلدك مثل الرجل؟
155 responses

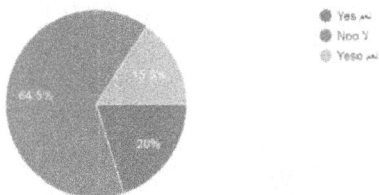

- Yes نعم
- Noo لا
- Yeso نعم

64.5% 15.5% 20%

Italy

11) Do you think women find a job in your country as men do?
216 responses

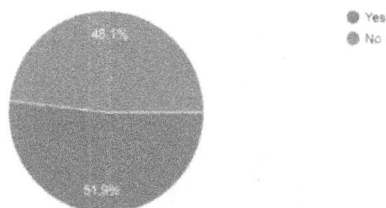

- Yes
- No

48.1% 51.9%

Ivory Coast

11) Pensez-vous que les femmes trouvent un emploi dans votre pays comme les hommes?
141 responses

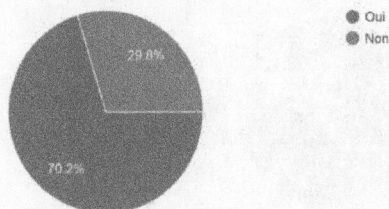

- Oui
- Non

29.8%
70.2%

Mexico

11) ¿Crees que las mujeres encuentran trabajo en tu país como lo hacen los hombres?
388 responses

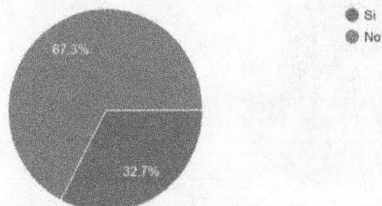

- Si
- No

67.3%
32.7%

Pakistan

11) Do you think women find a job in your country as men do?
198 responses

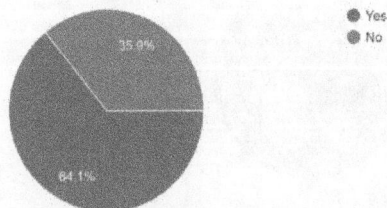

- Yes
- No

35.9%
64.1%

Peru

11) ¿Crees que las mujeres encuentran trabajo en tu pais como lo hacen los hombres?
229 responses

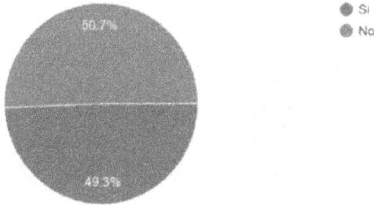

- Si
- No

50.7%

49.3%

Poland

11) Do you think women find a job in your country as men do?
176 responses

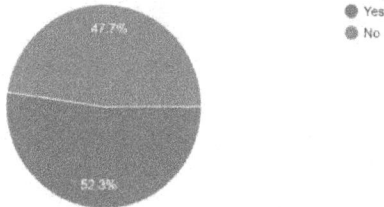

- Yes
- No

47.7%

52.3%

Tunisia

11) Pensez-vous que les femmes trouvent un emploi dans votre pays comme les hommes? 11) هل
تعتقد / تعتقدين ان المرأة تجد العمل في بلدك مثل الرجل؟
132 responses

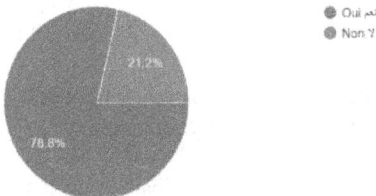

- Oui نعم
- Non لا

21.2%

78.8%

United States

11) Do you think women find a job in your country as men do?
153 responses

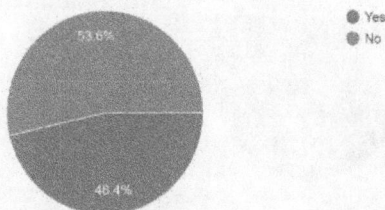

- Yes
- No

53.6%

46.4%

Venezuela

11) ¿Crees que las mujeres encuentran trabajo en tu pais como lo hacen los hombres?
132 responses

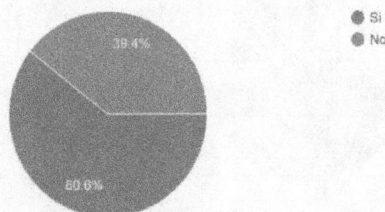

- Si
- No

39.4%

60.6%

When asked to explain the reasons for their answers, interviewees declare that they are convinced that there is a level playing field in the use of technology and the internet, but some differences prevail at work.

Here are some of the given answers, country by country:

Can you explain the reasons about difference between women and men's finding a job in your country?

CUBA - Menos oportunidades de trabajo y formación - Los hombres encuentran trabajo antes, por lo que pueden acceder a las tecnologías antes que una mujer que no es independiente. Los trabajos que puede encontrar una mujer acá en Cuba, son siempre de lo mismo, en las casas, limpiando, cuidando niños y ancianos... Otro tipo de trabajo es menos accesible para ellas - Las mujeres se deben encargar de la familia y del hogar...lo que supone renunciar a competir igual que los hombres en condiciones laborales o acceso a la tecnología - No hay diferencias ni discriminación - La tecnología está más al alcance de los hombres puesto que el mundo laboral en Cuba es de ellos - Muchas tienen Altos cargos en El governo, y Partido comunista - En muchísimos puestos de trabajo no quieren mujeres por el simple hecho que tienen que coger la baja por la maternidad y no quiren que la vida familiar intervenga en el trabajo.

Haiti - Les raisons ne sont autres que la réalité, c'est-à-dire le contexte socio-politique, économique et éducatif. Plus les gens (les femmes) vivent dans la misère, plus elles sont vulnérables et prêtes à satisfaire les désirs de leurs prédateurs - La technologie est maintenant à la portée de tous, surtout avec l'émergence des téléphones intelligents donc les opportunités peuvent être les mêmes - Parfois les femmes sont sujets à des harcèlement sexuels pour trouver un emploi et encore pire pour garder cet emploi, on pense souvent que notre intelligence dépend de notre vagin, c'est surtout une situation les plus abjectes et révoltant - Toutes les femmes ont le droit à l'internet, à un Android, à un ordinateur, mais en ce qui concerne le travail les patrons leurs posent des mauvaises conditions - Oui les femmes ont l'opportunité de travailler comme les hommes mais les conditions ne sont pas les mêmes. On voit en l'homme la compétence le plus souvent mais chez la femme qu'est-ce qu'elle a à offrir après sa beauté et ce qu'il y a entre ces jambes. On vous propose de prendre un verre avant d'avoir le travail - Il y a souvent la politique de la culotte - Jusqu'à présent les femmes ont du mal à trouver un emploi, parfois on les exigent un rapport sexuel en échange - La simple raison est que notre société garde toujours à l'esprit que la place de la femme n'est pas au bureau de quelque chose contre laquelle on a commencé à se battre. Parce que c'est difficile de trouver un travail sans que le patron vous demande de coucher avec lui - Les femmes ont le même accès à l'Internet et aux technologies. Mais dans la réalité du marché de travail les femmes restent minoritaires - Beaucoup de femmes professionnelles qui travaillent dans certaines institutions sortent avec le patron. Beaucoup sont harcelées et sexuellement abusées. Elles n'ont pas de choix parce que c'est le seul moyen de tenir un emploi - En matière de technologie je pense que les hommes et les femmes sont égaux en Haïti qu'avec un téléphone portable, tout le monde peut avoir accès à internet et postuler pour un avis de recrutement posté sur internet. Pour le travail c'est souvent compliqué parce que parfois les patrons font des chantages aux femmes, les harcèlent en échange d'un travail peu importe qu'elles soient compétentes.

India - Today both of them are getting education and they are competitive - If the person is qualified, they will be able to find a job regardless of their gender as far as i know - There is equal possibilities for both - Men are considered superior - Women are denied phones and internet in many houses as it might make her a spoiled girl or a loose character - In here women are supposed to do the household and remain in a safe zone - Yes the internet's and technology are helped the woman's developed - Women doesn't have the time or opportunity to explore technology as men do. They must take care of the household chores even if they're working. There is a discrimination against married and pregnant woman and mothers considering them for a job - Both are given equal chances - Women can also use internet services in our country but women can't get jobs like men - As the women education improved women are also able to find job and access internet.

IRAN - There are still many jobs that are only for men - In my opinion, women can find work like men and with lower salaries and wages - No woman in my country is ever in the same job position as a man, because she never has the right to choose freely in different positions, and secondly, that position may not provide sufficient security -Because wherever we go for the first job, our beauty, serotype and body are given points for the work ... The art of specialization in work has no meaning for a woman - Cultural and governmental restrictions - Job opportunities are not equal in engineering disciplines -They have made many jobs masculine. Like a mechanic ... an electrician - In freelance jobs, yes, like a salesman, being a secretary, but in jobs like government agencies, very few can work. It does not matter if it is a woman or a man. Even if they are educated, it is very rare for them to have a government job - Because rural women and disadvantaged areas are more under the pressure of custom and tradition, they are more confined to homes and less present in society, so they enjoy technology much less than men, they are usually engaged in housekeeping or having children. It also makes their working conditions more difficult due to the sexual abuse they receive in the workplace and the discrimination that is imposed on them for reasons such as pregnancy or menstruation - The Internet in our country has a filter and is completely controlled. Women cannot be elected and employed in the politics of the country - Women and men have the same access to technology, finding the perfect job is difficult for both - The payment for women is much lower than men - Some of the jobs these days just belongs to the man, like president, judge - The women of our country do not have authority. And they must be at the request of their husbands. The desire of the husbands is a priority and the desire of the women is not so important - Because in my country, I clearly see many women who have jobs - Our country has many female scientists - Many of the priority jobs are men, such as engineering – Islam - Because men are connected to the source of power and politics, they use the relationship more to create jobs for themselves and their relatives - About question 10 Fortunately, they have not yet found a way to separate men and women in the virtual world !!!! - Because most women in Iran are not independent and are dominated by men (father or brother or husband) and are not the final decision makers on their own issues.

IRAQ - As for work, there is more job opportunity for women in companies than for men - In terms of work, my country did not differentiate between men and women, but there are professions that require only men because women in terms of their physical strength are less than men - Women are treated by society as a housewife only, even if they reach the tops, and they do not have complete freedom to act, everything is limited - There are actions in our country that are forbidden for women - Technological freedom for men is greater than that of women - Because the government does not give equal opportunities - Because not all families in our country accept any work for women, accept some and reject some of them because of the societal nature - Because gender of Kirkuk doesn't let women do any work she want if she don't want to stand in front of her community or area or peoples near to her - There is no work that a woman cannot do - Yes, you can work like a man and sometimes you outperform a man at work – Many professions are still prohibited for women or socially unacceptable - We are an Islamic country, so many people refuse their daughters to work with another gender - As for self-employment, they are subjected to harassment and receive criticism from society, and it is difficult to convince relatives or relatives - In my society, a woman who works as a nurse is not respected, but they respect her if she is a doctor, and they do not respect the lawyer, and they think that this profession is only for men. As for women who work in restaurants, companies and shops, they consider them an offer in which you can be harassed, because if you do not want that, why work here - Now women can find job opportunities in every field, whether within their competence or outside their competence, with the exception of areas or professions that are difficult for women to perform physically and morally - Because most companies, especially private companies, require men - It is not permissible for a woman to work in a centre or a mall to take a not-so-sweet look at her, even though it is an honourable job, unfortunately this thinking - Because most of the bosses justify pregnancy and maternity leave for not hiring women.

ITALY - There is no gender distinction to work - From this point of view there is still some discrepancy, for example, here I have not yet met a woman working as a bricklayer! - There are still differences between men and women If a woman is highly qualified, she is hired as men - Because woman have children - I think women find a job in my country as men - Equal treatment - Currently, women and men have at their disposal the same tools, technological and otherwise, that they can use in order to achieve a purpose, including work. Unfortunately, they don't have the same opportunities to find work - Similar opportunities in access but not in growth - Women find work but with more difficulty - Sometimes recruiters ask women if they want to have a family and when they think to get pregnant – We have a fair constitution and law - Women are always placed in second place, as a reserve – Women have the same rights, in Italy these rights are highly respected - Power belongs to men - Today perhaps women have less difficulty in finding a job.

IVORY COAST - Tous les emplois ne sont pas autorisés aux femmes - Il y a des lois qui défendent le droit des femmes - Ils sous-estime la femme, son intelligence et sa capacité - Pour un homme on se base soit sur son CV soit ses relations pour une femme plus souvent sur son corps - Le harcèlement et le favoritisme dans le milieu de l'emploi - C'est pareil - Une femme mariée avec des enfants à moins de chance d'être recruté par rapport à un homme. De plus Il y'a plus de femmes analphabètes qui ne savent utiliser la technologie - Je ne penses pas que les femmes trouvent du travail aussi facilement que des hommes. Dans un premier temps sur le plan de la maternité des employeurs préfèrent embaucher des femmes plus viellent pour ne pas être confrontés au congé maternité ou autre. Ensuite d'autre employeurs embauchent des femmes plus jeunes dans le but de les draguer ou d'autres choses - Tout s'explique par des mentalités archaïques des Ivoiriens et des hommes qui refusent qu'une femme puisse avoir les mêmes opportunités qu'eux - Beaucoup de femmes sont analphabètes. Elles sont réduites au rôle de la gestion familiale.

MEXICO - Siempre nos etiquetan a las mujeres por tener hijos y no nos consideran para puestos de alto mando - Hay posiciones en que se prefieren a los hombres, incluso en entrevistas la laborales se les pregunta a las mujeres acerca de sus planes de matrimonio e hijos, esto es inconstitucional en otros países por ser altamente discriminatorio - Creo que en el ámbito tecnológico si es lo igualitario pero en el ámbito laboral si hay injusticia - Tenemos la Misma oportunidad de aprender pero no de ejercer - Hay trabajos que aquí en México sólo son considerados para hombres - El der madre limita mucho el que te tome en cuenta en puestos directivos - En muchas empresas prefieren hombres pues la mujer se embaraza - Podemos como mujer tener las mismas oportunidades laborales pero hasta el día de hoy los sueldos no son iguales en posiciones iguales y el poder escalar en empresas compitiendo con hombres es algo más q difícil, siempre basándose en q las mujeres nos embarazamos y tenemos otras prioridades. - A mi me negaron un trabajo por ser mujer, de manera explicita.

PAKISTAN - They are not treated equally due to social system and society's point of view Males always has an upper hand. And, job is difficult to find and job harassing is one of the biggest fear of women - In countryside area the education does not provide as men and the opportunity are large for men as compared to the women - Because in our society, it is not considered good for a woman to earn money by going out of the house. Is made a problem and obstacles are created in its way, or it is prevented from doing anything positive. Woman can find a job in our country as men do because every field has both vacancies. But the seats are minimum for women as compared to man - Women who want to work have a harder time finding a job than men, because people don't like women work in office - In our country all the women are not equipped with technology especially village woman - Yes in urban areas situation is different than rural. Technology is equally available to men and women. But rural areas somehow still have Orthodox mindset - Majority of the women are in workforce - Yes women can find jobs but not so easy.

PERU - Hay más trabajo para mujeres que para hombres actualmente - Hay las mismas oportunidades - Si por las leyes de igualdad de genero - Dan prioridad al hombre. Hay machismo - Todos somos entes pensantes - Las diferencias entre hombre y mujer ya no se dan en el ambito laboral, es inclusivo - Las empresas por mucho que hablen de igualdad de derechos y oportunidades, prefieren tener dentro de su fuerza laboral varones - Muchas veces si una mujer está embarazada la desemplean, y eso no es algo justo - El problema radica en que las mujeres ocupan empleos en sectores económicos peor pagados - Hay acceso a la tecnologia y el estudio pero en el campo laboral mas facilidades es para el hombre - Se ha llegado a la igualdad en el uso del internet pero en cuanto al trabajo aún las mujeres somos discriminadas por ser madres de familia.

POLAND - Being a specialist is not gender related - In our country it is told that there are some jobs that only men can do - Lots of women work and can find jobs as a men do. The development of technology means that we have greater access to it without dividing it by gender - For sure finding the job is very similar, but salaries are varied between men and women, mainly at the conservative components. The common question during interview is a question about children or the plans of having children (even though it's forbidden to ask about it). In more conservative regions smaller towns probably it's very difficult for women to get the management or high management job position - Sometimes it is harder for women to find better paid job because some of them are "only for men" - It is still believed that women should not perform "male jobs" such as: electrician, professional driver, construction worker, it is harder for women to find work in such industries - Internet access is equal, the employment situation is better than it used to be, but still not perfect.

TUNISIA - .En général la femme tunisienne n'a pas de chance comme les hommes d'avoir un travail - Nous ne trouvons pas de femmes occupant des postes de direction ou politiques en nombre suffisant, en plus du fait que les femmes sont vulnérables à l'exploitation sexuelle au travail - Mon mari ne me permet ni de travailler ni d'utiliser le téléphone portable - Parce que les entreprises veulent plus de femmes que d'hommes - Parfois, il est plus facile pour une femme d'obtenir un emploi que pour un homme, d'autant plus que les usines et les entreprises telles que l'agriculture, les restaurants, les marchandises dans les magasins, etc. sont des femmes - Les femmes sont plus susceptibles de travailler que les hommes - Parce que les femmes travaillent plus de temps et moins de salaire mensuel - Les femmes travaillent dans les ministères, l'administration, la médecine et même l'architecture - Dans certaines familles, vous constatez que les parents autorisent leur fils mâle à acheter un smartphone avant la femelle, et il a le droit de communiquer avec qui il veut sur les réseaux sociaux sans être surveillé, contrairement à la femelle qui est habituellement surveillée - Parce que l'homme ne permet pas à la femme de travailler.

UNITED STATES - The opportunities are there, but women have more barriers to break. With many industries being male dominated and having "boys club" culture, it is more difficult for women to capitalize on these opportunities compared to men - Men get better jobs - For a woman is still difficult to have some opportunities There are disparities. Particularly for women of colour in the U.S. They do not have technology, educational opportunities to improve employment, or health care - Blind auditions show that the results are different when employees know the sex of the candidate - yes but they are paid less - It really depends to the level of job. The higher the job the glass ceiling is more tangible - Technology is equal - Men are preferred - There are many fields, mainly in STEM careers, in which there aren't many women involved. Men are often favoured in these fields, and there is a great deal of sexism. It's not those women don't have access to technology that would help them get into these fields, it's that women are often discouraged from participating in them - Doors maybe open but glass ceiling is still real. Countless CEOs are men - They have equal opportunities - I do believe women and men have the same access to technology, however I don't believe that women are able to find jobs as easily as men. It's as simple as that, men are more likely to be hired for positions -

VENEZUELA - Si tienen el mismo acceso a la tecnología, aunque por la crisis económica que atraviesa el pais, hace que existe un internet con muchas fallas y si el empleo lo puden ejercer tanto el hombre como la mujer, la diferencia es la experiencia laboral y los estudios realizados, es lo que se toma en cuenta para laborar en las picad empresas que existen. Pirque lis cargos publicos son a dedos - Las empresas prefieren contratar hombres - El sexo no es restricción para optar a un cargo - nuestras leyes hoy en dia proteje a las mujeres como ser humano y tenemos los mismo derechos que los hombres - Muchas empresas prefieren hombres - No encuentran trabajo como los hombres porque permanece el machismo a la hora de decidir el perfil del cargo, prefieren a los hombres - El Internet en Venezuela no sirve y ya casi nadie tiene trabajo, ni va a los trabajos, es triste pero es difícil encontrar trabajo en Vzla y los que tienen uno, pasan las penurias para llegar a él, sin transporte público, ni gasolina, la inseguridad y tantas cosas - Se tiene muy poco acceso a la tecnologia, es difícil acceder a ella . No, para el hombre es más difícil! - Dada las condiciones en las que se encuentra el país la economía informal, el comercio y la construccion es la fuerza que mueve el pais y allí es requerida mano de obra masculina - Las mujeres tienen acceso a internet igual que los hombres, pero en cuestión laboral es más difícil debido a la Crisis en todos los niveles que atraviesa el país - A veces las mujeres consiguen mas acceso al trabajo

2. *Legal conditions for gender equality in having a successful career*

Also of interest are the answers that respondents provide about the possibility that women have a career as successful as men. Interesting, because if in some of the countries the affirmative answers to the previous question - women find work like men – are in a low percentage, such as Haiti, the possibility of being successful as men is considered obvious.

And so, on average in the fourteen countries considered, 77.8 percent answered the question in the affirmative, that is, more than three out of four respondents. The percentage in the Ivory Coast is impressive, where 96.5 percent of respondents are convinced, while in Peru is 88.6 percent, in Venezuela 87.8 percent; as well as in Haiti, with 85.5 per cent and in Mexico with 83 per cent.

They are therefore around the general average in Cuba, with 79.2 percent of positive responses; India, with 79.5 percent; Pakistan, with 77.3 percent; Poland with 76.1 per cent and Tunisia with 79.5 percent. Below the average, they are instead Iran, with 69 percent; Iraq, with 57.4 percent; Italy, where 68.1 percent of respondents answered affirmatively and the United States of America, with 62.1 percent.

Figure 12 shows a comparison between the different countries, with reference to the affirmative answers to the question about the chance for women to be potentially as successful as men:

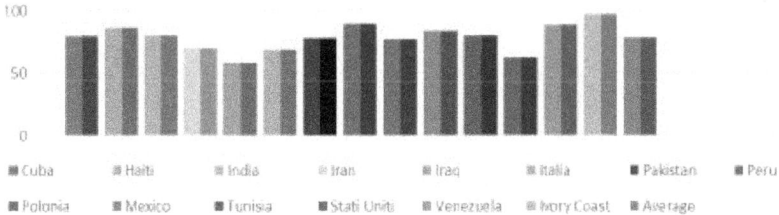

Figure 12. Possibility for women to have a successful in career as men -
Source: IWT Research.

Below (Figure 13) is the comparison, country by country, with the respective answers:

Figure 13. Do you think women can have a successful career in your country as men do? Y/N

Cuba

13) ¿Crees que las mujeres pueden tener una carrera exitosa en tu país como lo hacen los hombres?
120 responses

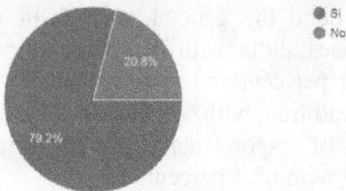

- Sí
- No

79.2%
20.8%

Haiti

13) Pensez-vous que les femmes peuvent mener une carrière réussie dans votre pays comme le font les hommes?
120 responses

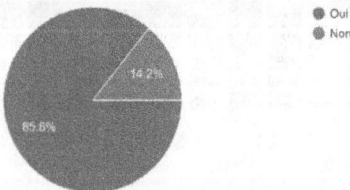

- Oui
- Non

85.8%
14.2%

India

13) Do you think women are able to have a successfull career in your country as men do?
190 responses

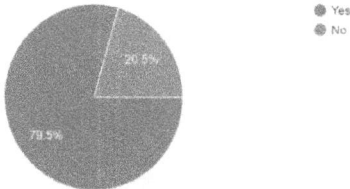

- Yes
- No

20.5%

79.5%

Iran

13) Do you think women are able to have a successfull career in your country as men do? - فکر می
کهید زنان می توانند مانند مردان در کشور شما حرفه ای موفق داشته باشند؟
100 responses

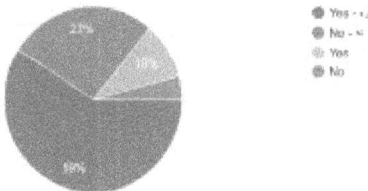

- Yes - بلی
- No - نه
- Yes
- No

23%

38%

39%

Iraq

13) Do you think women are able to have a successfull career in your country as men do? هل تعتقد (13
تعتقدين ان المرأة قادرة على الحصول على حياة مهنية ناجحة في بلدك مثل الرجل؟ /
155 responses

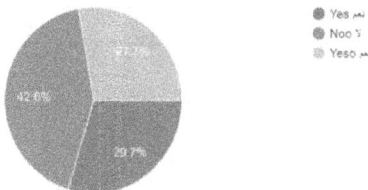

- Yes نعم
- Noo لا
- Yeso نعم

27.7%

42.6%

29.7%

Italy

13) Do you think women are able to have a successfull career in your country as men do?
215 responses

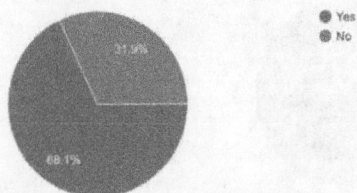

- Yes
- No

31.9%

68.1%

Ivory Coast

13) Pensez-vous que les femmes peuvent mener une carrière réussie dans votre pays comme le font les hommes?
141 responses

- Oui
- Non

96.5%

Mexico

13) ¿Crees que las mujeres pueden tener una carrera exitosa en tu pais como lo hacen los hombres?
388 responses

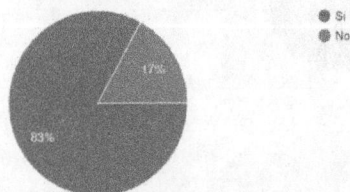

- Si
- No

17%

83%

Pakistan

13) Do you think women are able to have a successfull career in your country as men do?
198 responses

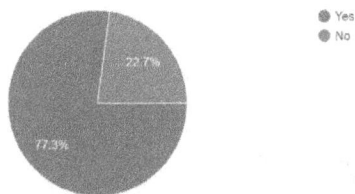

- ● Yes
- ● No

22.7%

77.3%

Peru

13) ¿Crees que las mujeres pueden tener una carrera exitosa en tu país como lo hacen los hombres?
229 responses

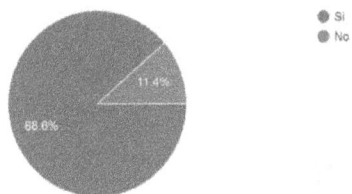

- ● Si
- ● No

11.4%

88.6%

Poland

13) Do you think women are able to have a successfull career in your country as men do?
176 responses

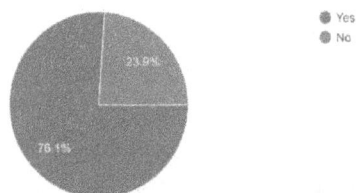

- ● Yes
- ● No

23.9%

76.1%

Tunisia

13) Pensez-vous que les femmes peuvent mener une carrière réussie dans votre pays comme le font les hommes? (13 هل تعتقد / تعتقدين ان المرأة قادرة على الحصول على حياة مهنية ناجحة في بلدك مثل الرجل؟
132 responses

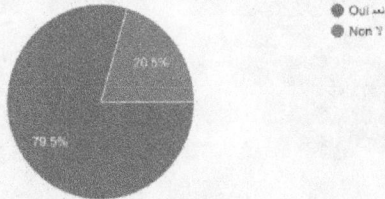

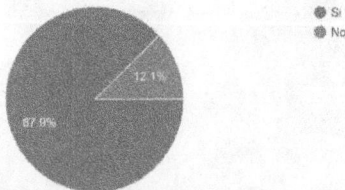

- Oui نعم
- Non لا

79.5%
20.5%

United States

13) Do you think women are able to have a successfull career in your country as men do?
153 responses

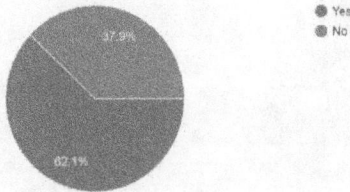

- Yes
- No

62.1%
37.9%

Venezuela

13) ¿Crees que las mujeres pueden tener una carrera exitosa en tu país como lo hacen los hombres?
132 responses

- Si
- No

87.9%
12.1%

3. *The role of law in finding a job*

What, then, are the conditions, the prerequisites for making a career in your own country? In this case, the IWT research provided for the possibility of selecting multiple answers or inserting additional answers to those indicated. In almost all fourteen countries, the largest percentage of respondents indicates "education" as the main factor to find a job and, overwhelmingly, to make a career. Only in Iran, Iraq and Italy, there was a prevalent majority of responses regarding personal skills.

Below (Figure 14), the analytical responses, country by country, on the conditions for a woman to make a career, according to the opinion of the interviewees from the different countries:

Figure 14. Conditions for a woman career development

Cuba

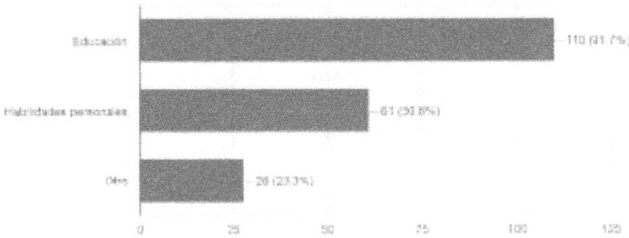

15) Segun tu, ¿cuáles son las condiciones necesarias para el desarrollo profesional de una mujer? Puedes elegir una o mas de las siguientes respuestas:

Haiti

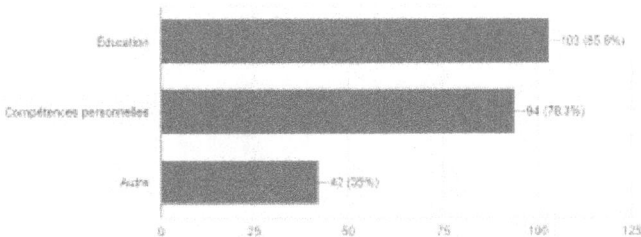

16) Selon vous, quelles sont les conditions pour une femme d'evolution de carrière? Veuillez choisir une ou plusieurs des réponses suivantes

India

15) According to you, which are the conditions for a woman for a career development ? Please choose one or more of the following answers
170 responses

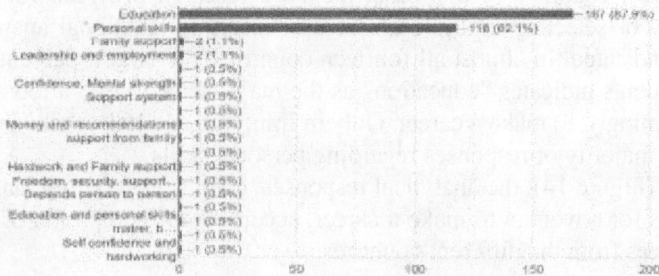

Condition	Value
Education	167 (87.9%)
Personal skills	118 (62.1%)
Family support	2 (1.1%)
Leadership and employment	2 (1.1%)
	1 (0.5%)
Confidence, Mental strength	1 (0.5%)
Support system	1 (0.5%)
	1 (0.5%)
Money and recommendations	1 (0.5%)
support from family	1 (0.5%)
	1 (0.5%)
Hardwork and Family support	1 (0.5%)
Freedom, security, support...	1 (0.5%)
Depends person to person	1 (0.5%)
Education and personal skills	1 (0.5%)
matter, b...	1 (0.5%)
Self confidence and	1 (0.5%)
hardworking	1 (0.5%)

Iran

15) According to you, which are the conditions for a woman for a career developrnent ? Please choose one or more of the following answers - به گفته شما ...پیشرفت شغلی چیست؟لطفأ یک یا چند پاسخ زیر را انتخاب کنید
100 responses

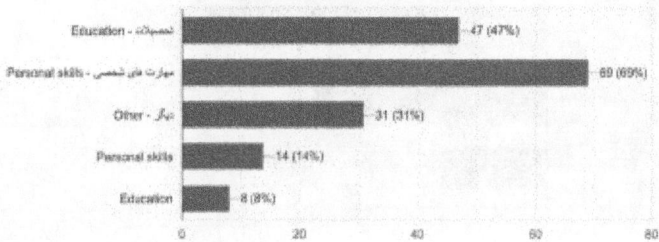

Condition	Value
Education - تحصیلات	47 (47%)
Personal skills - مهارت های شخصی	69 (69%)
Other - دیگر	31 (31%)
Personal skills	14 (14%)
Education	8 (8%)

Iraq

15) According to you, which are the conditions for a woman for a career development ? Please choose one or more of the following answers (15) حسب رأیك لـ...ور الوظیفي؟ الرجاء اختار واحدة او أكثر من الإجابات الاتیة
155 responses

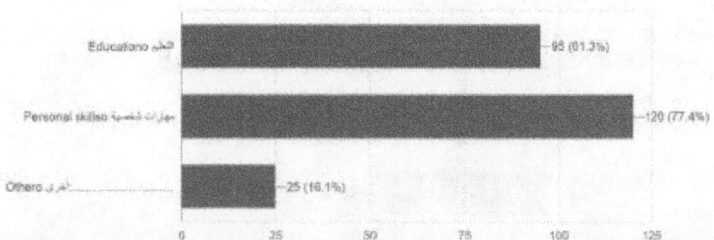

Condition	Value
Educationo التعلم	95 (61.3%)
Personal skillso مهارات شخصیة	120 (77.4%)
Othero أخرى	25 (16.1%)

Italy

16) According to you, which are the conditions for a woman for a career development ? Please choose one or more of the following answers

212 responses

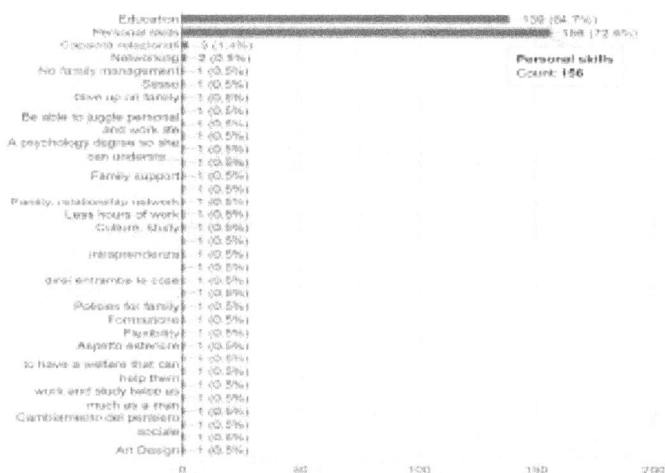

Ivory Coast

15) Selon vous, quelles sont les conditions pour une femme d'évolution de carrière? Veuillez choisir une ou plusieurs des reponses suivantes

141 responses

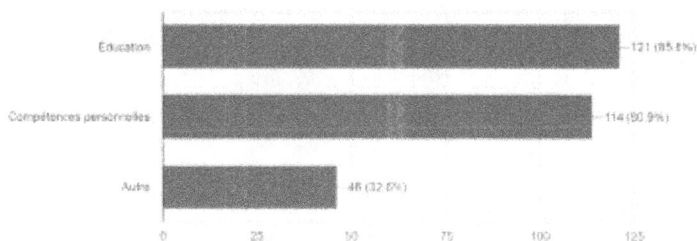

Mexico

15) Según tu, ¿cuáles son las condiciones necesarias para el desarrollo profesional de una mujer? Puedes elegir una o más de las siguientes respuestas:
388 responses

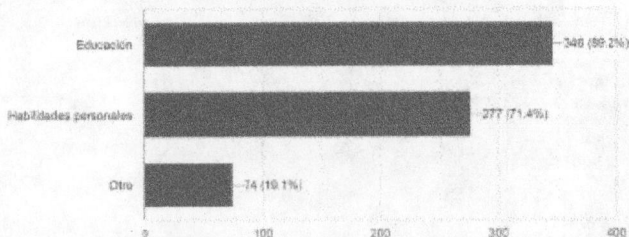

- Educación — 346 (89.2%)
- Habilidades personales — 277 (71.4%)
- Otro — 74 (19.1%)

Pakistan

15) According to you, which are the conditions for a woman for a career development ? Please choose one or more of the following answers
198 responses

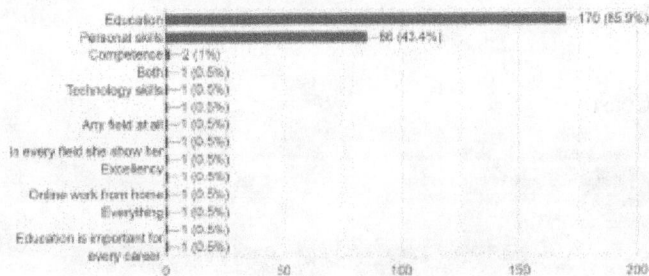

- Education — 170 (85.9%)
- Personal skills — 86 (43.4%)
- Competence — 2 (1%)
- Both — 1 (0.5%)
- Technology skills — 1 (0.5%)
- — 1 (0.5%)
- Any field at all — 1 (0.5%)
- In every field she show her — 1 (0.5%)
- Excellency — 1 (0.5%)
- Online work from home — 1 (0.5%)
- Everything — 1 (0.5%)
- Education is important for every career — 1 (0.5%)

Peru

15) Según tu, ¿cuáles son las condiciones necesarias para el desarrollo profesional de una mujer? Puedes elegir una o más de las siguientes respuestas:
229 responses

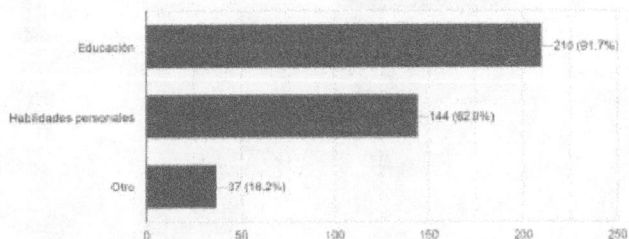

- Educación — 210 (91.7%)
- Habilidades personales — 144 (62.9%)
- Otro — 37 (16.2%)

Poland

15) According to you, which are the conditions for a woman for a career development ? Please choose one or more of the following answers
176 responses

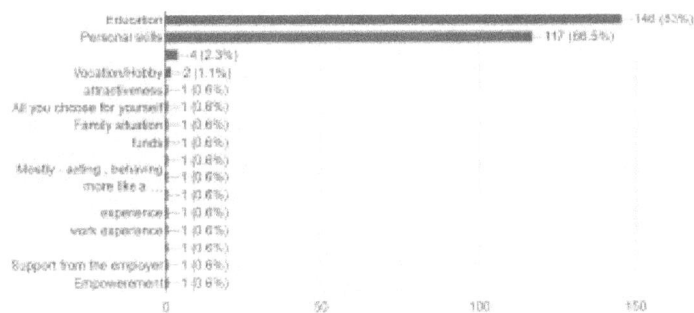

Tunisia

15) Selon vous. quelles sont les conditions pour une femme d'évolution de carrière? Veuillez choisir une ou plusieurs des réponses suivantes 15) ما هي الشروط التي يجب ان تمتلكها المرأة من اجل التطوير حسب رأيك / ك
132 responses

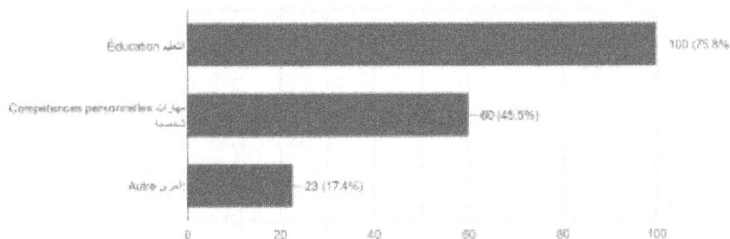

United States

15) According to you, which are the conditions for a woman for a career development ? Please choose one or more of the following answers
131 responses

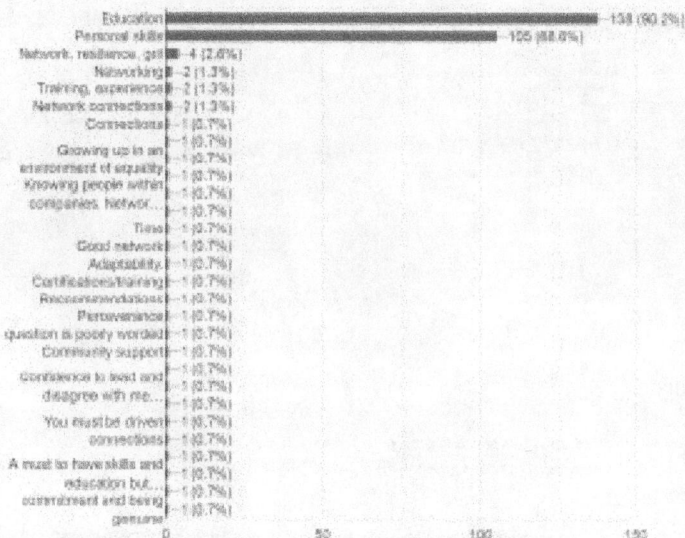

Venezuela

15) Según tu, ¿cuáles son las condiciones necesarias para el desarrollo profesional de una mujer? Puedes elegir una o más de las siguientes respuestas:
132 responses

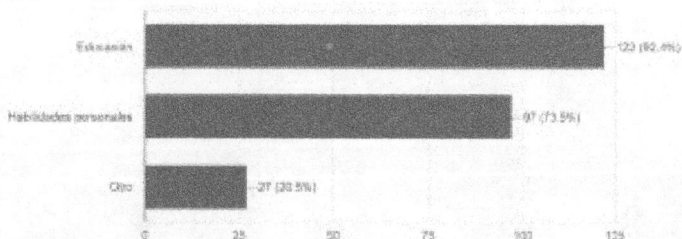

4. *Reconciling family and work: a socio-legal perspective*

Speaking of work, career for women recalls on the other hand the need to reconcile professional activity with family. Therefore, the further aspect deepened by the IWT research was that of the possibility of having support in one's own country to balance, to reconcile family needs and work.

On average, in the fourteen countries considered less than one in two respondents, precisely 46.4 per cent, believe there is adequate support for women to balance family and work. The country that seems to have a greater chance in this sense is India, where 62.6 percent of respondents expect a balance between family and work. The same happens in the Ivory Coast, where 58.2 percent are convinced; in Venezuela, where 56.1 percent considers it favourably; in Cuba, 55.8 percent is of the same opinion; while in Poland and Pakistan 55.1 and 51.5 percent of the interviewees respectively hold this opinion. Moreover, Italy is around the general average, also in this case just above or slightly below, with 46.5 percent, while in Mexico, 48.2 percent and in Peru, 43.7 percent, declare it. Well below the average, countries are also very different from each other. In fact, only 22.5 percent of Haitian respondents and 35 percent of Iranian ones believe that there is support for women in their own country to balance family and work; 31 percent of those in Iraq and 36.6 percent in the US.

Figure 15 below compares the affirmative responses of the countries considered.

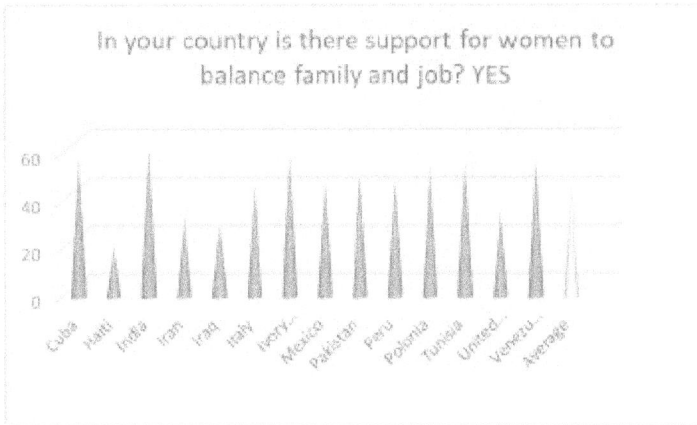

Figure 15: In your country, is there support for women to balance family & job? YES
Source: IWT Research

Following (Figure 16) are the complete data, country by country:

Figure 16. In your country, is there support for women to balance family and job? Y/N

Cuba

17) En tu país, ¿hay apoyo para que las mujeres equilibren la familia y el trabajo?
120 responses

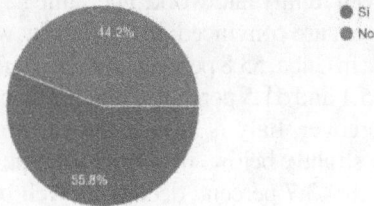

- Si
- No

44.2%

55.8%

Haiti

17) Dans votre pays, existe-t-il un soutien pour les femmes pour concilier famille et travail?
120 responses

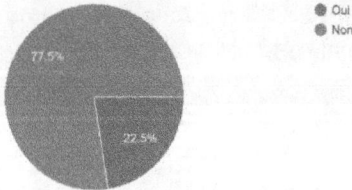

- Oui
- Non

77.5%

22.5%

India

17) In your country, is there support for women to balance family and job?
190 responses

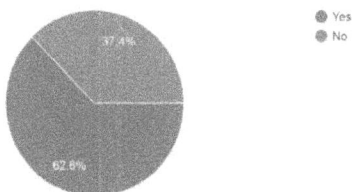

- Yes
- No

37.4%

62.6%

Iran

إيا در كشور شما از زنان براى - 17) In your country, is there support for women to balance family and job?
تعامل در خانواده و شغل پشتيبانى مى شود؟
700 responses

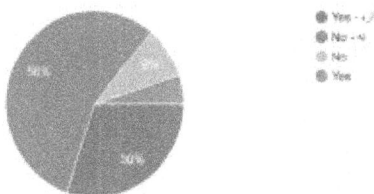

- Yes - بلى
- No - نه
- No
- Yes

50%

30%

Iraq

هل يوجد في بلدك دعم للمرأة (17) 17) In your country, is there support for women to balance family and job?
لخلق توازن بين الاسرة والعمل؟
155 responses

- Yes نعم
- No لا

69%

31%

Italy

17) In your country, is there support for women to balance family and job?
215 responses

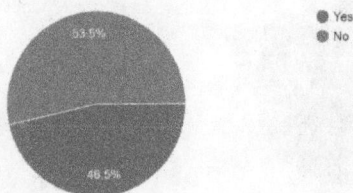

- Yes
- No

53.5%

46.5%

Ivory Coast

17) Dans votre pays, existe-t-il un soutien pour les femmes pour concilier famille et travail?
141 responses

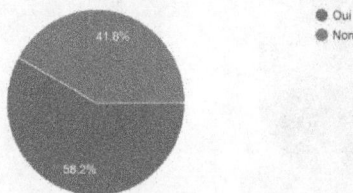

- Oui
- Non

41.8%

58.2%

Mexico

17) En tu país, ¿hay apoyo para que las mujeres equilibren la familia y el trabajo?
388 responses

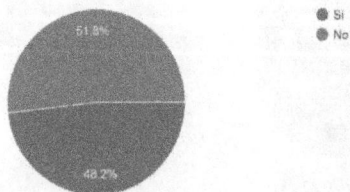

- Sí
- No

51.8%

48.2%

Pakistan

17) In your country, is there support for women to balance family and job?
198 responses

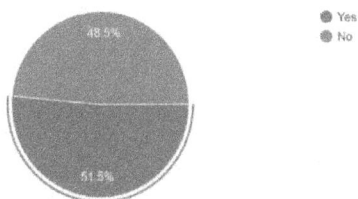

48.5%

51.5%

● Yes
● No

Peru

17) En tu país, ¿hay apoyo para que las mujeres equilibren la familia y el trabajo?
229 responses

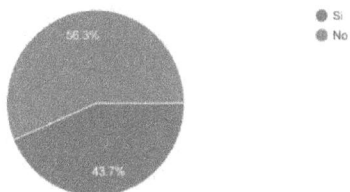

56.3%

43.7%

● Sí
● No

Poland

17) In your country, is there support for women to balance family and job?
176 responses

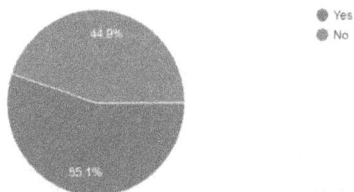

44.9%

55.1%

● Yes
● No

Tunisia

17) Dans votre pays, existe-t-il un soutien pour les femmes pour concilier famille et travail? (17 هل
يوجد في بلدك دعم للمرأة لخلق توازن بين الأسرة والعمل؟

132 responses

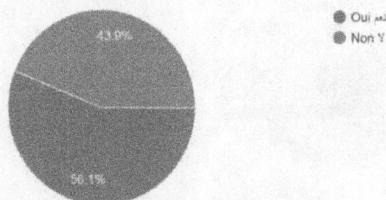

- ● Oui نعم
- ● Non لا

43.9%

56.1%

United States

17) In your country, is there support for women to balance family and job?

153 responses

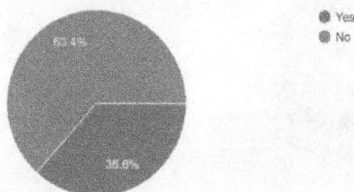

- ● Yes
- ● No

63.4%

36.6%

Venezuela

17) En tu país, ¿hay apoyo para que las mujeres equilibren la familia y el trabajo?

132 responses

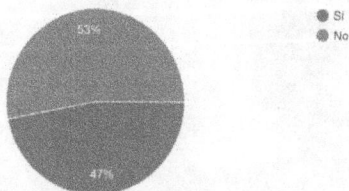

- ● Si
- ● No

53%

47%

5. *The right of internet*

If, as we have seen above, the orientations are different, in the various countries considered in the research, regarding the aspects highlighted so far, a profile that is instead common is that relating to the possibility for women to access technology - especially on the internet - in their own country in the same way as men.

The interviewees reply, on average, that women have the same possibility of accessing technology, and the internet, to an extent equal to 74.65 per cent: three out of four respondents believe that in their country there is no difference between women and men in the ability to access the internet.

Below, Figure 17 shows a comparison between the different countries in reference to the affirmative answers on the equal use of the internet between men and women:

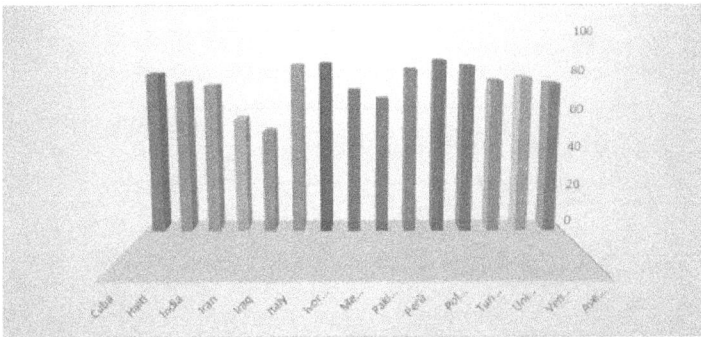

Figure 17. Equality between men and women in technology and internet's use.
Source: IWT Research

Even 85.8 percent of respondents in Poland are convinced of this; in the Ivory Coast, 84.4 percent; in Italy, 83.8 percent; in Tunisia, 83.3 percent; in Peru, 81.7 percent and in Cuba 79.2 percent. Only one in two believe that there is equal access in their own country in Iraq, exactly 50.3 percent, and a little more in Iran, where 57 percent are of the same opinion. They remain on the threshold of the Haiti average, with 75 per cent; India, 73.7 percent; Mexico, with 71.1 percent; Pakistan, 66.7 percent; United States, 75.8 percent and Venezuela 77.3 percent.

Below Figure 18 shows the country-by-country data:

Figure 18. Women have the same access to technology,? Y/N

Cuba

10) ¿Crees que hombres y mujeres tienen el mismo acceso a la tecnología - como Internet - y las mismas oportunidades gracias a las tecnologías en su país, también en la fuerza laboral?
120 responses

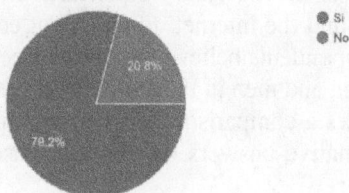

- Si
- No

20.8%

79.2%

Haiti

10) Pensez-vous que les hommes et les femmes ont le même accès à la technologie - comme Internet - et les mêmes opportunités grâce aux tec...ns votre pays, y compris sur le marché du travail?
120 responses

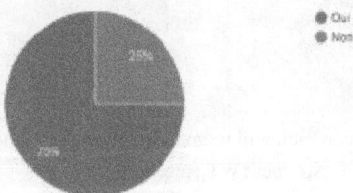

- Oui
- Non

25%

75%

India

10) Do you think men and women have the same access to technology - such as Internet - and the same opportunities thanks to technologies in your country, also in the labor force?
190 responses

● Yes
● No

Iraq

10) Do you think men and women have the same access to technology - such as Internet - and the same opportunities thanks to technologies in your countr...العاملة الفرى في وأيضا بلدكم في التقنيات لتلك الوصول من
155 responses

● Yeso نعم
● Noo ٧

Italy

10) Do you think men and women have the same access to technology - such as Internet - and the same opportunities thanks to technologies in your country, also in the labor force?
216 responses

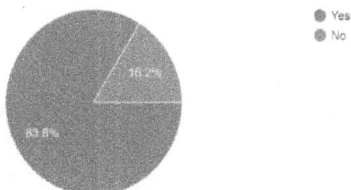

● Yes
● No

Ivory Coast

10) Pensez-vous que les hommes et les femmes ont le même accès à la technologie - comme Internet - et les mêmes opportunités grâce aux tec...ns votre pays, y compris sur le marché du travail?
141 responses

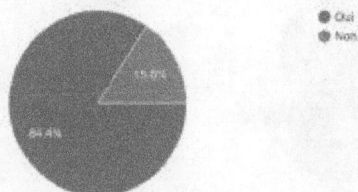

● Oui
● Non

15.6%

84.4%

Mexico

10) ¿Crees que hombres y mujeres tienen el mismo acceso a la tecnología - como Internet - y las mismas oportunidades gracias a las tecnologías en su país, también en la fuerza laboral?
388 responses

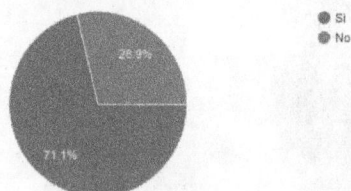

● Si
● No

28.9%

71.1%

Pakistan

10) Do you think men and women have the same access to technology - such as Internet - and the same opportunities thanks to technologies in your country, also in the labor force?
198 responses

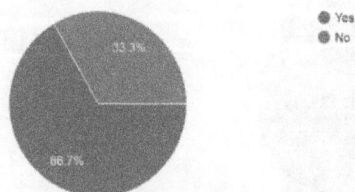

● Yes
● No

33.3%

66.7%

Peru

10) ¿Crees que hombres y mujeres tienen el mismo acceso a la tecnología - como Internet - y las mismas oportunidades gracias a las tecnologías en su país, también en la fuerza laboral?
229 responses

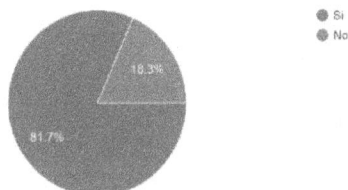

● Si
● No

18.3%

81.7%

Poland

10) Do you think men and women have the same access to technology - such as Internet - and the same opportunities thanks to technologies in your country, also in the labor force?
176 responses

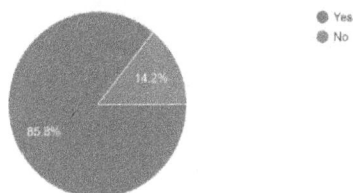

● Yes
● No

14.2%

85.8%

Tunisia

10) Pensez-vous que les hommes et les femmes ont le même accès à la technologie - comme Internet - et les mêmes opportunités grâce aux technolog...؟هل تعتقد أن الرجال والنساء لديهم نفس الوصول لتلك التقنيات في بلدك، وايضا في القوى العاملة
132 responses

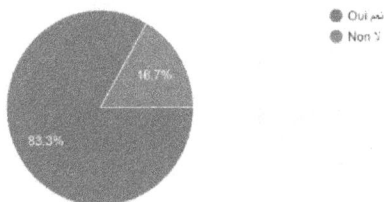

● Oui نعم
● Non لا

16.7%

83.3%

United States

10) Do you think men and women have the same access to technology - such as Internet - and the same opportunities thanks to technologies in your country, also in the labor force?
153 responses

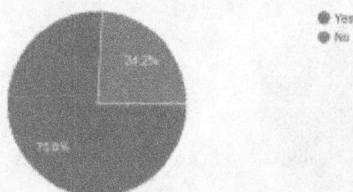

- Yes
- No

34.2%
75.8%

Venezuela

10) ¿Crees que hombres y mujeres tienen el mismo acceso a la tecnología - como Internet - y las mismas oportunidades gracias a las tecnologías en su país, también en la fuerza laboral?
132 responses

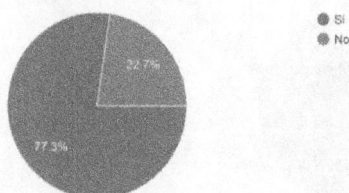

- Si
- No

22.7%
77.3%

Iran

10) Do you think men and women have the same access to technology - such as Internet - and the same opportunities thanks to technologies in your coun...
ن به لطف فناوری های کشور شما و همچنین نیروی کار دارند؟...
100 responses

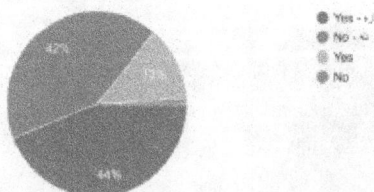

- Yes - بله
- No - نه
- Yes
- No

42%
13%
44%

But it is with reference to the issue of domestic violence that the greatest difficulties for women emerge, in almost all the countries considered, as it will be explained in the following chapter.

CHAPTER IV
MALE DOMINATION
AND WOMEN DISCRIMINATION

1. Violence against woman: the result of atavic unequal power relations between women and men

In the awareness that stereotypes contribute not only to the risk of weakening judicial action but also to the secondary and tertiary victimization of women, our project investigated the cultural and normative matrices of the legal system for the protection of women from gender-based violence, to identify and analyze the stereotypes and prejudices inherent in the social representation of violence.

Gender-based violence is linked to unequal relationships between men and women, reflected, legitimized and reproduced by culture, permeated by stereotypes and prejudices and introjected from childhood through socialization (Saccà 2021). It's a culture that is reflected in the ways in which institutions and various social actors deal with the violence suffered by women, helping to produce or reproduce the underlying conditions (Tay, Ior 2009; Richards et al. 2011). From a sociological point of view, gender-based violence is a social phenomenon, linked to the relationships of force, roles and forms of relationship that society establishes for people (Saccà 2003, 2021; Monckton-Smith 2012). It's a cultural phenomenon on too because the way of perceiving relationships between genders is the basis of the male predisposition to use violence against women and of society to tolerate such violence (Merli 2015).

According to the Istanbul Convention (2011), violence against women represents a violation of human rights and a form of discrimination (Article 3 letter a) and it is mainly consumed in intimate relationships (Article 3 letter b). That is in the presence of an emotional relationship, such as marriage, coexistence, sentimental relationship. It explodes when this relationship is interrupted and includes physical violence, psychological violence, economic violence, committed sexual violence from partner or former partner.

This is one of the most relevant topics of the IWT investigation. The impressive data recorded by our research reveals that in the fourteen countries considered – as a general average - nearly six respondents out of ten, exactly 57.1 percent, say they have suffered or know someone who has suffered from domestic violence. In some of the countries the result is even more alarming: 78 percent of those interviewed in Iran declared it; 74.2 per cent in Iraq; 72.7 percent in Mexico; 70.5 percent in Venezuela; 66.7 percent in Haiti and Tunisia and 66.4 percent in Peru. Apart from Italy, where there is a percentage of "yes" equal to 24.2 percent, the rest of the countries presents percentages still significant: in Cuba, 44.2 percent claims to have suffered from domestic violence or to know people who have suffered from it; 51.1 percent declares it in India and Ivory Coast; in Pakistan, it's the 43.4 percent; in Poland the 46 percent and in the United States the 45.1 percent.

In Figure 19, below, the comparison between the fourteen countries regarding the affirmative answers to the question "have you ever suffered or know someone or someone who has suffered from domestic violence?":

Have you ever suffered or know someone who suffered for domestic violence?
YES

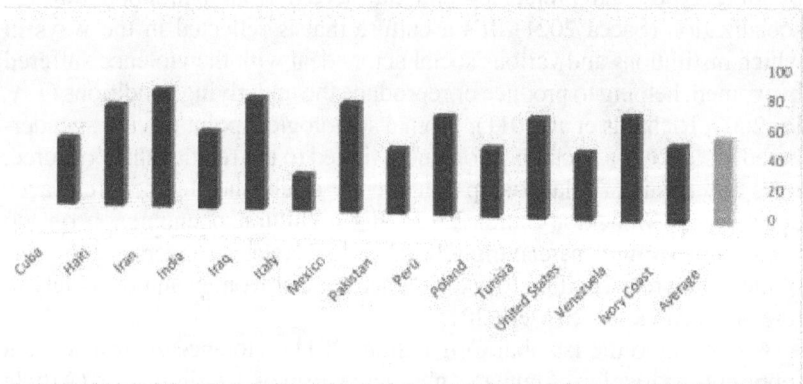

Figure 19. "have you ever suffered or know someone who suffered for domestic violence? YES". Source: IWT Research

It is such a deep-rooted plague and so difficult to eradicate, yet it has only relatively recently emerged as a scientific problem.

The expression "gender violence" is infact introduced in the international theoretical and political language only starting from the IV UN Conference on Women (Beijing 1995). It allows the emancipation of subjectivities that seemed by nature destined for social subordination. Equally recent is the use of the expression "femicide", used for the first time by Russell in 1992 and taken up in 2003 by Lagarde, with reference right to the numerous cases of killing of women in Mexico. This concept, by the way, became part of the public and academic debate in Italy only in 2008, thanks to the jurist Spinelli. The entry into the common language of these expressions is therefore to be understood as the sign of an ongoing cultural change. There are several studies that focus on the ways in which language reflects and produces stereotypes and which invoke a language non-sexist and respectful of the dignity of the person (Sabatini 1986, 1987; Cavagnoli 2013; Robustelli 2016, 2018).

The contemporary methodology refuses *a priori* to treat violence simply as a problem of public order, framing it on the contrary as a cultural issue and social responsibility, opening innovative ways of intervention inspired by operational concreteness. Investigate these actions and methodologies in order to identify good intervention practices and make them widely available and accessible to public debate means also to recognize the silence and fear that is hidden behind certain situations even in giving anonymous answers to an online questionnaire. For this reason, we believe that the percentage of those who "prefer not to answer" is relevant: on average in the countries considered by the IWT project it is 8.4 percent, with percentages that vary significantly from country to country. Thus, for example, there are countries such as Pakistan, Haiti and India where the number of those who prefer not to answer is two-digit percentages, respectively 20.2, 11.7 and 18.4 percent. However, the percentage is also relevant in other countries such as Cuba, 9.2 percent; Iraq, 9 percent; the Ivory Coast, 9.2 percent and Tunisia, 8.3 percent. Interestingly, some countries where the percentage of those who prefer not to answer is quite low - such as Mexico (3.1 percent), Iran and Venezuela (3 percent) - are among those where it is recorded the highest percentage of affirmative replies: as seen above, respectively 72.7, 71 and 70.5 per cent. On the contrary, if you add up the percentage of "I prefer not to answer" in countries where it is quite the percentage of 'yes', very high such as in India, Iraq, Pakistan, and Haiti, percentages arrive between 63 and 83 percent of respondents.

Ultimately, among those who claim to have suffered domestic violence or to know who has suffered it and those who prefer not to respond, the average figure is 65.5 percent in all fourteen countries considered.

Figure 20 compares the indicated data:

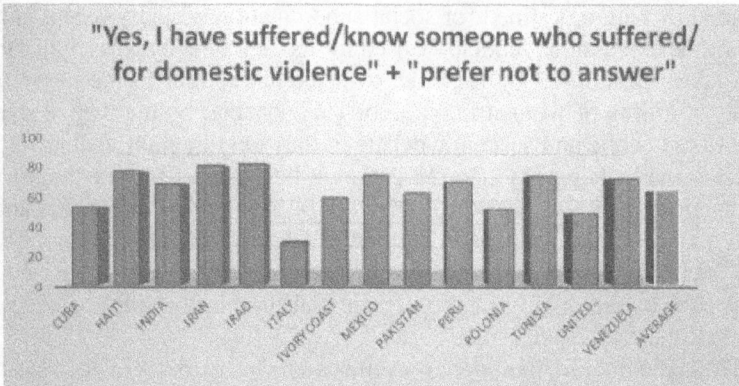

Figure 20. "Yes, I have suffered or know someone who suffered for domestic
violence" + "prefer not to answer". - Source: IWT Research

From a geographical point of view, then, high percentages occur for
the summation variable of the answers "yes" and "I prefer not to answer"
in the Caribbean and South American countries - apart from Cuba - that
is Haiti, Mexico, Peru and Venezuela; in those of the Middle and Central
East, such as Iran, Iraq, India and Pakistan; and in the two African countries
of Tunisia and Ivory Coast. In short, only the United States remain below
50 percent, with a percentage of 49.7 percent, and Italy with a percentage
of 29.3 percent, while Poland is at 51.7 percent.

Below Figure 21 shows analytical data for each of the countries
considered.

Figure 21. Have you ever suffered or know someone who suffered for domestic violence?

Cuba

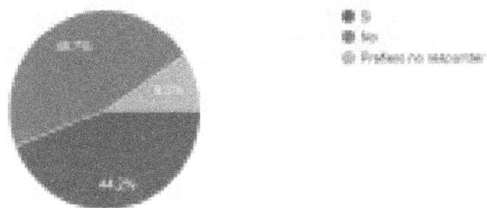

Haiti

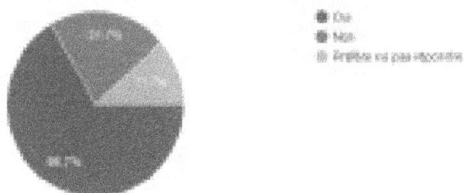

India

1Y) Have you ever suffered or know someone who suffered for domestic violence?
100 responses

- Yes
- No
- Prefer not to answer

Iran

19) Have you ever suffered or know someone who suffered for domestic violence? - ؟ را کسی آیا تاکنون
؟ اید شناخته یا برده رنج خانگی خشونت خاطر به که - 180 responses

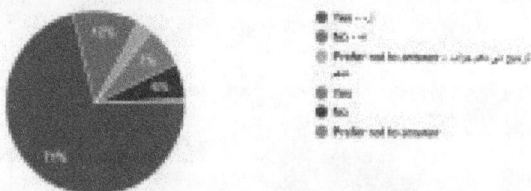

- Yes – بلی
- No – خیر
- Prefer not to answer – ترجیح می دهم جواب ندهم
- Yes
- No
- Prefer not to answer

Iraq

19) Have you ever suffered or know someone who suffered for domestic violence? 19) ان او سبق هل
؟ المنزلي العنف امرض اشخاص تعرفین او لمعرفین او تعانیت
166 responses

- نعم Yes
- Y لا No
- Prefer not to answer اجب ان لا افضل

Italy

19) Have you ever suffered or know someone who suffered for domestic violence?
215 responses

- Yes
- No
- Prefer not to answer

Ivory Coast

19) Avez-vous déjà souffert ou connaissez-vous quelqu'un qui a souffert de violence domestique?
141 responses

- Oui
- Non
- Préfère ne pas répondre

Mexico

19) ¿Alguna vez has sufrido o conoces a alguien que sufrió por violencia doméstica?
380 responses

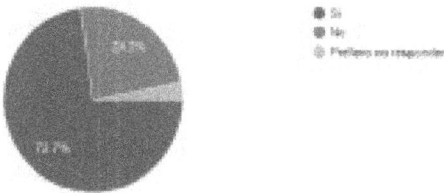

- Sí
- No
- Prefiero no responder

Pakistan

19) Have you ever suffered or know someone who suffered for domestic violence?
266 responses

- Yes
- No
- Prefer not to answer

Peru

19) ¿Alguna vez has sufrido o conoces a alguien que sufrió por violencia doméstica?
239 responses

- Sí
- No
- Prefiero no responder

Poland

19) Have you ever suffered or know someone who suffered for domestic violence?
179 responses

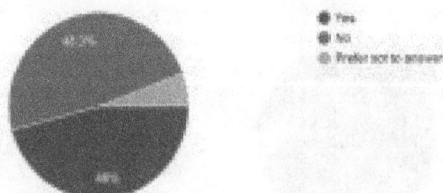

- Yes
- No
- Prefer not to answer

Tunisia

19) Avez-vous déjà souffert ou connaissez-vous quelqu'un qui a souffert de violence domestique?

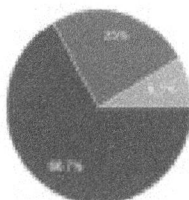

United States

19) Have you ever suffered or know someone who suffered for domestic violence?

Venezuela

19) ¿Alguna vez has sufrido o conoces a alguien que sufrió por violencia doméstica?

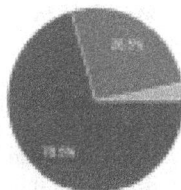

2. *"Donnons le monde aux femmes, elles en feront un paradis* ☺☺☺ *!"*

Although the debate on the social representation of gender inequality in the media is still not widespread in some countries, mainly from the studies carried out in the area of gender violence, the tendency of the national media to transmit a distorted representation of violence emerges. Albeit with praiseworthy recent exceptions (see Manifesto di Venezia, 2017), it is told as a private fact, rather than as a problem of collective relevance. Stereotypes and gender prejudices concern media narrative, but also justice. Just think of the distorted representations of domestic violence that are derided from "relatives" or the defensive strategies of the accused aimed at supporting the victim's unreliability or conduct.

But suffering from injustices and even the violence suffered, does not take away the hope for a better future of those who responded to the IWT survey. As one of the respondent from Haiti believes everything is possible for women, even change the world in a paradise: "Donnons le monde aux femmes, elles en feront un paradis ☺☺☺ !"". In all the countries considered, the expectation of see recognized the importance of woman today is affirmed and rightly claimed as indicated below.

Is it important being woman today? Why?

CUBA - Porque las mujeres tienen sabiduría, destreza, paciencia, criterio propio, autodeterminación, saben lo que quieren - Siempre lo ha sido, más que nada para asegurar que la especie no se extinga - Si, por la maternidad - Hoy y siempre. La mujer aporta a la vida y al mundo en general tantas cosas que para la mayoría de los hombres pasan desapercibidas, que de no existir "esto" no tendría sentido - No es importante. Simplemente puedes nacer mujer, hombre o alguna variedad trans. Somos todos seres humanos - Somos necesarias - Si, porque aunque no lo reconozcan podemos cambiar muchas cosas - Somos el futuro de la sociedad - Es fundamental que haya mujeres, su forma de ver las situaciones, o su sensibilidad para hacer un mundo mejor... - Es importante ser mujer porque tenemos cualidades diferentes a los hombres y junto a ellos formamos un equipo fantástico - Es importante ser mujer hoy y conseguir plenitud de derechos, que por ser mujer tú vida laboral y familiar no cambie, que se normalice la conciliación familiar - Las mujeres somos integrales, fuertes y con mucha resiliencia jjjjj - Si, Gracias a la mujer sussiste la familia - Todos son importantes, tanto hombres como mujeres. Mantenemos un equilibrio - Si, las mujeres cambiaremos el mundo y a los hombres mes preocupa - si tenemos los mismos derechos hay igualdad y consideraciones en diferentes programas - Un enorme privilegio - La mujer cubana sufre de escasez en algunas cosas necesarias además a pesar que en Cuba no hay mucho machismo aun mantenemos la labor doméstica y el cuidado de nuestros hijos más que los hombres - Lo considero muy importante desde todos los aspectos de la vida - Creo que ser mujer ha sido siempre importante, la diferencia es que hace unos años no se valoraba como hoy en día - Las mujeres en la sociedad actual somos ejemplo de inteligencia y fortaleza, lo que se ve reflejado en la capacidad para superar las adversidades ante la discriminación de la somos objeto, a pesar de que se considere una sociedad igualitaria y tolerante aún existe un núcleo de personas machistas, que nos mantiene en la marginación; pasan por alto que las mujeres asumimos obligaciones, lo que socialmente no es valorado, ya que pues se asume que esto es un deber de la mujer, por el simple hecho de ser mujer, lo que no entienden es que este rol no es fácil, si tomamos en cuenta que las mujeres tenemos aspiraciones, anhelos y metas que se ven obstaculizadas al ser las encargadas de dirigir el hogar, pues nos absorbe casi por completo - Si, porque lo es todo en un hogar - Sin es importante ser mujer en este mundo que vivimos, Dios nos escogió desde el principio para ser la compañía y la base de todo en la familia ,cuando eres mujer debes sentirte feliz ya que fuiste elegida por Dios llevar una tarea de dar luz a un hijo, de día a día cuidarlo, alimentarlo, enseñarlo, educarlo y viviré con el cada vivencia que Dios pone en su camino, Feliz de ser mujer soy única y repetida tengo tanto derecho que el hombre ,no mejor ni pero que nadie más bien soy una mujer con los mimos derecho en mi sociedad como otro ser viviente - per essere una persona che porta amore in su grembo - La gracia, encanto femenino impulsa cualquier proyecto, pone más empeño y no impone, involucra a los demás para el desarrollo constante. Así soy yo - Para demostrar que podemos!!!! - En Cuba realmente es una oportunidad - Eso me parece muy bien ,en Cuba se le da gran importancia a la mujer - Porque podemos ampliar en conocimientos, cultura, desarrollo, ser madre, trabajar, estudiar, lograr grandes propósitos...- Es igual de importante que ser hombre. hemos dado la educación y la vida a las generaciones futuras - Porque las mujeres en Cuba, tienen todo el apoyo gubernamental - Por supuesto, es un orgullo - Si porque tenemos que prosperar como mujeres - Ser mujer es puna condición, como la de ser hombre, no se es más importante. Somos iguales - Es muy importante ser Mujer hoy, porque nosotras con nuestra capacidad e inteligencia damos nuestro granito de arena para una mejor sociedad, somos escuchadas que es lo más importante, porque siempre tienen en cuenta nuestras opiniones, nos hemos ganado que se nos respete, admiren y valoren, somos un eslabón fuerte en nuestra sociedad - Es importante identificarse mas alla de un genero. Pero es gratificante ser mujer - Porque si enciendo el pilar fundamental para la educación de los hombres - Sin mujeres no existiría la Humanidad... - Super importante - Mi madre es mujer, mi esposa es mujer, mis hermanas son mujeres y son primordiales en mi vida. También mis amigas son mujeres al igual que mis compañeras de trabajo, con las que trabajo codo con codo como iguales - La mujer y el hombre en Cuba pasan trabajo, más en esta etapa de pandemia y con un bloqueo que arreció en el gobierno de Trump.

HAITI - Oui elle est importante pour devenir une femme parce que les femmes est un poteau mitan - L'importance d'être femme est incontestable et ce depuis toujours. La femme symbolise la vie, la bonté, la tendresse et la joie. Malheureusement, elle n'est pas toujours respectée dans un monde dirigé par des hommes en grande partie. Oui, c'est important d'être femmes aujourd'hui pour faire bouger les choses à tous les niveaux - Parce qu'elle donne la vie - Elle est très importante - Oui, cela est très important. Les Femmes sont l'alpha de la naissance, elles sont sensibles et protectrices, elles incarnent l'humanité et la douceur - Oui. Haïti par son histoire a connu des femmes extraordinaires. Elles jouent un rôle capital dans le développement de la société Haïtienne. Elles doivent certainement lutter pour se faire respecter, pour ne plus être réduite aux tâches ménagères. Mais c'est vraiment important d'être une femme en Haïti - Un artiste Haïtien dénommé Jean Roosvelt a chanté la phrase suivante dans une chanson "donner le monde aux femmes" - La seule femme nommée présidente d'Haïti a été réputée pour être la plus crédible. Donnons le monde aux femmes, elles en feront un paradis. ☺ ☺ ☺ - On ne trimballe pas les Femmes une Femme reste une femme dans tous les pays du monde quel que soit pauvre ou riche noir ou blanc C'est le fait d'être une Femme ☻ - Nous sommes la vie ! - Ça devrait l›être, mais certaines sociétés comme Haïti nous donnent l›impression qu'être femme est un châtiment - Oui. Car les femmes jouent un rôle important dans la société haïtienne. Elle seule arrive à concilier travail et foyer et parfois étude. Elles sont très courageuses nos femmes haïtiennes - Oui, puisque nous les femmes sont des moteurs de toute société sans nous elle n'y a pas de société - Oui il est important d'être femme aujourd'hui puisque c'est indispensable à la société et que les hommes à eux seuls ne peuvent pas vivre et gérer le monde. C'est une vie complémentaire. - Oui sans nous il n'y aurait pas d'hommes nous donnons la vie la plupart du temps les hommes s'enfuient dès qu'on leur dise qu' on est enceinte - Oui, et même très important, car les femmes jouent des rôles importants dans des activités humaines - Parce qu'être une femme c'est être le complémentaire d'un homme. L'homme ne saurait exister sans la femme - Parce que la femme est la mère et maman. Sans elle le monde s'arrête - Oui les femmes sont importantes autant que les hommes -Oui c'est important d'être une femme - Les femmes sont très importantes tout comme les hommes, je suis pour la non-violence sur l'espèce humaine en générale. La violence est dès deux cotés ...- Les femmes sont tellement intelligentes, elles donnent vies, elles sachent concilier travail et famille. - Pour moi c'est important : lorsqu'on s'aime réellement, qu'on s'approuve et QU'on s'accepte tel que l'on est tout fonctionne dans la vie. Même que de fois dans nos vies il y a des difficultés, les épreuves mais de fois ça nos fais grandir - Être une Femme ouï. Je prends le soin d›écrire femme avec la lettre majuscule. On ne peut pas former une société avec seulement des hommes. En outre, toutes les femmes peuvent impliquer dans les activités de développement du pays. Je n'aime pas la question de quota des femmes. Cependant, il suffit que les femmes possèdent la compétence requise. La matière grise qu'on a besoin pour développer un pays n'a rien à voir à une question de sexe - Parce que la femme est le pilier d'un foyer - On donne la vie je pense que c'est important - Il est surtout important d'être un être humain conscient des injustices. Homme ou femme, ce n'est pas important si vous pratiquez l'injustice ou la promeut - Pour être mère des enfants - Très très important !!! - Oui. Parce-que les femmes sont des êtres doués d'une capacité extraordinaire, elles sont sensibles - Oui. Les femmes savent comment diriger et comment bien diriger ! - Oui. Sans la femme, la vie n'aurait aucun sens - Il est important d'être humain parce qu'on a besoin de tout pour faire un monde. Cependant les femmes doivent continuer le combat et montrer qu'elles sont capables de mener au même titre que les hommes - Oui il est important d'être une femme. Parce que sans la femme nous ne pourrons pas réaliser des choses qui est très indispensable dans la nature. Tout d'abord on peut dire la femme c'est le mère de notre communauté, dans ce sens il est important d'être femme pas n'importe quelle types de femmes, mais une femme qui connaît exactement c'est quoi le monde de la femme, leurs importances etc. - En dépit de toutes les maltraitances, harcèlement dont sont victimes les femmes haïtiennes je crois que c'est important d'être une femme en Haïti... il n'y a que les femmes qui peuvent concilier, études, travail et famille... la plus grande histoire de démocratie fut donnée par une femme, elle a organisé les élections les plus honnêtes et démocratiques qu'Haïti ait connu.

INDIA - There is no new life on earth without women - Surely it is important - Without women, how can there be men?? - I don't think it is important being woman today, but whatever the gender you belong to, you must respect each other as a human being. And my policy is "Give respect and take respect" - Yes. Definitely. Because there are certain things only a women can do - Yes. I'm proud of that being a woman. Woman is a friend, sister, mother and a first teacher of their children - Yes, it is. Because it is about time that we show the world that we can do whatever we want - Being a woman today means using your voice to empower others to create positive change. Women today realize that helping other women achieve their aspirations is just as important as achieving their own - Yes, women are essential - Definitely yes. As there are some unprescribed restrictions, we are more challenged. It's nice to be charged like this to achieve something we are not supposed to - Being born and living happily is important.... gender doesn't matter - Women are important. They are equal to men. They have equal freedom like that of men. Being a woman. The role of women today has changed better - Only a woman can be a mother - Definitely yes. Women contribute so much to this society. Just a little liberation, support and positive mindset will let them show up more. Laws are supportive, attitude of people and their own family must change. Saving money for a girl's marriage should change to saving money for her studies - It is important being human - It's important. Or else there won't be a next generation - Yes, women are the epitome of strength love, sacrifice and courage. women are now self-sufficient, financial independent and aware and they have also attained immense success in different fields like sports, politics etc - Yes, women can bring many changes in families as well as in the society - Yes, of course. I'm so proud of being a woman, because she is the future - Yes, both the men and women should be considered as the same and in an equal manner - Yes, women or men, it is not the gender, but each personality deserves due importance trespassing the time periods i.e., past or present each life has importance and role of its own in this world - Women's have the major role in the development of the nation. And they must get the same chance, same opportunities that get by the men - Yes, it is important being women today because these are the basic things based on women – I'm prover to be a woman. I'm willing to change our attitude towards women being a woman so it is very important to being a woman today from my prospective - Yes, it is important being women today because they become success in their career - Yea it is very important thing – Of course. Women are the best beautiful thing in our world. She can do anything. But the world doesn't think the worth of a woman. I am proud to be a woman - Yes. Men can handle Job and family together from old generation. It is because Women the wives of the Men are at home, taking care of the other half (family) to balance a perfect lifestyle. It is rare that the opposite happens – Equally - Yes. I am very proudly saying that being woman is very important. Woman has a unique quality. Women are equal with men. I think there is no difference between them -Nothing just for a balance in the society - Being a woman is a big deal. Compared to today's society, being a woman is never confined to one corner and should also be a platform to express all their own personality abilities. Today 's world needs to become a society where women are never limited to being a woman. Today there are women who suffer a lot more persecution but this the time to change everything - It's no matter being a woman or man... behave like a human being, that's the importance. There are things that you can get from rule books, statistical research... those things must be analysed based on the data from authentic source. attitude analysis is a different genus - Women are the power - Women have a unique role and contribution for the betterment of the humanity - (It is important, A'sN) -Yes. The sensibility and sensitivity help to keep mankind from not falling and failing - I don't think so - Yes because there are many things to do for the society as being a woman - Today women faced more problems in our society or country. It is important being woman today. Today she gives more important. Women's gives freedom, free education, and free employment opportunities. Let's educated the women's – Yes, it's important being woman today for showing strength and power of a woman - The one who create can create world - Yes because women's are the power full one in the world - Nothing particular but just for a balance in the society - Yes. It is not easy to live as women, but struggle and self-motivation makes it possible through respect in society.

IRAN - A woman is the pillar of the family and can bring happiness to everyone - Not only is it important but it is also very difficult because of the cultural, political and social discrimination - Lots of responsibility - It is important because being a woman is the most beautiful event in life, but this beautiful event has been forgotten for women - Absolutely yes - Importantly, the presence of women alongside men is beautiful - Both the idea of weak death and the laws of inequality in the country diminish the importance of women - Yes, of course - a woman has different roles at the same time, mother-in-law, and an independent woman, and I think it really plays an important role - Yes, because women are probably as much more influential than men in the flourishing of society. Women are no different from men - Being a woman is important. If women are not, the burden of society's feelings will collapse. The necessary support for different situations will be lost. Being a woman is as important as being a man - Yes, because women have the power to change the future - Not being a woman is a great power - Being a woman has always been important. Women raise children and the next generation must be able to be educated and be strong and free - Yes, it's important, it's very important ... I enjoy being a woman, but unfortunately, I am in a society where women have no value. Clerical society and culture want a woman only to give birth and enjoy a man - Yes, because it helps the community a lot - It is important because it is the main pillar of educating and encouraging children and a woman society - Yes, because it is the main foundation of the family - From the beginning of humanity until today, being a woman is and is important because half of the society is made up of women, which is the basis of family existence and human survival - Yes, because really, if a man is successful because of his mother, sister, wife or daughter and all the women in his life - Yes, because the role of a woman is very important because a woman is the foundation of the family and plays an important role in raising children - It is very important because the foundations of a family of a society revolve around the women of that society and the men of the future and today will not be complete without the presence of women - Yes, because governments need to be able to care about women as much as men – No - Yes, it is very important. As we know, women managers, politicians, planners are smart and accurate, and without a doubt, with their cooperation, the world will progress more - No ... it is important for a woman to be capable - No, there is no difference between men and women. So being a woman and being a man are not different in the present age - Even though we are moving forward, I do not think so. Women are not important in society - Today, being human is more important ....- No, trust human beings is important - Yes, because in recent years the capabilities of women in all fields have been supported and used, I am proud to be a woman in a country whose security is better than the rest of the world - A woman is a wonderful person. In terms of emotions. Being a mother. And that he can work and be happy even if he is single - Yes, in my opinion, a woman is the main pillar of the family and a creature that gives joy and excitement to the happy community. Without women, there will be fewer smiles in the world - Yes, a woman is the mother of society. If not a woman, the pillar of society is gone - In my opinion, being a woman, or rather a mother and a daughter, gives life expectancy to the society, and the existence of happy and capable women has a great role in the cultural development and education of the society - Yes, because in the family and in the community, men share in the work side by side and do things well - I don't think it's important to be a woman or a man, it's important to play the role we have in this world well - Yes. But if it is not an abuse - Being a woman has always been and will always be important - Also gender is not important it is important being human, strong and update your knowledge - It is very necessary for the emotional growth of the society - It is important that men have no women - Yes. Women are the source of good management and prudence all over the world. Because it reproduces, nurtures and educates. So, a good and advanced society revolves around women (if it pays principled and correct attention to women) in that society. The learned woman is an ideal and desirable society - Yes, because it educates the next generation, and this training is effective for generations to come.

IRAQ - Not in this backward society - Yes, women are half of society. Without women, there would be no life at all - No, because of the difficulty of life - Because it is more powerful and more giving today, women are practical, serious and present better than men - It is important for me to be a woman today to control many things such as domestic violence, the way children are dealt with, marriage at an early age, and many more..- Yes, because I am the secret of life - Yes it should be - Definitely to develop a family - Of course! I'm proud to be Iraqi woman who can work for the best future for all Iraqis - Yes, to prevent the community from being lost - Yes, and successful in my field of work and my family, perhaps I will be a hand capable of reforming the next generation - Yes, it is important and most important for me to be a woman, because even in the Holy Qur'an, women's affairs are presented in more than ten chapters, including Surat An-Nisa. The woman is not only half of society, but rather she is a whole and everything is based on it. Women have great importance - Yes / society would not exist without women - Yes, it is important because it is women who create a successful future generation - Yes, because we live in a purely tribal society, and many uneducated women need education by educated women. And many things and rights that she is ignorant of, and this exposes her to violence by a member of her family or her husband, however, she must have a free voice and have an effective impact on society in order to be respected, and thank you - Yes, I think that, by the grace of God, I am better than many dependent men who do nothing - Why should I not be a woman while I work? God, the Exalted, the Majestic, made a woman great and placed Paradise under their feet, and the Messenger described them as bottles, and likewise he found a home and serenity with a woman and others... A woman is a treasure whose giving does not cease, and his energy is not exhausted - Yes, of course, in order to prove my presence in society and achieve my ambition - It is important to be a woman today because I am successful in everything - Being the nanny of the house and half of the community, I have great abilities and energies in my daily tasks and the job if I have them - naturally! A woman is a great being with stamina and creative skills that are twice as much as a man (in my opinion), and her presence in society is very important, no less important than the presence of a man, but unfortunately she is a victim of wrong and unjust customs and traditions that were established hundreds of years ago and are still applied to them - Yes, because women are half of society, and children are the other half - I am proud that I am a woman because I create life through my birth and raise a generation that stands next to men in all fields, so I cherish my femininity - Of course, it is important because of the development taking place in life, and because women represent three quarters of society - Yes, because

I have confidence in the whole community - Yes, because women are half of society, despite all the negativities and despite all the pitfalls, but the woman remains the first in everything and troubles the development of herself - It is important, and I do not find any shame in this. It is enough that the woman is a mother while she is raised, the source of tenderness and tenderness, and an important being in the family. A home without women is devoid of life. - I am important as a woman as much as there is no limit - Yes / because women, despite everything, are special - Yes. A strong woman has her full rights like a man to be given vision, work and the right to choose in her life, and to give awareness and moral support to women housewives to be strong in character and create for themselves a life worthy of them...- Yes, to help develop my community - It is not important to see him as a man, there is no difference between them - Yes, but you must be strong and your family support you - Yes, for the sake of self-realization and for the sake of serving my country and the people of the country - Yes, I can be a woman and spread awareness and reduce ignorance -Yes, it is very important, and we need women leaders in society who know how to pay for themselves from the social and legal point of view as well - Being a woman, I am half of society, even if I do not find the opportunity today to reveal myself, the day will come - In our society today, it is important for women today to document their existence.. because true beauty stems from when she perseveres for herself and achieves her goals and ambitions - Being a woman in an Arab society is very difficult, but women are still struggling to obtain their rights. The next one is better, God willing - Yes, it is important.... in order to continue living and not depend on anyone 💜 - Yes, it is important to be a woman today.

ITALY - Yes, it is important ... the woman is always a fundamental figure in work and in the family - She is like being a man - In my opinion, women manage to bring a sort of balance ... so regardless of the fact of being proud of being a woman, for me, women are essential in any circumstance - Being a woman is important today, a woman as a human person first of all - Men and women are equally important - Yes for the different prospective of life - Yes, we are smarter - Yes. To improve society - Donna is everything - It is always important to be a woman, to be a woman must mean to be free - Yes! Generation needs to go on - Yes. Because women can be whatever they want despite adversity - Because the women give their lives - It is important because women are the engine of the world - Because the women are more proactive - being a woman is just as important as being a man, there is no difference between the two genders - Yes, if they have different, important and complementary skills - Yes, because we must assert who we really are - Of course!!! Women have a sense of poeticism and can do many things at the same time - Woman is evolution - Yes. Many things are changing, and our society is becoming more and more inclusive and equal - Because we women have an edge - It will always be important, society is made of and based on both men and women: it could not exist without one of them - Sure! It is important because being a woman enriches our country with a precise and high-quality work service and at the same time allows Italy to be one of the countries with a high birth rate and where the family remains one of the most important values!! - Yes, the woman is the engine of everything - It's important to be human, regardless the gender, which by the way is one of the stupidest social constructs. Obviously one can say we are important because we give birth, or because we balance men with issues created by patriarchal education, or because we are beautiful, but it's all offensive, measuring the meaning of our existence by how we can serve the men's world - It's nice to be a woman!!! - Mother and worker - yes, it is important to show that women are more than what others think - Because their role and social responsibilities, both in the community and within the family, are reflected in the community - Women ca do several things at the same time and probably even better than men - Being a woman is a challenge that worth to be lived - being a woman is important because women, if supported by the state in providing the necessary services to make it easier for them to enter work in all fields, know how to be able - It is important to be a woman today because we are the force that moves the world - Today, however, being a woman also means fighting to be yourself, to have your independence, your rights, your job - I think it should not be important, meaning that it should have the same importance as that of men, but we are far from that, so what's important for women right now is for their needs to be heard and met - Women have many skills that men do not have because of their role in society - Because the woman has achieved many goals even if she had to elbow to get there with will and intelligence - Yes, because you are an important pillar of society - The woman has the ability to manage work and family - Yes. Women are expected, and used, to manage at the same time all aspects of life, from work to family, and they are capable to 'treasure the experience' from one field to another. Regarding the excellence, I strongly believe in gender equality, so I don't think that men are better than women and vice-versa. I believe in competence, honesty, skills, independently from gender - Yes, because we can make a change for the better - The woman was created to complete the man, today as in every time his presence in society is important and of great value - yes, because we can change the world - Women are the most beautiful thing in the world and life! - It is important, and it has always been. Also, man is equally important - yes because we are the future - Of course!!!! The woman is the cell of the family, of society: you corrupt the woman, and you have corrupted society! Don't take women into consideration and you will have a society and an inhuman future! - Complete preparation in all areas - Being a woman today is important because today more than ever we have the awareness and the ability to fight for women's rights - I don't think it is important. It could be just a fact - Yes, I'm a woman and happy to be - Donna is family obviously, because maybe women is the same of man and she can understand the children or adolescent's reality - To fight for a better future -Yes it is very important. The woman is the foundation of society, the family rests on her. Her laborious and often silent contribution from her is fundamental for a harmonious and more humane society.

IVORY COAST - Oui c'est important d'être une femme. Parce que c'est la femme qui donne la vie sans elle la vie n'a pas de sens - Il est important d'être femme car Dieu a vu l'importance de la femme pour un homme et pour l'humanité, la femme maintient l'équilibre de notre monde, alors je souhaite encore bcp de filles conscientes - Oui, une femme consciencieuse qui veut changer les choses, le dogme surtout - Oui. La femme est le socle et le pilier de la famille. Une femme responsable garantit le succès des enfants et l'amélioration de la société - Oui déjà parce qu'on aide à l'évolution de la population, important parce qu'on est plus intelligente et parce qu'on a beaucoup à prouver dans ce monde pour pouvoir Adon mieux s'émanciper. - Oui, la femme est indispensable en tout - la chance d'être femme aujourd'hui est mieux, car avec l'arrivée de leur émancipation, les hommes comme a baissé sur le marché et les femmes prennent la relève ... mais pas en Afrique, tend que on aura des dirigeants alphabètes, non intellectuels se combattent sera inutile - Oui, car on dénombre beaucoup de qualités au sexe féminin - Tout sexe doit être important - Oui, parce que la femme c'est la vie en effet c'est par la femme Dieu passe pour donner la vie à un être humain donc je pense que juste pour sa c'est hyper important de être d'une femme car c'est merveilleux de donner la vie - Oui parce que les femmes sont également fortes et compétentes donc c'est une fierté aujourd'hui - Oui aujourd'hui, c'est très important pour moi d'être une femme, car ainsi, je pourrai montrer à toutes ces personnes qui sous-estiment encore la femme, qu'être une femme, c'est avoir une très grande force pour briser les mythes de la vie, merci - Oui de la même manière qu'il est important d'être un homme - Oui dans certains cas il y'a beaucoup d'avantages d'être une femme - Une femme c'est le futur de la société - On ne décide pas, on naît femme - Très important d'être une femme aujourd'hui, vu leur rôle dans la société. Que ce soit en zone rural ou urbaine, ce sont elles qui soutiennent les familles, éduquent même si cela doit se faire à deux (Père-Mère). J'ai envie de terminer mes propos en disant ceci, la société de demain dépend de la femme d'aujourd'hui. Vous voulez une meilleure société demain commencez par les femmes aujourd'hui - la femme est un vecteur de cohésion sociale elle assure un certain équilibre dans la société moderne elle est indispensable a l'épanouissement de la famille - Être une meilleur femme sais de travail de plus essais de mieux avance de par se prend la tête et de prouvé que nous pourrons mieux dépasse les homme et mieux fait leur boulots avec plus de respect ,et plus responsabilité en assumant tout avec humilité - Autant que l'homme la femme a des aptitudes qu'elle pourrait valoriser pour se faire une place dans la société - Être une femme est d'abord c'est une grâce et privilège mais souvent c'est un combat ,une lutte contre certains violence - Homme ou femme cela importe peu il faut travailler et son travail sera récompensé - Il est très important d'être une femme aujourd'hui car elles réussissent tous – Les femmes ont des droits au même titre que les hommes □□ - Oui parce qu'il y'a plus d'opportunités pour les femmes que les hommes - Oui oui C'est important d'être une femme parce que la femme à beaucoup de privilège et Est beaucoup privilégié que les hommes – Bien sur - Il est important d'être une femme. Le mariage est l'union d'un homme et d'une femme du mariage nait la famille base principalement de

la société. La femme donne la vie. Elle intervient dans la création de richesse
- Oui parce-qu'elle sait diriger et gérer son temps - Évidemment, la femme est
le centre de tout développement - Oui Être une femme donne accès ! - Oui, la
femme participe à la vie sociétale - Très important parce-que la société en a
besoin pour son équilibre - Il est important d'être une femme car ça contribue
à son épanouissement personnel et à son autonomie - Pour moi il est important
d'être une femme parce que la femme est beaucoup valorisées pas seulement
dans son ménage mais aussi et surtout sur le marché du travail. Je pense même
qu'il est plus facile pour une femme d'avoir accès à un travail qu'à un homme
- Aujourd'hui il ne suffit as seulement d'être une femme l'important c'est
d'être une femme avec des ambitions, des connaissances, et une détermination
afin de pourvoir être indépendante - Oui c'est important d'être une femme
aujourd'hui.Car la femme aujourd'hui est valorisé respecté et elle est aussi
libre de s'exprimer dans la société d'aujourd'hui - Oui par ce que tout comme
les hommes elles sont superbes et très intelligentes et donc important pour le
développement économique et technologique de la côte d'ivoire - Oui, il est
important d'être une femme aujourd'hui car c'est un challenge.

MEXICO - Si, por qué estamos en una época de cambio - Siempre lo ha sido
- Por que somos libres - Para mi el género que somos es importante seas mujer
u hombre - Somos el pilar de la sociedad - Si, abren puertas que hace años
eran imposibles de abrir para otras mujeres - Para mi es importante ser un
ser humano responsable, respetuoso, con valores, trabajador con principios
seas hombre o mujer. No podemos generalizar que todos los hombres son
malos ni que todas las mujeres son abnegadas. Yo estoy orgullosa de ser
mujer - Siempre es importante ser mujer, si bien es cierto físicamente somos
diferentes a los hombres, nuestras capacidades pueden ser. Iguales o mejores
y eso no nos debe hacer más o menos importantes, creo que tanto hombres
como mujeres tenemos la misma importancia - Somos parte fundamental para
el desarrollo d Este mundo - Por supuesto una sociedad equilibrada necesita
tanto de hombres como mujeres - Si, nosotras somos bastante importante para
los hombres pero es bastante importante que luchemos por la justicia que mu
país desgraciadamente no nos da - Sí, eres la razón de ser de nosotros los
hombres, sin ellas no seríamos nada - Porque puedes hacer una diferencia -
Porque Dios creó hombre y mujer y ambos se complementan - Si es importante
ya que somos muy creativas, inteligentes, buenas, con muchas habilidades al
igual que los hombres y tiene que haber justicia en totalidad porque podemos
hacer un gran cambio en el mundo - Siempre lo ha sido, las mujeres estamos
en constante deconstruccion, sabemos percibir lo que es correcto de lo que
no con mucha facilidad, estamos generando un cambio en la actualidad muy
importante y es importante ser parte de la historia que se está cambiando - Es
tan importante como ser hombre - Es importante ser mujer. Yo soy mujer y
me gusta el rol que tengo y las oportunidades de estudio y ejercicio de mi
carrera. Pero ha sido igual de importante la presencia de hombres y mujeres
en mi vida que me han apoyado y enseñado. Es importante que se les dé el
valor a las personas, hombre y mujer, así como oportunidades y trabajos bien

remunerados - Claro que sí, porque debemos demostrar que somos capaces de todo - Porque vamos a arreglar y colaborar para un mejor pais, mas balanceado y democratico - No hoy, siempre; simplemente porque es quien genera la vida y somos tan capaces como los hombres para todo - Porque aportan mucho a la sociedad: otra visión y sensibilidad, otra forma de tomar decisiones y de discernir - Porque de nosotras depende la educación de las futuras generaciones - Por que siento que las mujeres tienen las mismas capacidades y cualidades de un hombre siendo capaces de ocupar altos cargos dentro de la política y de las empresas. Tomando en cuenta que hace 10 años ni si quiera era bien visto que una mujer ocupara un buen cargo - Todos valemos igual - Si porque somos fuertes, emocionales - Si es importante yo pienso que las mujeres van a tener una contribución importante en salvar este mundo del desorden que traemos - Las mujeres pueden llevar una vida dentro, siempre sera importante ser mujer. Hay muchas cosas que los hombres pueden hacer, pero tambien muchas que las mujeres pueden hacer mejor - Cada quien vino a este mundo para aportar su granito de arena - Si es muy importante ser mujer hoy, ser mujer significa procrear, dar vida - Definitivamente. Nuestra aportación a la sociedad es muy valiosa e imprescindible - Si, porque somos la base de la familia. Es decir generalmente ella es la responsable de la educación de los hijos - Somos la fuerza de las familias, mayor conocimiento y cultura - No sé si realmente sea importante - Porsupuesto, ya que somos el sustento de la misma - Si, porque gracias a nosotras, el país sigue creciendo y desarrollandose - Si, somos igual de importante que los hombres - Sí es importante pero al igual es difícil serlo - Siempre ha sido importante, solo que hoy en día se ha tomado más en consideración los derechos de las mujeres - Demasiado, las mujeres pueden hacer muchísimo más de lo que la ignorancia y el machismo le hace creer a la sociedad - Claro que es importante, como también lo es ser hombre. Ambos nos necesitamos y se necesitan en este mundo, con nuestras diferencias para poder complementarnos. Seamos equitativos ante la ley con sus derechos y oportunidades, pero complementarios socialmente, apreciando los diferentes rasgos - Si, porque la sociedad no sería lo mismo sin las mujeres y tenemos una función muy importante en el mundo - Sí. Para cambiar el status quo - Sí es importante porque le damos peso a nuestra sociedad y debemos seguir haciéndolo - Si, debemos abrir camino para las que vienen!!!

PAKISTAN – Yes – No - I don't know - Yes, because it's all about women's career - Yes but not most - Yes, being a woman is important because they are born free, and we are born to be real not perfect. They have their own identity, and they are born with a beautiful status as a woman - Females must fight for survival - Without women, men are nothing - Yes. Women has same or even more potential than men if given opportunity and access to resources - It's my responsibility to share my views. Yes, it's so much important being women today because with a woman culture society and our country can't progress. Can't survive - Yes, it's important because without a woman any country in the world can't make the proper progress that they deserve that why it's important - Yes, being a woman is important. Especially an educated woman is more important than just being a woman. Because an educated woman raises educated children for her family and country as well - If Allah created you a woman, then nothing else matters. Women are their own kind of beautiful creature. It's important because of balance in genders - Existence is the image of colour in the universe - Without strong Women not built strong Nation - No matter. Male or female. If you try your best results are also best - The central role of women in society has ensured the stability, progress and long-term development of nations. Women, notably mothers, play the largest role in decision making about family meal planning and diet - Women must be educated is it important for our nation, generations and our country – Yes, absolutely, it is very important because women are a necessary element of the society as men are .and it is their first and foremost right to claim equal rights and opportunities to men - A society without women don't progress. women country development an important role. If we want to give best career so we should give education to a women it is a basic thing - Yes, women is the holder of the next generation because no women no society - Yes, we also get benefit on many places for being a woman - Yeah It's very important to be a woman as history gives us vivid vision about this fact that a well-managed woman can give rise to a well-managed family - Being a women plays a very important roles and if she gets the opportunities same like man she can be the Reason of success for country - Because both gender are necessary for each other - To be a woman is not an option... It is a blessing - Yes! (. No reason for why) - So we can continue making progress in work and for generations too - Because women are strong and caring 💜 they have been very supportive of her family - Yes because country can't work without women - Without women there is nothing - Yes it is important because men cannot survive without females – Yes, because a woman is kind hearted and hardworking than men and also shows responsible behaviour according to your personal and practical life - Yes because woman play a great role in up bringing of man - As I explain it's not important you are a men or women it's a time to improve themself a successful person - Because being a women you have less responsibilities then men - Yeah due to her right skills or education - Women work like man. Women have also many qualities like men. They also done work like men - Woman are important part of our society - Because nowadays women are working along a man - Woman can manage everything family and society - There is no such importance of gender i believe but more of a good human being - women play a key role in every aspect of life and society – Yess !! It is stated that progress of any nation is by women – Yap, I am honoured that I am a woman - If your women work side by side with men you can change the nation - Yes because woman plays many roles in our society - Past, Today or the future women are as important as men - it is important to be a woman because our Islam has given us priority and respect but unfortunately our country men are not following it - In this society, woman face many difficulties about their respect - Yes but with respect ,dignity ,aesthetics and ethics - Women are the beginners and pedestrian to any family - I don't think so because being women you have to face more huddles - Yes it is important to show that we are not less than man - Being women is important because without women no society no personal skills - Yes because woman are the backbone in our society . Women are very hardworking than man - Being women is important as men. Because universes incomplete without a man or without women - Being women in our country is not easy - Yes because women have great contribution in all sectors of life - Not today but every day. Women are the entities who give birth and carry on the circle of life. Woman can or will do wonders.

PERU - Claro que si es el equilibrio del hombre y parte fundamental para el desarrollo de la humanidad - La mujer tiene un rol muy importante hoy en dia en la sociedad con los mismos derechos e igualdades de trabajo que los hombres, Pero hay que recalcar que todavia existe la discriminacion en nuestro pais - Soy hombre.. sin embargo el papel de la mujer al igual que el hombre en oportunidades está equilibrado, los 2 géneros tienes la capacidad de lograr lo que uno se propone! – No - Si, porque brindan el equilibrio en nuestras vidas, familias, trabajo - Por qué las mujeres hemos demonstrado lo que somos capaces hoy en día y si nos esforzamos más seremos lo que nosotras queremos - Somos emprededoras y sacamos adelante a nuestro hijos - Es muy importante ser mujer.La mujer tiene ciertas capacidades y habilidades innatas ,que la hacen especial y única - Si ya que somos tan valiosas como los varones - Orgullosa de ser Mujer - Porque somos pieza clave en cualquier ámbito. Y tenemos las mismas capacidades que los hombres - No, por qué todos somos iguales - Siempre será importante, pero no saben valorar lo suficiente a las mujeres en muchos aspectos - Sí. La mujeres somos tan capaces como un hombre de ejecutar distintos puestos de trabajo y de actividades en general - Si, porque ahora hay mujeres luchadoras y profesionales que hasta an superado a los hombres - Creo que si, las mujeres tienen habilidades humanas que podrían permitir el desarrollo de muchas cosas, ya sean empresas, proyectos, la ayuda de personas. Sin embargo, hombres y mujeres podemos ser un complemento del otro y equipo - La mujer no se hace problemas resuelve mas rápido todo lo que se presente - Por supuesto. Las mujeres damos vida!!!... Cosa que un hombre no puede hacer!! - La mujer puede y tiene otra manera de ver las cosas es más detallada y profunda - si por que todos somos iguales - Si porque nos valoramos - Si, ya que el rol de mujer es importante para nuestra sociedad y siento que ahora es más valorada que antes - Si, la mujer es la pieza fundamental en la familia es necesaria aún más que el hombre para su propia familia por ser la columna de su hogar abogada de sus hijos - La mujer es la persona que trae vida a la tierra y por ello debe ser más que respetada - Somos la mejor creación del mundo - Por supuesto!! La mujer es lo mejor que Dios a creado junto al varón (que no es menos importante) realiza grandes cosas y logra grandes cambios en la sociedad. Forma un buen equipo humano si se lo permiten, creo -y no es que me considere feminista- pero si hubiera un 90%de mujeres conductoras el tráfico en la ciudad bajaría y habría más orden!! - Por supuesto porque nosotras debemos de asumir un rol muy importante en esta sociedad, ayudamos en la toma de decisiones y el único rol que no se puede compartir con un hombre es el de ser madre, ya que las mujeres fuimos especialmente

creadas para concebir - Es importante ser hombe o mujer - Si, porque la mujer
puede tener múltiples oficios y puede cuidar de su familia - Dios lo dispuso así
y formamos cabeza del núcleo familiar cuando nos casamos y también como
solteras podemos ayudar en muchos ámbitos a consolidar un país mejor donde
nuestros niños puedan crecer y vivir sus sueños somos iguales de inteligentes
que el sexo masculinon - Si, para demostrarles a los hombres que las mujes
podemos hacer muchas cosas - Sí, la mujer es el complemento del hombre. No
sólo en el hogar, también en la sociedad - Si la mujer siempre a sido importante
ella es la ayuda idónea del hombre - Si, porque el aporte de las mujeres en la
familia y la sociedad es importante para un mejor desarrollo y progreso de
todos - Muchas veces hay mujeres que son cabeza de hogar y a la vez es madre
y amiga para sus hijos es una equilibrio perfecto - Sí, porqué hoy en día gracias
a la mujer peruana que sacan adelante a sus hijos sin un padre al lado, vemos
mucho esfuerzo y dedicación - Indudablemente, porque participa en todos los
asuntos que le conciernen a mi pais - Bueno para mi si, porque gracias a ella da
la vida a un nuevo ser - Si formas parte de una sociedad igualitaria - Claro que
es importante, la mujer con el pasar de los años ha demostrado que es capaz de
realizar cualquier reto que se les interponga, dejando con la boca abierta a todo
el mundo - Siempre es importante ser mujer, el rol de una persona en la sociedad
siempre es importante para hacer crecer a la sociedad, independientemente del
generó que se sea - Sí , ya que gracias a una mujer es que nacemos y recibimos
el cariño – Todos somos importantes influye mucho nuestra formación - Si muy
importante - El género de una persona no debería sumar o restar importancia
para su contribución a la sociedad - Si, porque somos parte fundamental en la
sociedad.

POLAND - Very important - Without women world couldn't exists so women
must head the difficulties that world consequently gives them - Yes! To fight for
the rights and well-being future generations - Being woman today is important
to change the world and try to improve it - being a woman is important and you
need to prove that you are mentally strong to be successful - Yes. I think that
women need to show that they are as strong and independent as men. And they
can take care of themselves, need to be shown to the new generations - I don't
know - Yes, it is important to be woman today, especially in this world. There
are a lot of people, that think that the rights are not equal for men and women,
but the truth is that they are not open minded. It would be enough to look at
today's rights and at those from 100 years ago, the difference is big and notable.
People should not complain about today's rights, because they are the same
for both men and women - being a woman is extremely important. women are
the foundation of the development of society and the world - we must fight
for a better life for us and for women in countries where their situation is even
worse - Yes, it is. Women must fight with variety of problems and difficulties
- It is important. Like in whole ecosystem - there is place for variety. It is
good to be different and to inspire each other. Women are very need especially
nowadays, their strength is hidden in vulnerability, flexibility and sensitives.
I can't imagine world without woman - strong and clever woman! - Because

women are strong and can fight for themselves - Yes, it is very important. We need to fight for future generations of women - Obviously it is important to be woman nowadays because they need to show the world that being woman doesn't mean that they are weaker than man - It is important to be a woman. women should develop and fulfil their dreams just like men - Being a woman is very important. Women are the future of this world - Yes, we need to show that we are also strong - Without women the world cannot exist at all so the last question is silly - Of course, every person is equally important in every aspect of life. The psychological division of the sexes represents a balance in the conduct of both parties. Each side is important in social and cultural life - Yes, as a woman i think it's important to fight for women's rights. For our generation and future generations, we can't be silent! - Being a woman is a psychological condition, you can't tell if it's important or not, because it's biology - Being a woman in our time is very important. We women are the ones who are more responsible and sensible in making many decisions. We are the moms, and we are the ones who know what is best for our children. We have that maternal instinct that men lack - It is very important to be a woman, women in our time are independent, they fulfil themselves professionally and reach high positions at work. They often must share work responsibilities with parenting - I think being a woman is important. women must show that they are not worse to men and are successful just like them - Very important, a woman is a sign of strength - Nowadays it is important to be a woman, to show that the weaker sex also matters and is able to achieve success whether at work or in everyday life. Being a woman is a great privilege, which also often makes life easier - Yes, we need to show that we are strong no matter what - yes because the world needs women - it is important but sometimes is harder than be a man - Yes, being woman today in Poland is very important. I think that because last year show us how much it is - A woman is the strength of the nation - I think so Women, even though they have a more difficult path to success than men, can achieve impressive results in science, sports, etc. This makes them unique - I think this is very important, this breaking down of barriers and beliefs that women are weaker than men. Women are a strength; they deserve to be treated equally - I believe it is important to be a woman these days. However, women play important roles, and they too can be very successful, just like men. The function of a woman is very extensive nowadays - Being a woman is important nowadays, despite the hardship of performing this role, we must remember that we are strong beings who are capable of "great things". Not in my country - Yes, because without woman it's impossible to create a family - Important as a man. Both genders are equal. Fanatic feminism is not a good option. Misogynism too - To fight for a better future for next generations - I don't know, I'm not a woman - The woman turns around the world! - I don't know how to be a man, but I feel good with this who I am - It' s important because woman is also a mum, so we create a new life – Yes. It is very important. The most important thing is only women can be mothers.

TUNISIA – Non - Oui, c'est important pour élever les générations futures - Il n'y a pas de différence – Oui - Une société sans vision ne réussit pas - Oui, mais dans un pays autre que la Tunisie - Non, ce n'est pas important du tout, en tant que femme, je n'ai plus aucune différence ni valeur, que ce n'est qu'une machine -Bien sûr, je suis fière d'être une femme qui réalise ce qu'elle veut - Oui, pour créer un équilibre dans la vie, et dire que les succès les plus importants ont été menés par une femme, ou derrière elle par une femme - Heureusement que je suis une femme parce que les femmes sont beaucoup plus intelligentes que les hommes - Le statut de la femme ressemble à celui des minorités bien que de fait numériquement les femmes sont supérieures ou égales aux hommes c'est à dire qu'elles sont tolérées et la tolérance n'est pas la certitude - Les femmes en Tunisie sont capables de s'imposer et de faire avancer la société - Les femmes doivent disparaître pour que les hommes survivent seuls dans ce monde - C'est important parce que c'est une grande partie de la société et qu'il y a un équilibre dans tout dans la vie - Je suis homme et je remercie dieu de l'être - Sans la femme, l'homme n'aurait pas été créé - D'une femme dans une société j'ai peur de l'équilibre et de la créativité dans la vie - Parce que les femmes sont la moitié de la société - Je suis (…), étudiante en deuxième année d'un baccalauréat en génie des méthodes chimiques à l'Institut supérieur d'études technologiques du palais Hilal. Je suis fière d'avoir créé une femme avec de nombreuses ambitions et d'en avoir réalisé quelques-unes. J'appartiens à une famille qui me soutient pour atteindre mes objectifs. Avec respect et confiance, du moins de mon entourage, ma famille, ma ville.... - En tant que militante de la société civile, même si c'est une expérience faible, je vois des femmes présentes et fortement dans la vie associative, sans oublier leur présence dans les postes décisionnels.....- Oui .la femme est plus active Dans la vie quotidienne - Oui, pour diffuser sa voix et pour la fierté d'être Femme - Oui, sans gêne...- il n'y a pas de différence - Parfois j'aimerais être un homme - oui très important - Oui, car je crois que les femmes sont persévérantes et capables de réussir plus que les hommes, ambitieuses et s'accrochent à l'atteinte de leurs objectifs - Parce que je suis la moitié de la société - Oui c'est très important - Les femmes ont plus de droits que les hommes - Oui, j'ai dit avant qu'une femme vaut mieux qu'un homme - Pour les tunisiens oui, la femme sert à faire des enfants et rester chez elle - Oui, parce qu'il n'y a pas de vie sans femme - Les femmes créent l'équilibre naturel, l'équilibre émotionnel, les femmes sont la beauté, la tendresse et l'amour - Une femme est la mère, la patrie, la sœur, la maîtresse, la collègue et l'amie - Bien sûr important - Il est important pour une femme aujourd'hui de tout vivre : force, faiblesse, beauté, perfection, liberté, injustice, fatigue, confort et vie... Une femme peut vivre mille sentiments en une heure, ce qu'un homme ne peut pas faire en toute sa vie - Ni plus ni moins qu'être un homme - Oui, et avec fierté, car aujourd'hui les femmes ont un grand rôle à l'intérieur et à l'extérieur du foyer - Bien sûr, il est très important pour moi d'être son commandement car Dieu m'a créé aussi pour que l'univers soit équilibré et remercié - Je suis une femme parce que j'ai été créée pour être une femme - Je suis fière d'être une femme parce que j'ai réalisé ce que certains hommes n'ont pas réalisé aujourd'hui en termes de responsabilité et d'équilibre de pensée et de conscience parce que je me suis réalisée et que je me suis mise à la place où je voulais être - Bien sûr, parce qu'il n'y a pas de vie sans femme - C'est important que les femmes continuent de lutter pour leurs droits - Oui, les femmes ont un rôle actif dans la société et ne sont pas moins importantes que les hommes - Les femmes sont importantes parce qu'elles sont l'épine dorsale du foyer et de la famille - oui, c'est important d'être une personne qui respecte tout les autres hommes ou femmes - Ce n'est pas important parce qu'il n'y a pas de différence de droits et de liberté entre les femmes et les hommes - J'ai été victime de violence de la part de mon père, de mon frère et de mon mari, et maintenant j'ai trois filles. Je suis très intéressée à être une femme qui essaie de changer la mentalité d'accepter la violence et de créer une nouvelle façon de penser - Les femmes sont une école pour construire une société et un peuple - Pour moi, je suis resté un homme pour pouvoir mieux choisir mon style de vie et le changer pour le mieux sans restrictions - L'importance des femmes en Tunisie réside dans leur fécondité et leur capacité à donner naissance à des hommes et non à des femmes – Non, parce que je suis né homme - Oui parce que je suis une femme – Pas nécessairement – Non, ce n'est pas important pour moi d'être une femme.

UNITED STATES - Yes, it's important for women to strive for equality and success and to champion equity and equality for future generations. Just as important for men to prioritize and be allies in this fight - Women make the world better - Yes, only the woman can change this country - Yes, women can provide a novel perspective to approaching issues - Absolutely! Let's just normalize it. I can bring humans into the world! - Yes, provide wider perspective in job place - God made both women and men. Both are needed. I know that my purpose on Earth is wrapped up in the fact that I am a woman, and I must work with that to carry out God's will for me - Yes. We have a voice and need to be proactive in bringing about change, sharing our experiences and listening to others - Women power - Women have the participative leadership style and collaborative skills now needed in the workplace - Power to the women - We are better - We can make the world better - We make the difference - Well, someone has to make baby - Well is important today as always, the point is how to achieve real equality - Today, as always in the past history, women mostly have been protectors of life within the planet while men created tensions and conflicts - We can be better than men - Important is an understatement. Being a woman today means fighting for those coming tomorrow and leading the way for future generations. Not only for women but for the whole society. Being a woman today is being a game-changer and modifying the current narrative that says being a woman means being weak, opinionated, and selfish—creating a newer version of that narrative where the word woman is a synonym of resilience, advocacy, support, and perseverance. Because being a woman today means standing up when everybody tells you to sit down. It means speaking up when the whole world is trying to silence you. Being a woman today means nothing can stop you, and nothing will stop you if you keep raising your voice - Yes. Woman changed this county - We can work hard - It is extremely important being a woman today because women will shape the future of the world - Yes, it's important, we're strong capable and are capable of leadership - Yes. The world is a more beautiful place when we demonstrate feminine virtues - Yes. It is important to be a woman today, and to advocate for women's rights, so that things can be better for everyone moving forward - It is extremely important being a woman today. We must stand up for each other and defend each other when people or society are trying to suppress our voices. The recent #MeToo movement is an example of this solidarity. Women are making their voices heard and supporting each other through their shared experiences - We can make a difference - Yes, there is the need for women to contribute not only to family life but to the world at large as well - It is important, to see the unique beauty, skills, and strength that women can bring to the world; it is important to see that women complement men, and they should work in harmony with them towards a better world - We have a different viewpoint from the men - Women need to advance - Of course. We are professionals, leaders, nurturers and we are breaking ceilings, even if they are slow to break - Both genders are important. They complement each other the world needs both - always has been important, nothing special about today - Yes, women are our mothers, sisters, aunts. They are equally and sometimes even more capable than men to make decisions and make things happen, if just they are given the opportunity. Unfortunately, there are biases, inequalities, discrimination, preconceptions, and even self-beliefs than prevent women from thriving - We have the power to change many things for the best - Yes. I think it is more important than ever. If more women were in charge, I think there would be less violence and conflict - As important as being a man - Of course it is important to be a woman today, because we need women. Humanity cannot function without the other - Women must fight - Yes, it is. Sadly, it should not even be a question to do if real equity between sexes really existed - Women are needed - Well, I certainly like being a woman. And I try to be a good role model to my two daughters - Women need laws to help them - Women need to make the world better - Yes it most definitely is. Women help society move forward in a very specific way. We cannot ignore the unique qualities that women possess while at the same time we cannot limit women to specific roles in society - Yes, to be there for our families and continue to pave the way for other women - Women need to step up - It is important to stand up for our rights as strong women of this country so that the generation of women below us know their rights and worth!

VENEZUELA - Por supuesto que es importante porque la mujer es el motor del hogar para que exista una familia debe existir un hombre y una mujer y detrás de un buen hombre existe una buena mujer, la mujer es la que siempre va a estar a la vanguardia del hogar para educar a los hijos para ayudar a levantar al hombre en el momento que flaque pero al igual el hombre el bastón de la mujer en el momento de una debilidad - Si porque demostramos que podemos ser lideres, empresarias como los hombres, que podemos llegar hasta el mas alto nivel como ellos - Siempre ser mujer es importante.. si nosotras no habría vida - Hoy y siempre!!! porque soy Mujer - Las mujeres proporcionamos balance, ternernura, pasión por la vida - Si es importante, representamos una parte importante en la sociedad , en la familia Y en la iglesia, fuimos dignificadas con Jesús cuando busco que se respetará, el pasaje de la hemorrodiza o cuando justo fue su aparición en lo a Resureccion a lo a mujer, no podemos olvidar que somos de la misma naturaleza del hombre pero dimos diferente no se trata de competencia cada uno tiene sus competencias , Dios no se equivocó somos complemento no podemos vivir pensando que somos autosuficiente somos necesarios ambos. Estar claros nos crearon hombre o mujer - si es un regalo de DIOS haber nacido mujer - la importancia de ser mujer es ser mas humana y sentimental, puede abarcar roles en el hogar, en el estudio y en lo laboral, ser mujer es ser mas libre y decidida - Es tan importante como ser hombre, solo que los aportes deben ser equilibrados - Siempre ha sido más que importante, la mujer es vital para la familia, lo laboral, hasta para que un país avance; la mujer es un pilar fundamental e irremplazable en la sociedad - Importantissimo somos el empuje en una sociedad, sabemos dar oportunidades y podemos cumplir con todas nuestras espectativas y obligaciones lo demostramos día a dia,en la Familia, politica (cuando nos lo permiten), trabajo somos el equilibrio siempre y con una fuerza sobrenatural ...! - Siempre es importante ser mujer, ambos sexos son necesarios para la continuacion se la especie humana - Si. Porque Somos un potencial futuro y podemos dar otras vidas al futuro - es muy importante ser mujer, pero considerando que el hombre es hombre y mujer es mujer, el tema de la igualdad de genero que esta ocurriendo en varios países, esta algo desenfocado al fin que debería tener - Tan importante como ser hombre - Mucho, porque la base de una sociedad es la familia y la familia no solo es papá, mamá e hijos, es papá bueno, amoroso, educando con amor y rigor; y también una madre que sea escuchada, capaz de entender todo lo que pasa a su alrededor, y empoderarse de cualquier rol y enfrentarse a cualquier circunstancia. Esa madre dará un gran ser humano a la sociedad, será emprendedora, culta y hábil para enseñar a vivir por su misma experiencia, la sociedad que todos soñamos - En todas partes del mundo, la igualdad de género es un derecho humano fundamental. Promover la igualdad de género es esencial en todos los ámbitos de una sociedad sana: desde la reducción de la pobreza hasta la promoción de la salud, la educación, la protección y el bienestar. La mujer es muy capaz y habilidosa y cuando se proponen algo lo logran y sin ella no se podría engendrar un nuevo ser - Sí para mí sí...porque me conecta con la espiritualidad que hoy día con tal pandemia me exige el momento histórico - Ser mujer, es ser parte de la vida, del amor y de la esperanza, las mujeres podemos llorar y reír, al mismo tiempo que damos consuelo, Ser mujer hoy es sinónimo de la Voluntad de Dios en Venezuela - Yo como mujer me considero una persona importante - Es igual - Claro que es importante, porque es la mujer la que realmente lleva y conduce a la familia, es importante su rol y que ella misma lo aprecie - Si, es una lucha que estamos ganando - Hoy y siempre, la mujer debería tener más protagonismo en la toma de decisiones - Cada Genero sea masculino o femenino es importante no en vano somos creación de Dios somos el equilibrio de la vida... nuestra capacidad de supervivencia , de innovación , de crear , de amar, de respetar entre otras ...es importante en nuestro planeta - Para la mujer venezolana, implicarse en la defensa de la igualdad ha sido una tarea titánica en todos los ámbitos sociales, en un país que atraviesa la mayor crisis económica y social de su historia. Pero a pesar de las condiciones actuales, en Venezuela la mujer lucha y se supera a sí misma diariamente, sin abandonar el objetivo de cumplir un papel fundamental en la reconstrucción del país - necesario los dos géneros en el mundo, ambos en conjunto construyen un pais.

These relevant considerations and suggestions re-emerge in the analyses and the experiences carried out on the territory by academics, scholars and researchers from the fourteen countries examined, as highlighted in the next chapter.

CHAPTER V
EXPERIENCES AND COMMENTS
FROM THE TERRITORIES

1. *The Americas*

The gender-based wage gap in the United States has narrowed in recent years, but disparities remain: national median earnings for civilians who worked full-time, year-round in the past 12 months was $53,544 for men compared to $43,394 for women, according to the U.S. Census Bureau's 2019 American Community Survey (ACS). There are a multitude of factors that may contribute to earnings differences between women and men not only in US: age, number of hours worked, presence of children, and education. The types of jobs women and men hold, and the earnings difference among these occupations also contribute to gaps in overall earnings.

The paragraph collects the comments and analyzes of those who conducted the research "The Importance of being woman today" not only in US but in the three Americas - North, Central and South - exactly United States, Mexico, Cuba, Haiti, Venezuela and Peru.

1.1 *Commentary on the US Survey about the importance of women in society (Maria de Lourdes Dieck-Assad[1])*

Women have increasingly shown the world that they can undertake much more than their traditional role at home, both in developed as in developing countries. Society does not question their role as housewives, mothers, housekeepers, and caring for parents or older relatives. About

---

1   Economist, dean Emeritus of EGADE Business School of Tecnologico de Monterrey in Mexico, was the Inaugural Vice President for Hemispheric and Global Affairs at the University of Miami in Florida, USA, served as Ambassador of Mexico to Belgium and Luxembourg and as Chief of the Mexican Mission to the European Union and Permanent Representative to the European Council (2004-2007).

50% of the world's population are women and there is also an increasing number of households led by women, but at the same time we witness the feminization of poverty world-wide, and continued complaints about discrimination and violence against women. Women all over the world have entered the labor force, either forced by the economic needs of their own family or their extended family, or simply because they want a better life for all and have the talent and the education to pursue a job and a career as well as raise their families and improve their social and economic status.

This commentary will describe the US results of the Survey on the Importance of Women in Society whose purpose has been to understand what the respondents (85% women and 13,7% men) think of role of women, the challenges, the needs and the importance of being a woman in the Country. We will present here the highlights and the key issues raised by the respondents to the Survey. Before starting with the Survey results, we will present some figures to get a picture of the size and some characteristics of women's population in the US.

Women in the US- some key data.

US has a total population of 331 million people (2020), of which women represent 51.6%. According to the Census Bureau, the distribution of women by race is 60% White, 18.5% Hispanic or Latino, 13.4% Black or African American, 5.9% Asian[2] Women represent 47% of the labor force and 64% of them are between 25 and 54 years of age[3].

On the other hand, women in the labor force have higher education attainment than men. The percentage of women between 25 and 64 years of age, with a college degree quadrupled between 1970 and 2020 (from 11% to 47%). So, in 2020, 47% of women have bachelor's degree or above. For men, this percentage is 40%[4].

The labor force participation rates[5] of women is 56%, and almost 68% for men. Now distinguishing those who are fathers and mothers, the participation rate is higher for fathers than mothers, 90% for fathers and less than 75% for mothers. The unemployment rate is higher for women at 8.3% in 2020 and 7.8% for men (2020 data affected by Pandemic), and it is higher for Black Americans and Hispanic, both for men and women. The

---

2   census.gov/quickfacts/fact/table).
3   US Bureau of Labor Statistics. Population Survey 2020, US Department of Labor, Women's Bureau.
4   Ibid
5   Defined as the women 16 years or older who are working or actively looking for a job.

unemployment rate is higher for women than for men, at any educational
level. However, the higher the educational level of women, the lower the
unemployment rate. Mothers always have higher unemployment rates than
fathers[6].

Women's earnings are lower than men, but the disparity seems to have
been reduced, since the rate of women's earnings to men were 62% in 1979
and went up to 81% in 2018. So, the trend seems to be going well. On the
other hand, there is evidence that among full-time working individuals,
more women (3.8 million) than men (3.1 million) lived below the poverty
line in 2017[7].

The Survey- highlights of results. Hard to be a woman – and why.

The Survey's answers reveal that there is a sentiment that it is hard to be
a woman in the US society. About 60% of the respondents believe so. The
key reasons for their answer are related to job/employment conditions and
perspectives, women' status/stereotypes in society, the lack of respect of
their rights, discrimination, traditional women roles and income pressures,
and the cultural context.

Regarding Employment/job conditions.

It is repeated by many respondents that the job market is not a plain field
where each person, men, or women, get their fair share according to their
qualities, capacity and contributions to the workplace. Among respondents
54% say that it is not possible for women to find a job like men do. The
reality the Survey's respondents present is that women get a lower pay for
the same job, that it is harder to attain certain jobs in specific fields, and
that even if qualified, women need to justify themselves much more than
men do in the same situations, and that there is a clear limit for women with
children in terms of escalating the job ladder. There is the perception also
that the higher the job level, the glass ceiling is greater and more tangible.

It is interesting that 62% say that women can have a successful career
as men do. But they say that women must work harder and be able to fight
many fights. On the other hand, it is mentioned that men must also be
educated about the role and worth of women, that is, they must provide the
spaces and conditions given that they are majority group and with higher
paying jobs in the job market.

---

6   Ibid
7   Ibid

When asked about the change in labor market conditions in the last 10 years, 33% of respondents say that a lot has happened and are optimistic, 36% say they are not optimistic, and 32% say they are less optimistic.

Regarding the job market, but specifically focused on the jobs in the public sector, 67% of respondents answer that women can participate in public roles (politics). They attribute the limitations to the presence of factors such as bullying and sexism, societal barriers, and the fact that they always must work harder to be as successful as men in the public sector. Respondents recognize that women gradually are participating more in politics, but it is still hard for them, and they are no doubt a minority.

Regarding women's social stereotypes.

A great number of respondents mention the problem of discrimination, the threats to women and to their families, and sexual abuse and toxic masculinity as threats against women. Women in general, according to survey, are still seen as the responsible party for family raising, so children continue to be their key responsibility. However, some say that there is now more conscientization about the need to change and pay attention to discrimination issues, and that women with children are at a disadvantage to be able to get a better life for them and their own families.

But some respondents mention that there is gradually a greater belief in society that the role in the in family must be one of shared responsibility between partners husband and wife. However, it is also mentioned that when there are broken families, women always keep more responsibilities.

Regarding technology access for women.

Avery high percentage of respondents say that women do have access to technology, 76% say so. However, in their comments they qualify this statement pointing out to the fact that it is higher income households that have the access, and hence poor communities have a disadvantage here. Technology can help women to find out job possibilities, but such possibilities are reduced for women without the access. The role of education is also brought up in this question, as a condition that enhances the impact of technology in the lives of women. Women who have more education and skills are more able to take advantage of technology for whatever need they might have, being it finding a job, finding childcare, improve their skills and their education, and any other service they might need.

Government or company support.

Regarding the support of the government to advance the status and role of women, 52% say it is not enough, but 33% say that current support is fair. It is mentioned that some laws and diverse policies are helping but still slowly. It is mentioned that it is very important to support women who have children. It is expected that respondents would stress this fact, because throughout the survey, the issue of the needs and disadvantages women with children have, are mentioned when referring to the job market and opportunities, and when discussing the women's heavier responsibilities, especially when families brake. If we put this together with the lack of access to technology for certain groups with disadvantages and the lack of good jobs, lower-income women are confronted with immense needs and little support from society or from government.

Violence against women.
45% of respondents say that they know someone that has suffered it. It is less than 50%, but it is already too many! The reality women face with violence, being it domestic violence, or violence in the job place, or even in the streets, is overwhelming. It does not seem that respondents believe the government is doing nearly enough about this in favor of women.

Some positive prospects.
Within the responses, there are signs of hope for women's role in society, since many respondents admit there are positive changes within society, within the job market and government, but they recognize that changes are too slow. They focus on those women that have achieved power who are helping this cause, that they promote conscientization of society and of the young ones, and they are working for the incorporation of initiatives to protect and help women, both legally and in communities, specially promoting more education opportunities for women, more strongly for those with greater disadvantages.

The respondents are also asked to cite the conditions for women to develop professionally, and 90% mention education as the main condition. 69% also mention personal skills, but if we think deeply about this, both education and personal skills have to do with knowledge acquisition and training. In the minds of the respondents these are the essential elements for women to open new spaces for themselves in the job market and in general as human beings. In this matter, it is also mentioned the need for society, and particularly the government to provide women the resources and initiatives to become more skilled and with better education opportunities, which also means the access to technology and job information.

Regarding why it is important to be a woman.

The Survey asked why it is important to be a woman, and most respondents, one way or another, mention all the character and personal features that women bring to society. They state that women are an asset to society, with skills and values that are unique, that women are uniquely able to provide participative leadership styles and collaborative skills, that they can be game changers and modify the current narrative about their weakness. Respondents state that women need to continue fighting for women's roles and rights in employment and society to help future generations of women. They need to stand up when "all tell you that you must sit down" and they should do it if needed. They say women need to contribute to family life but to the world at large as well, which will make women transcend any career boundaries.

Final Comments.

The Survey reveals the sentiment that women's role and support within the US society has improved, and opportunities have opened, but in general, the view is that it is still lacking force and not enough. There are still issues of discrimination in the labor market, lack of support for women with children, and a greater disadvantage for poorer women. They agree there are more women in power, both in the companies and in government, but not enough yet. However, these women are fighting and becoming examples for other women, mostly for the young ones. Technology seems to be accessible if the family has the resources, but this is not the case for poor families, who are in a disadvantage because they lack a tool that can help them get more skills, education, and jobs. And finally, it is important to see the consistency between the Survey respondents' comments and what US statistics reveal about women's challenges and lack of justice in terms of access to the same jobs for same qualifications, and to same pay for same job and responsibilities. Education and skills are no doubt recognized as the highest in the list of elements for women at all levels to improve their social and economic conditions and to help their families and to help their Country. Data also shows that working women have been very dynamic in advancing their education, but again, poorer women have less resources to do this, hence the need for government and society's support. The other aspect that is present in the answers to the survey is the lack of justice in terms of violence against women, which needs to be addressed to preserve the sanctity of a very valuable resource and member of society, that is, women. Something that is clear is that women can be a great resource for producing value for the Country, and if not given the opportunity, the right one, the Country is wasting valuable resources.

One or more respondents said: *"Without women there is no human race…."* And I would add, that without the proper care and attention to women's needs and potential, there is not a better future for society.

1.2 *Some reactions to the results of the Research Questionnaire "The Importance of Being Woman Today" in the United States of America (Maria Galli Stampino[8])*

Interpreting the results of a survey whose responses represent a minuscule sample of the population in any given place is always challenging. Nevertheless, from my point of view (an Italian woman transplanted to the US over thirty years ago), there are some striking elements in the replies to the research questionnaire "The Important of Being Woman Today" as far as those from the United States of America are concerned.

I was struck by how evenly divided respondents are in their replies to the initial, and foundational, question: "Is it difficult being woman today in your country?" A majority (58.8%) believe that it is, but I am surprised that 41.2% of respondents believe that it is not. This bifurcation is evident in the answers to the second question, in which respondents were asked to explain the reasons for their choice: terms like "discrimination," "sexism," "misogyny," and "gender norms and stereotypes" recur, as do "same rights" and "more opportunities and freedom then [sic] in other countries around the world." So much in these responses is determined by an individual's experience, as made explicit by some participants: personal histories and past events are invoked to underscore how the present, while imperfect, represents an improvement over the yesteryear.

Another important trait that was evident to me is the belief in and reliance on the legal system, on policies and their implementation, or the lack of both. Interestingly, the word "law(s)" appears 23 times and the related "legal(ly)" three. It appears that even in the face of slow progress, or recent blows, to legal protections, respondents accept and trust that a system is possible that will protect and champion their rights as women. This is also borne out by the replied to question 7: "Generally speaking, according to you, the policies of your country about women are…?" 52.3% of respondents selected "Not enough" and 32.7% "Fair." Only a small minority indicates that such policies "Do not exist." Overall, the belief

---

8   University of Miami, FL, US.

in the legal system is strong. One more point to emphasize, as I conclude considering this facet of the results, is that this survey reflects the times in which it was administered is clear from the comments that the "Supreme Court [is] heavily weighed now conservative and against women's rights" and legal "Gains for women and minorities gained under the Obama administration have been eroded."

In keeping with concerns that emerge more readily within a Western culture, another frequent theme has to do with workforce equality, both in terms of pay (a term that recurs 20 times) and of responsibilities. One answer encapsulates this recurring concern: "Per above, the men don't feel the guilt of choosing work over family. It is expected and ok for them to do so. If they are involved as a father in their kids [sic] school and activities, it is a bonus. Don't get me wrong, it is great, and my husband is great, but if he can't make it to something for the kids, he does not feel the guilt that I and most working mother's feel. If we choose family first, we are looked at as not giving our all to our jobs. There is no way to meet expectations at both and it always feels like you are choosing." Many respondents feel torn between expectations and ambitions or recognize that women around them are struggling with these tensions. In other words, culture in the US seems to demand different levels of engagement in the home and in the workplace from men and women.

One responder included the following as part of the answer to the second question: "I have experienced the ability to chase what I want to chase and freely make choices here in the Us [sic]. Much to do with the fact that I'm white and have an education." This reflects an awareness of the many facets that compose our identity as well as how people perceive each one of us—the concept of "intersectionality." Coined by law professor and theorist Kimberlé Williams Crenshaw in 1989, intersectionality is a powerful tool within the US context because it allows to examine how various identity elements combine to shape our experience of the world as well as how the world responds to each one. I submit that this concept and the analyses it supports and promotes will become more and more central in socio-cultural contexts that used to be uniform, at least superficially, and that have been changed by migratory fluxes—Italy among them. So-called second-wave (which lasted about twenty years, starting in the early 1960s) feminism in the US was criticized by both women of colour and poor and working-class white women for emphasizing elements that were not germane to their life experience (e.g., many blue collar women already worked outside their homes, in order to make ends meet) and for ignoring others that were part and parcel of the lived of under-represented minorities and disadvantaged women (e.g., the stress on abortion rights did not take into consideration the forced sterilization campaigns foisted on women of colour and women suffering from physical or emotional ailments). Crenshaw's concept of "intersectionality" allows for consideration of overlapping social identities, some of which may be empowering, while others may be oppressive.

Other responses also point the way to a more nuanced view of gender, moving away from the man – woman binary juxtaposition (which is nevertheless prevalent, given how the questionnaire is phrased). In replying to question 6, "Please can you explain the reasons of your answer to Question n. 5?" ("Being Woman in your country is different from being man"), one respondent states: "Obviously there are still some stereotypes and ideas that can limit a woman, but at the same time with the LGBTQ+ and other movements trying to "equalize" everyone by removing gender, soon there may not be a difference at all." While I am not as optimistic as this person as to the time frame of any movement away from a binary conception of gender, it is nevertheless notable that one of 153 respondents has brought up what is in essence a vast philosophical difference vis-à-vis a traditional understanding of genders in Western cultures.

In fact, this respondent's belief in an accelerated time frame for change is not supported by the opinions expressed by others. The adjective "slow" appears six times, including, in response to question 9, asking for an explanation to answer to question 8: "From 1=nothing to 5=a lot, according to you, compared to 10 years ago, women's conditions in your country have changed, not only within the workforce?", the following peremptory answer: "Very slow changes." Some respondents believe that change took place at a more accelerated pace in the past (for example, still in answer to question 9, "The big jump was 25 years ago"). There is a generalized awareness that, at least in the US, things are markedly better than they used to be, but that perception leads to opposite conclusions; here I would like to juxtapose two answers to question 2, one that states "It's not as difficult as it was for women living in decades/centuries of the past, but sexism/misogyny is still prevalent in society today and holds many women back" and the other "it was more challenging in the past but now people are basically treated fairly, men and women."

Another salient trait shared by several responses emphasizes the sense of physical fear that still pervades women's life experience. "Violence" appears five times, "fear" four, "rape" two. Several respondents express the perception that their everyday life is forcefully shaped by their gender, when it comes to the risks to their bodies as well as to what it is possible to them. One answer to question 9 stands out to me: "As a new mother, I am primarily looking at this from that perspective and it's difficult to determine what it was like ten years ago. Also, I have lived in many states and policies vary drastically across the nation (USA)." As this new mother states, there are large differences in how we go through life across the span of our individual experiences, depending not simply on our chronological age, but crucially on whether we have given birth or not, how long before, under what circumstances, and so on. Some of these responses bear powerful witness to the physical, embodied quality of our existence—precisely what past women at times fought against. We are vying to reach a balance of sort between equality of opportunities and possibilities on the one hand, and biological elements on the other. It is precisely the latter element that is brought to bear in some responses that are fall in what I would describe as an ideologically conservative camp. The fact that there is a biological difference is brought to bear four times, in answers to questions 6 and 9: "There is a biological, mental and physical difference. Men were created in a certain way and women in another;" "the genders are different biologically, so they are different. this is a silly question, to be very honest;" "this question really makes no sense - biologically men and women are different. What is there to add?" and "women are treated as are men, obviously there are biological differences".

There are also much more conservative answers that border on the combative. The one that stands out to me is in answer to question 2: "Women are in power and control everything." This response is so pithy and devoid of context that it simply makes a claim that is not born out by facts (such as number of women CEOs, in Congress, in State legislatures, Presidents of universities and non-for-profit organizations, etc.).

Perhaps because of some traits shared by many respondents or the fact that this questionnaire was shared through university listservs (which is also evident in the answer to question 4: "What is your main activity?", to which 30.7% identified "Study"), education is the most frequent answer among those in response to question 15: "According to you, which are the conditions for a women for a career development?" 138 respondents our to 153, selected "education," while 105 chose "personal skills." The other options were selected by many fewer respondents (four or less). I interpret these results to indicate that responders believe in self-reliance and self-improvement above all else, including networking. Could this indicate a limitation in how women still think about themselves, as individuals rather than as a group?

The questionnaire closes with a richly evocative question: "Is it important being woman today? Why?" Respondents leave no doubt as to their enthusiasm for bringing about change for themselves and for the future. Even those who think that the present and the future are no different from the past express their enthusiasm for specific womanly traits that have and will continue to have an impact. Two responses stand out to me, for different reasons. One states: "Women provide a prospective on life that is life-affirming, community oriented, and overall, more inclusive and conflict free, which is precisely what humanity needs today." This respondent moves the narrative beyond the "women are givers of life" cliché and matches what women have traditionally been valued for to the difficulties that many societies encounter in the present. The other offers the following: "Being a woman today is being a game-changer and modifying the current narrative that says being a woman means being weak, opinionated, and selfish—creating a newer version of that narrative where the word woman is a synonym of resilience, advocacy, support, and perseverance. Because being a woman today means standing up when everybody tells you to sit down. It means speaking up when the whole world is trying to silence you. Being a woman today means nothing can stop you, and nothing will stop you as long as you keep raising your voice." This answer encapsulates traditional misogynistic views (women must be silent, women must be subject to the will of others) and transforms those into strengths for the present and the future, for the betterment of all humanity, beyond gender and stereotypes.

One more point that I would like to make: while the results of this questionnaire are interesting in themselves, the fact that responses were collected in a variety of countries will increase its impact when responses are considered within a comparative framework. For example, question 10 asks: "Do you think men and women have the same access to technology – such as the internet – and the same opportunities thanks to technology in your country, also in the labour force?" The responses collected in the US overwhelmingly (by a ratio of 3 to 1) are in the affirmative. I imagine that respondents in other countries might have had a different reaction, and this is fertile ground for analysis, study, policy making and actions.

Reflecting on these questions and responses, I am pushed to reaffirm our commitment to understanding, listening, and opening our horizons, while being ready to act. Humans must come together to take care of each other and of the planet, and we need everybody's traits, skills, and gifts to promote mutual support, the identification of past wrongs, their redressing, and a continuous desire to grow.

1.3 *The Importance of Being Woman Today in the United States of America (Musonda Kapatamoyo[9])*

Introduction.
In a qualitative study of women's reactions to how society treats them in various sectors such as professional and home settings, the researchers produced a large data set from which the following findings and conclusion are made.

Findings.
The research is anchored by one overarching question "is difficult to be a woman in your country?" Respondents answered this question by drawing from their own experiences or those of people close to them. In this analysis, the answers are clustered into six major themes. To answer the main question, 58.8% or respondents agreed that it is difficult being a female in America, while 41.2% did not. The demographic data showed that respondents were comprised of 41.2% women between the ages 18-30 years old; 34.6% between 31 and 58 years old, while respondents in the last group of 24.2% comprised of women over 56 years old. As observed in the chart below, the spread showed a variety of experiences especially in form of professional interactions since 62.1% of respondent are involved in some income generating occupation. Only 3.3% reported not working currently employed.

4) Which is your main activity? You can answer one or more of the following options
153 responses

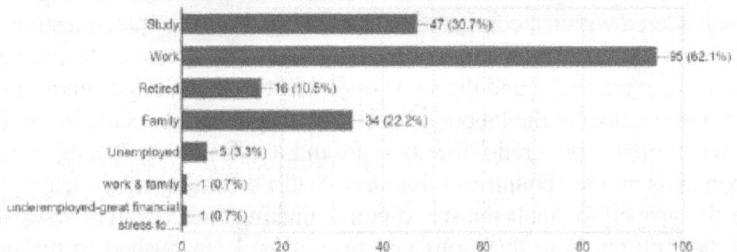

Study — 47 (30.7%)
Work — 95 (62.1%)
Retired — 16 (10.5%)
Family — 34 (22.2%)
Unemployed — 5 (3.3%)
work & family — 1 (0.7%)
underemployed-great financial stress fo... — 1 (0.7%)

Further, 85% of the respondents agreed that women and men are different, while 15% did not. This question may have confused some because it can be looked at from many angles. For example, some may emphasize differences in biological terms, while others may look at abilities that both males and females possess. The respondents also ranked policies aimed at women as 32.7% fair and 52.3% as not enough. There were some respondents that would not answer question for lack of clear knowledge about the policies in question.

8) From 1=nothing to 5=a lot, according to you, compared to 10 years ago, women's conditions in your country have changed, not only within the worforce?
153 responses

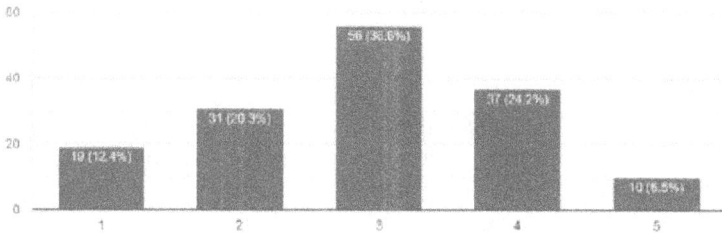

The above chat shows the perceptions of improved conditions over time. Most respondents agree that conditions are getting better. As stated in the introduction, these are lived experiences from which the women could draw comparisons over time. The perception of improved conditions is operationalised in the perceptions towards access to technology. 75.8% of women stated that they have as much access to technology as men, and that this technology affords them the same opportunities as men to the labour force. In addition, 53.6% compared to 46.4% said they were just as likely as men to find employment. On the job, 62.1% stated that women can have a highly successful career just as men do. 37.9% did not this this was the case.

Public life is a major concern to women of all ages since policies are generated in that space that involve every one of them. When quired about whether women are allowed to participate in public life, especially pilots, a large majority at 66.7% said yes, while 33.3% disagreed.

The overwhelming majority (90.2%) said education is key to career development for women. Despite this affirmation of the role of education career advancement, many women (63.4%) said that it is hard for them to balance family and jobs. The qualitative answers shed more light on this dichotomy.

Domestic violence is a very disturbing phenomenon. 51% of the respondents, fortunately responded that they have not been victims. However, 45.1%, which is a substantial number, reported being victims, with the rest refusing to answer that question.

Methodology for analysis.

This analysis uses thematic analysis. I found the responses to associate with the following themes. These are 1) rights; 2) justice; 3) bias; 4) opportunities; 5) effects; and 6) not difficult

Common themes.

1) Rights

Some respondents stated that women and men have the same rights in every respect. However, others made remarks that focused on the legal rights that get debated in legislatures and courts around the country. For example, one stated that

> "In terms of justice, some women observed that the justice system, especially the conservative justices appointed by former President Trump, were hostile to women's health and reproductive choices."

or

> "Four years of the Trump administration. Supreme Court heavily weighed now conservative and against women's rights."

The above statements are example of many similar ones.

2) Justice

Some respondent said "unfair laws" exist. For example, another said

> "Women are conditioned by society to take countless precautions to avoid being attacked by men — and if they are attacked, all too frequently, the perpetrator is given a lenient sentence or not held accountable."

Another stated

"But I think it can be difficult sometimes for a Christian/Catholic woman in regard to the pressure for their bodies--abortion, birth control, etc."

3) Bias

Some respondents have observed biased towards them. For example, one stated that

"There are still gender norms and stereotypes that make it more difficult for women to be successful in the workplace and puts pressure of them to take parental/family roles that are not equitable."

This kind of bias leads to discrimination.
Another stated that

"While gender norms are starting to be viewed a bit more critically, they still play a role in women's lives, and it can be particularly difficult for women when their goals do not align with these norms. For example, it can be difficult for women to be taken seriously in STEM fields, especially when they are outnumbered by men. Additionally, toxic masculinity and rape culture pose a serious danger to women"

A third respondent stated

"Non-stop struggle going against societal silent norms and expectations. I think being a woman today in the USA means having to explain yourself after certain things/situations in which men are never questioned. As an example, if a woman gives a different opinion or her point of view she can be is described with adjectives like ''opinionated'' ''aggressive''. But when a man shows the same behaviour, we never question that behaviour, we just say they are being leaders. In this sense, I believe there is A. an implicit bias and B. a sense of double standards within society. It is hard to get into a career in my field of study due to the overwhelming male presence and underwhelming female presence.

The result of the biases is that women often must prove that they are just as qualified as men.

4) Opportunities

Some respondents were very optimistic, stating that "Women are given opportunities to grow and succeed," and "we have more opportunity and freedom then in other countries around the world." another stated that

"In my personal experience, when I was a young woman and started my career, I did face some age discrimination. Otherwise, being female has not been difficult. I feel as if I have the same opportunities as men."

Although 62.1% stated that women can have a highly successful career just as men, several qualitative statements gave examples of when women felt they had fewer opportunities.

"Men dominate many fields, corporate boards, and leadership roles still. We still do not have a female President though at least we have a VP. It's disappointing that worldwide woman still cannot lead in the Catholic Church. Progress is good but slow."

Another stated

"Women are told that they can choose whatever they want for their lives. But what this really means is that women should make themselves "like men" by shutting down their reproductive system with birth control, by advancing in their career, by putting off marriage and/or children, and by finding childcare and continuing their career after children. The "option" for woman to pursue a feminine desire of caring for home, family, and neighbour does not exist, and women are belittled for making such a choice."

The result of the disparate opportunities is the observable wage gap mostly, and politics and religion; occupations largely controlled by men.

5) Effects
There are several effects on women as result of biases and dished opportunities. These include "salary gap (generally in all jobs), especially in STEAM fields women's work is considerably."
One respondent stated that

"In terms of effects, most women said they were discriminated against based on gender, age, and perceived lack of ability. For example, some said women are taken less seriously in STEM fields where they are outnumbered by men."

Other effects manifest in lack of protection; having too much labour to do (especially domestic); and doing it without much help. Others are ageism, hardships of being a single woman, and lack of economic mobility
A respond stated that

"There is pressure to excel in the workplace and be the perfect involved mother. There is much more pressure placed on working mothers in this respect than on working fathers."

In the same vein another stated that

"Men are still viewed as having more important status, so their voices are given more credence. Women have more responsibilities. Men are generally paid more, and the men I know do not ever feel unsafe doing anything alone."

6) Not difficult

The last theme is a collection of anecdotes about why it is not a difficult thing being a woman in America. Some said that "women are in power and control everything." without qualifying this statement, it is hard to know whether it was meant in jest. However, it sets an opportunistic tone for respondent that had a positive outlook. One of them said It is not difficult because in the metropolitan area in which I live women have a better lifestyle and parity than in many other areas."

Another respondent stated that

"I am just speaking from personal experience. I haven't ever had a difficult time because I was a female. I know others have, but that has not been my life."

Another that

"Most married men today help with household chores and child rearing than in the past. Some husbands are the chief cooks or even house husbands while the wife is the major bread winner. Employers are looking for potential employees who can be an asset to their company regardless of gender."

One respondent stated that difficulties do not discriminate

"I think broken families, addiction, unemployment, poverty, sexual abuse, etc. affect individuals irrespective of gender because they are human issues. I know certain studies show higher rates of males or females affected by certain issues and I wouldn't disagree with that; but how deep personal pain goes and the fact that all people have challenges because we are human does not make me feel like it is necessarily harder to be a woman in my country right now."

Some respondents identified intersectional between several women characterises. For example, by stating that

"Hard for this as a yes or no question but I have experienced the ability to chase what I want to chase and freely make choices here in the Us. Much to do with the fact that I'm white and have an education."

1.4 *Commentary on the Mexico's Survey about the importance of women in society (Maria de Lourdes Dieck-Assad)*

Women have increasingly shown the world that they can undertake much more than their traditional role at home, both in developed as in developing countries. Society does not question their role as housewives, mothers, housekeepers, caring for parents or older relatives. About 50% of the world's population are women and there is also an increasing number of households led by women, but at the same time we witness the feminization of poverty world-wide, and continued complaints about discrimination and violence against women. Women all over the world have entered the labor force, either forced by the economic needs of their own family or their extended family, or simply because they want a better life for all and have the talent and the education to pursue a job and a career as well as raise their families, as well as improve their social and economic status.

This commentary will describe the Survey's results for Mexico, whose purpose has been to understand what the respondents (80% women and 20% men) think about the role of women, the challenges, the needs, and the importance of being a woman in their Country. We will present here the highlights and the key issues raised by the respondents to the Survey. Before entering to the Survey results, though it is appropriate to get a picture of the size and some characteristics of women's population in Mexico.

Women in Mexico- some key data. Mexico's population in 2020 was 126 million people, of which 51.2% are women. The largest population group is between 10 and 19 years of age, 21.7 million, between 0 and 9 years, 21 million, and between 20 and 29 years, 20.4 million. So, more than 50% of the Mexican population is under 29 years of age, which make this a very young Country, with all its advantages and implications for the future.

The rate of labor force participation[10] for women has increased from less than 20% in 1960 to about 40% in 2017. Latest data seem to reveal that in 2019 the participation rate for women was 45%, but it was 77% for men. Women's participation is very low even as compared with Latin America (LA), since most LA countries have a participation rate for women above

---

10   Participation rate is the% of women 16 years or older that are working or actively looking for a job.

50%. On the other hand, women in Mexico have been gaining in the educational level. Recently, working women's education levels are higher than men. But the workload for women is heavier than for men, since they are now participating in the labor force, but continue to have the family responsibilities to a large degree[11].

The higher the education degree, the higher the participation rate of women. The participation rate of single women is much higher than that of married women, at any level of education. But interestingly, single women with a university degree have a participation rate of 95% but compares with the one for married women that is only 70%. On the other hand, the difference in the participation rate of men and women is larger in poor families, and families where both man and wife work are more likely in higher income families than in poorer ones. Education is a determining factor for women's participating in the labor force, and hence the need to ensure supporting the poorer ones, in their access to educational opportunities.

According to a World Bank report, if women would have the same participation rate as men, the per capita income in the country would be 22% higher[12].

The Survey- highlights of results. General acceptance of women in society: survey results overwhelmingly show that in Mexico it is hard to be a woman. About 80% of the respondents believe so. The key reasons for this answer are related to job/employment conditions and perspectives, women' status/stereotypes in society (patriarch-based), machismo, the lack of respect of their rights, discrimination and feminicides, traditional women roles and income pressures, childbearing conditions, and the cultural context.

Regarding Employment/job conditions: It is repeated by many respondents that the job market is not a plain field where each person, men, or women, get their fair share according to their qualities, capacity and contributions to the workplace. It is interesting to notice that most Survey´s respondents are between 18 and 56 years of age, and 62% are in the workforce. Among respondents 67% say that it is not possible for women to find a job like men do. The Survey's respondents comment that there is not salary-equity for the same responsibility and qualifications of

---

11   Data from: ONU study. La participacion laboral de la mujer en Mexico. Naciones Unidas México. Diciembre 2020 onu.org.mx/ la-participacion-laboral-de-la-mujer-en-mexico/
12   World Bank Group. Reporte: La participación laboral de la mujer en México. 2020.

women vs. men, where women are paid less even if they have the same responsibility and the same qualifications for the job. The respondents also state that in general there is a lack of opportunities for women in the job market, and harder to attain jobs in specific fields, even if qualified. The issue of discrimination against women in the job market is repeated by respondents, and they also mention that women need to justify themselves much more than men in the same situations, that women do not get the same recognition as men do and that there is a glass ceiling when trying to be promoted, and an even harder barrier for women with children to escalate the job ladder.

On the other hand, some have the perception that opportunities are already growing for women, although slowly, but mostly after demonstrating their talent and capacities. Actually, 83% say that women can have a successful career as men do. But they state that the key for this is women's education and personal skills to relate in the job market.

When asked about the change in labor market conditions in the last 10 years, 41% of respondents say that a lot has happened and are optimistic, 43% say there are not so many changes and are not so optimistic, and 16% say they are less optimistic. Why? Because women are still seldom considered for executive positions or high-level government positions, although it is mentioned that there are a few more for mid-management positions. Women fight for their positions, but it is said that the role of women has become more complex because of their responsibilities at home, and hence it is harder to be successful in both home and workplace.

Regarding the job market, for jobs in the public sector, only 56% of respondents state that women can participate in public roles (politics). They attribute this to the presence of factors such as a lot of discrimination from the population to see women as candidates, specifically they state that *machismo* is very deep in Mexico. However, they also state that some women are gradually participating more in politics, when this was practically impossible in the past.

Regarding women's social stereotypes: the respondents in a great way mention the problem of discrimination, mistreatment of women, patriarchism, violence, femicides and social injustice against women. Women in general, according to survey, still are seen as the responsible party for family raising, so children continue to be their main responsibility. It is mentioned that companies and employers in general rather hire men than women with children, in part because of women's limitations to travel, which sometimes arises as part of the job. So, women with children are at a disadvantage to be able to get a better life for them and for their own families. It is also said that some women have been able to participate in the job market due to some job-equality laws, but still very limited.

Regarding technology access for women: a large percentage of respondents say women do have access, 71% say so. However, in their comments they qualify this statement pointing out to the fact that even having such access, the job options are much more limited for women for many reasons, including discrimination, having a family and/or children, having the belief that women are less capable, not wanting to deal with women for other stereotypes, etc. One respondent even gives an example that in many families if there is money for one computer only, it would be given to the son, not to the daughters. So even within inside the families 'environment, daughters are treated differently, so it seems, being placed second after sons.

Government or company support: regarding the support of the government to advance the status and role of women, 66% say it is not enough, only 10% say that current support is fair and 11% say that the current policies are incorrect. It is mentioned that some laws and diverse policies are helping but still slowly. It is mentioned that rights have been acquired for women in the job market, but at the same time women are limited to take advantage of them because they have remained with the responsibilities of family caring to a much larger degree.

Violence against women. 73% of respondents say that they or someone they know has suffered it. The reality women face with violence, being it domestic violence, or violence in the job place, or even in the streets, is overwhelming. From their answers it seems that the issues of feminicides, machismo, traditional roles for women in family, and superiority by men, are all contributing to the violence against women. Only 48% state that there is support for women to balance family and work.

Some positive prospects: within the responses, there are signs of hope for women's role in society, mainly the women who have obtained education and are being able to find good jobs. These women are becoming examples for others. Some legislations have been passed to help reduce discrimination against women in the hiring process, but the respondents say that the implementation will take time.

The respondents are also asked to cite the conditions for women to develop professionally, and 89% mention education as the main condition. 71% also mention personal skills. This reinforces previous answers and comments by respondents, that education is key, and even more important when Mexico has still such a young population.

Regarding why it is important to be a woman: most respondents one way or another mention all the features that women bring to society as special to them, for example, a responsible, respectful, dedicated human being. Although they say both men and women must have such qualities, and that a balanced society needs both. They state that they are human beings very responsible, respectful of others, diligent, with principles. Furthermore, women's creativity and intelligence are to be highlighted in the current context where these are needed so much. Women, they state, can perceive what is right, generate changes, are sensible and visionary, have empathy, educate future generations, and make decisions based on all these qualities. Many respondents visualize women as the force of the family and say that without women there is no strong family, and without family there is not society. There are ample answers that portray the need for a balanced society that needs both men and women at home and in the workplace.

Final Comments. It is very surprising the low participation rate of women in the labor force in Mexico. It is the lowest in Latin America, except for Guatemala. The reasons for such low participation rate are clearly portrayed in the Survey's answers to the different questions. Issues of discrimination in the job market, lack of support for childcare, the struggle that women must be treated fairly in terms of opportunities and of salary, the need for opportunities for women's training and education (at all income levels, mostly the poor), and the need to find a way to balance family and work in a society that is still very traditional regarding the duties of women at home.

Clearly through the Survey, the subjects of discrimination, violence and femicides, lack of resources to help with childcare, are noteworthy. And data from Mexico, World Bank and United Nations confirm that the situation for women in Mexico is improving but mostly in the higher income, higher educated women. The law is still not to the level to ensure the equality and justice for women in the marketplace, as has been expressed by the respondents. There are small improvements, but their enforcement is questionable. For lower income women, the key issue of support for childcare seems to be the most important in order to allow more women to engage in work and/or in education or skill acquisition that can improve their options. Women also lack the backup of the law, the justice they deserve to protect them against violence.

There is a clear loss that the Country bears because of the low participation of women in the labor force: according to the world bank report, if women would increase its participation to the level of men, the Country's income per capita would be 22% higher. This is telling us that if all those existing barriers for women participation in the job market are taken away, women's contribution to the well-being of the Country would be very significative. But it would need the will of authorities and leadership in all sectors of society. And besides the economic benefits that are being foregone, the qualitive aspects of the participation of women are also recognized in the Survey: their talents and unique vision are lost if they are not able to participate in the labor force according to their capabilities. Finally, I would like to end with these respondents' comments which are worth repeating and reflecting on: "They visualize women as the force of the family and say that without women there is no strong family, and without family there is not society... women are human beings very responsible, respectful of others, diligent, with principles. They are sensible and visionary, have empathy... Women's creativity and intelligence are to be highlighted in the current context where these are needed so much. Women can perceive what is right, generate changes, and contribute to educate future generations... which constitutes the future of the Country".

1.5 *La importancia de ser mujer hoy en Cuba (Ivan Castillo Ledo*[13]*)*

En el estudio fueron encuestados 120 personas de ambos sexos, de la totalidad de respuestas el 60.8% refiere no ser un problema ser mujer en Cuba, las razones planteadas por los encuestados fueron disimiles, entre las que se destacan las relacionadas con la situación económico social que vive el país en estos momentos, según las opiniones dado por la Pandemia y por la política de los Estados Unidos recrudecida en el gobierno de Trump. Todavía existen manifestaciones de machismo (hegemonía del sexo masculino) y violencia doméstica que dificulta el desenvolvimiento femenino, hay quienes plantean que a pesar de existir una Constitución todavía se necesitan otras regulaciones jurídicas que protejan a la mujer. Por otra parte, hay quienes plantean que la mujer tiene los mismos derechos que el hombre, son respetados sus criterios, además que existe en Cuba leyes, artículos, decretos que apoya a la mujer donde le dan la potestad que sus palabras sean escuchadas. Ante la sociedad mantiene es apoyada por el gobierno, las mujeres pueden ocupar el mismo trabajo que los hombres, además tienen oportunidad de ocupar cargos directivos y las escalas salariales son iguales para ambos casos. A pesar de las dificultades se mira siempre hacia adelante expresado en opiniones como esta: "En

---

13   Policlínico Raúl Suárez Martínez, Rodas, Cuba.

Cuba las mujeres son muy luchadoras, fuertes y valientes, madres que caminan siempre hacia adelante y que a pesar de las dificultades del país siempre saben adaptarnos a la situación, la vida en Cuba es muy difícil, pero a pesar de todo salen adelante".

Del total de personas encuestadas el 17.5% correspondió al grupo etario de 18 a 30 años, el 32.5% al grupo comprendido por mayores de 56 años y el mayor porciento con 50% los comprendidos entre 31 y 56 años. De esta forma 66 encuestados para un 55% son trabajadores, igual cantidad representaron los retirados y estudiantes con 17 personas para un 14.2%, menor porciento representó los desempleados y otras categorías ocupacionales.

En cuanto a las opiniones referidas a ser mujer es diferente a ser hombre, las respuestas resultaron muy similares, un 50.8% considera que si resulta diferente y un 49.2% no lo manifiesta así. Las razones expuestas que explican estas respuestas están dadas por la percepción individual que se tiene, la mayoría expresa que las diferencias existen en cualquier latitud del planeta, en Cuba específicamente aún se muestras actitudes de este tipo, lo que se pretende es evitar que estas diferencias lleven a situaciones injustas, también se responsabiliza a la familia en cuanto a la educación sexista de los hijos, esto repercute en la visión global de este fenómeno. Otros criterios muestran que las mujeres tienen los mismos derechos y deberes que los hombres, la opinión de una mujer cuenta, pueden ocupar cargo que sean de hombres ya que se tiene la misma capacidad que ellos. La mujer no se siente en Cuba despreciada al contrario se siente protegida, segura, también se agrega "somos felices aquí y compartimos nuestra vida personal y laborar con los hombres, nuestros compañeros de lucha".

Atendiendo a la percepción que se tiene en relación con las políticas sobre la mujer el 51.7% las consideraron justas, un 21.7% como insuficientes, mientras que un 15.8% las consideran incorrectas y un 10.8% expresaron no saber.

El acápite relacionado con el criterio comparativo en relación con el cambio de las condiciones de la mujer en Cuba respecto a 10 años atrás se encuentra que el 32.5% considera que ha cambiado mucho, un 26.7%% considera cambios no tan significativos y el resto de los encuestados expresa que los cambios han sido mínimos. En cuanto a las razones que argumentan estas respuestas se obtuvo que a pesar de han existido cambios estos han sido tan de prisa que no se percibe si se está haciendo bien, por otra parte, se plantea que se ha avanzado mucho en materia de igualdad sobre la cuestión de la maternidad y la ayuda a la mujer trabajadora, aunque aún hay cosas que mejorar. También ahora las mujeres gozan de total independencia del hombre, ya que son libres de "trabajar donde decidan, vivir con quien queramos, amar a quien elijamos y decidir sobre nuestro cuerpo". Otros platean que el progreso hacía la igualdad de género en el ámbito laboral se está consiguiendo poco a poco, mejorando sustancialmente en los últimos años. Otras opiniones resaltan la política del país en este sentido refiriendo que "con El Triunfo de la Revolución se mejoro la situación de la mujer", "...en estos años la mujer ha jugado un rol protagónico en la sociedad, no solo como fuerza laboral sino que estamos en todos los frentes de batallas, en todas las organizaciones de masas como son, FMC, CDR, CTC, UJC, PCC, teniendo una destacada y activa participación, demostrando cada día de nuestra capacidad", "...han cambiado para bien, ya que las mujeres hoy en día juegan un papel fundamental en la familia y la sociedad, es un privilegio ser una mujer cubana, me siento orgullosa de serlo y de vivir en esta Cuba bella", "...han cambiado en comparación de hace 10 años atrás, para mejorar y en beneficio de la mujer, en especial de la mujer trabajadora, el estado defiende nuestros derechos, ya no somos mujeres marginadas en la sociedad, gracias a nuestra revolución", "... la Revolución Cubana ha empoderado a la mujer, realizamos las mismas funciones que los hombres, se nos respeta, nos valoran y siempre cuenta con nosotras, con nuestra organización de masas, la FMC fundada por Vilma Espín, destacada luchadora y defensora de los derechos de la mujer".

Respecto al acceso a la tecnología y a las oportunidades laborales referidas a la propia tecnología, se encontró que el 79.2% opina que se tienen los mismos derechos a diferencia de un 20.8% que creo lo contrario.

En cuanto a las oportunidades laborales el 57.5% opina que las mujeres encuentran trabajo al igual que los hombres, mientras el 42.5% opina diferente. En este aspecto se obtienen respuestas muy interesantes afirmando que "las mujeres tenemos el mismo derecho a la tecnología como Internet ya que podemos visitar páginas y sitios web para informarnos de las noticias y búsquedas que necesitan para uno estar preparados, las mujeres encontramos trabajo más fácil que los hombres ya que tenemos la misma capacidad y fuerza y voluntad que ellos, somos mejores y más dedicada y responsables".

Por otro lado, se plantea que la tecnología es algo comercial, no entiende de sexos, los trabajos sí que dependen de personas y por lo tanto la mujer por su condición tiene menos oportunidades.

Pero son reiteradas las respuestas que muestran que en nuestra sociedad hombres y mujeres tienen los mismos derechos a tener acceso a la tecnología y las mismas posibilidades de empleo que los hombres. Pero se hace necesario destacar una respuesta que explica cómo "en Cuba los avances tecnológicos llegaron muy tarde, solo algunas personas pudientes lograban tener acceso a internet, esto se debía a la situación económica y política que tiene el país. Hace como unos 5 o 6 años es que se ha logrado que el Internet llegue a todos y no existe diferencia en cuanto al acceso a tecnologías para hombres y mujeres, cada uno es libre de acceder. El problema más grave en este ámbito es la situación económica del país porque o no existen los medios tecnológicos o no hay suficientes recursos para acceder a ellos. La fuerza laboral también está muy organizada, hay libertades de acceder al trabajo que quieras y recibes un salario igual al del hombre según las responsabilidades o desarrollo profesional que tengas. En la educación, debido a que todos los estudios son gratuitos, al culminar la carrera universitaria o alguna formación superior te ubican en un puesto de trabajo tanto a hombres como mujeres y durante un año trabajas sin cobrar, serían como unas prácticas o lo que normalmente se conoce en Cuba como "trabajo social", al finalizar ese año puedes continuar en ese trabajo o te ubican en otro. Pero en un principio no tienes que buscarte algún puesto laboral".

Las respuestas concernientes a las oportunidades de acceso a una carrera exitosa, de los 120 encuestados el 79.2% respondió afirmativamente, a diferencia del 20.8% que tuvieron respuestas diferentes. Con relación a la participación en la vida pública, especialmente en la política, el 74.2% refirió que se tienen oportunidades mientras que el 25.8% respondió de forma contraria. Por otra parte, los criterios referentes a las condiciones necesarias para el desarrollo profesional de la mujer 110 encuestados para un 91.7% respondió que la educación es una condición necesaria, seguido de 61 para un 50.8% que manifestó que son necesarias las habilidades personales.

Los encuestados plantearon que el esfuerzo y la tensión que exigen los cargos en las mujeres son superiores por las muchas otras responsabilidades que tienen que desempeñar dentro y fuera del hogar. Es, por tanto, indispensable un cambio sociocultural que conciba la igualdad de responsabilidades en las tareas cotidianas de la vida familiar, lo que supone no sólo potenciar la creación de condiciones generales dentro de la sociedad que sirvan de plataforma para este propósito, sino trabajar en la esfera educacional y cultural con vistas a preparar tanto al hombre como a la mujer en principios auténticos de igualdad en el marco de la familia. Otros plantean que las mujeres pueden tener carrera exitosa como los hombres ya que tienen los mimos conocimientos y pueden superarse y lograr obtener carreras exitosas, las mujeres pueden tener cargos públicos, y además pueden dirigir ya que tienen carácter, fuerza, voluntad para llevar una carrera política con buen empeño. También se refiere que la educación es la base que usa cada país para enseñar, instruir, formar y adiestrar a la mujer en la sociedad y que sepa como trabajar, dirigir y exigir donde quiera que este, la educación es cultura que se debe llevar a cada lugar o sitio que pueda ir, ya que es quien le permite desarrollarse en cualquier ámbito que se encuentres.

Se expresa que la mujer en Cuba pueden tener una carrera éxitosa al igual que los hombres, porque no se nos limita para poder realizarla, con inteligencia y capacidad logran triunfar en todo lo que se propone.

Las mujeres con el paso de los años se han introducido en los diferentes ámbitos de la sociedad y con ello a la política le han dado un giro y perspectiva diferente dada por las capacidad que tienen para dirigir diversos aspectos debido a sus capacidades intelectuales.

En el acápite relacionado con el equilibrio familia-trabajo, el 55.8% contestó que se existe equilibrio y se tuvieron un 44.2% de respuestas diferentes.

Se hace necesario destacar que en el presente estudio el 88.3% lo constituyeron representantes del sexo femenino, esto es reflejado en la multiplicidad de respuestas. Al indagar sobre la presencia de violencia doméstica hubo una representación mayoritaria del 46.7% que refiere no existir este flagelo, mientras que no menos importante el 44.2% de respuestas que considera que si existe, un 9.2% prefirió no responder.

Finalmente se hace referencia a la importancia de ser mujer hoy y las razones por lo que lo expresan van en diferentes direcciones, se refiere que las mujeres en la sociedad actual son ejemplo de inteligencia y fortaleza, lo que se ve reflejado en la capacidad para superar las adversidades ante la discriminación de la son objeto, a pesar de que se considere una sociedad igualitaria y tolerante aún existe un núcleo de personas machistas, que mantiene en la marginación; pasan por alto que las mujeres asumen obligaciones, lo que socialmente no es valorado, pues se asume que esto es un deber de la mujer, por el simple hecho de ser mujer, lo que no entienden es que este rol no es fácil, si tomamos en cuenta que las mujeres tienen aspiraciones, anhelos y metas que se ven obstaculizadas al ser las encargadas de dirigir el hogar, pues las absorbe casi por completo.

Otras comentan que si es importante ser mujer en este mundo que se vive, Dios las escogió desde el principio para ser la compañía y la base de todo en la familia, "cuando eres mujer debes sentirte feliz ya que fuiste elegida por Dios llevar una tarea de dar luz a un hijo, de día a día cuidarlo, alimentarlo, enseñarlo, educarlo y viviré con el cada vivencia que Dios pone en su camino",. "Feliz de ser mujer soy única y repetida tengo tanto derecho que el hombre ,no mejor ni pero que nadie más bien soy una mujer con los mimos derecho en mi sociedad como otro ser viviente".

Es muy importante ser mujer hoy, porque "hemos dado muestra de que somos fuerte como sexo, desde la familia en la crianza de nuestros hijos formando valores para el bién de la sociedad, en nuestros centros de trabajo nos escuchan y valoran nuestras opiniones, así como en otros frentes de batalla, hemos sido capáces de estar en la primera línea, la mujer con su actitud y valentía es muy importante para el desarrollo de una sociedad más justa y por un mundo mejor, que sí es posible".

Expresiones masculinas concluyen: "mi madre es mujer, mi esposa es mujer, mis hermanas son mujeres y son primordiales en mi vida. También mis amigas son mujeres al igual que mis compañeras de trabajo, con las que trabajo codo con codo como iguales".

1.6 *La lutte des femmes en Haïti (Alandre Nandie Menelas[14])*

Historicité de la lutte des femmes en Haïti: bilan et réalisation. L'histoire contemporaine de la condition féminine en Haïti débute officiellement en mai 1865, dans la ville du Cap-Haitien, dans le quartier de la Fossette, lorsqu'une révolte urbaine et populaire éclate, mobilisant majoritairement des femmes issues des couches aisées. En effet, si les femmes haïtiennes ont toujours pris une part active dans les combats pour le respect des droits humains en général, cette date marque un tournant dans leurs revendications qui dépeignirent pour la première fois leur velléités d'être vues et entendues comme individus et citoyennes à part entière, et non comme des mineures qui passeraient de la tutelle du père, du mari puis du fils. Celles-ci lutteront jusqu'à la fin du siècle pour soutenir la cause de l'égalité entre les sexes.

La lutte fut de longue haleine, cependant, elles parvinrent, du moins sur le papier, à obtenir gain de cause. En 1934, la Ligue féminine d'action sociale (LFAS) est officiellement créée. Les membres de cette organisation militaient en faveur de l'avancement physique, moral et intellectuel des femmes haïtiennes en les sensibilisant sur leur responsabilité sociale. Elles réclamaient notamment l'ouverture d'écoles pour filles, un salaire égal pour un travail égal et la reconnaissance de l'égalité civile et politique. Elles mettront sur pied un journal, La voix des femmes, afin de propager leurs idées. Ces idées étant jugées subversives par le gouvernement de Sténio Vincent, la LFAS est bannie seulement deux mois après sa création.

---

14   ISNAC, Centre de Formation en Communication et en Administration, Port au Prince, Haïti.

Le gouvernement qui succédera lui permettra de reprendre ses actions en 1941. Près de quatre-vingts ans de lutte acharnée, ponctues de mort et de torture de certaines militantes, la constitution de 1950 accorda le droit de vote et d'éligibilité aux femmes haïtiennes, après deux échecs en 1944 et en 1946.

Des parlementaires progressistes comme Jean Price mars et Dantès Louis Bellegarde œuvrèrent pour l'adoption du texte. Ce n'est, cependant, seulement qu'à partir des élections de 1991, premier scrutin démocratique du pays, que les femmes votent réellement, toutefois le respect effectif des droits de la femme en Haïti demeure une vraie gageure.

La conjoncture sociopolitique sociale et économique fait partie de l'obstacle à la pleine jouissance des droits fondamentaux de la personne, y compris les femmes.

La violence faite aux femmes est perpétuée par des attitudes et des pratiques discriminatoires à l'égard des victimes. L'un des facteurs qui contribue à un sentiment général de tolérance à l'égard des actes de violence constitue une violation des droits de la personne, qui devrait déclencher l'obligation l'État de prendre une action pour prévenir ces abus. En outre les victimes et les personnes vivant dans les communautés les plus affectées n'ont pas bénéficié de l'intervention de la justice pour la plupart des abus ou des violations souffertes au fil des ans. Cet état de chose nourrit le climat d'impunité et un sentiment de tolérance envers cette situation. Un autre facteur qui contribue à la culture du silence entourant les actes de violences exercés contre les femmes, tels que la violence sexuelle, est la stigmatisation par la société que causent ces crimes.

S'il est vrai qu'avec l'aide des organisations féministes dans le pays et avec le Ministère à la condition féminine, beaucoup de choses se sont améliorées (une plus grande fraction de la communauté féminine issues de toutes les couches de la société, poursuivent des études supérieures par exemple), ces dernières années nous avons assisté à une recrudescence du bafoue ment des droits des femmes. Elles sont de plus en plus victimes de discrimination et de violences, entre novembre 2020 et mai 2021 plus de 10 féminoïdes perpétrés par leurs partenaires confirmés ont eu lieu en raison des difficultés à obtenir un emploi et des obstacles à leur participation à la vie politique réelles. On compte plus d'hommes dans les cercles dirigeants politiques, sociaux et familiaux ; ceux-ci estimant que le pouvoir est une affaire masculine. En dépit du fait que les femmes représentent plus de 52% de la population, les hommes occupent majoritairement les postes électifs. Mis à part les difficultés des femmes haïtiennes à intégrer le marché du travail et de la politique, elles font face a beaucoup d'autres problèmes tels: les abus sexuels de tout genre, des hommes qui n'assument pas leur paternité (la grande majorité des femmes élèvent seules des enfants parceque le géniteur qui l'a enceinté lui a fait comprendre que l'enfant n'est pas de lui, ou parce qu'elles vivaient chez une sœur, une tante ou avec sa mère dont le mari leur a fait subir un viol, voire plusieurs, mais nie tout en bloc)…On trouve aussi des femmes obligées d'abandonner leurs rêves parce qu'un conjoint le leur a imposé, ou certaines ayant été la proie de prédateurs sexuels au prétexte que les vêtements que portaient les victimes étaient une invitation flagrante à la consommation. Ici en Haïti la femme n'est pas maitresse de son corps, la notion de viol conjugal n'est pas reconnue par les principales entités, gardienne de la "morale" : l'église, la famille et l'État, elle n'a pas le droit de dire non à son mari si elle ne se sent pas capable ou d'humeur à avoir des rapports sexuels avec lui, tout simplement parce qu'elle est mariée et que son corps appartient à son mari.

Le poids du patriarcat traditionnel est tellement lourd dans notre culture que la majorité des hommes haïtiens se croient tout permis juste à cause de leurs attributs phalliques, et de fait malheureusement certaines femmes, pour ne pas dire beaucoup, se plient à ces abus établis comme la norme. On entendra souvent des mères s'enorgueillir d'avoir un fils pour tirer des coups pour elles, ce qu'elles considèrent comme une vengeance pour les calamités endurées, se révélant en fait n'être qu'une perpétuation d'un cycle vicieux millénaire, On assiste également à fémicides commis par des femmes se disputant l'attention d'un homme, dont le but n'est, somme toute, que de garnir son tableau de chasse.

La question des droits politiques sensibilise les partis politiques afin de permettre une participation égale des sexes aux cercles de décision. Certaine organisation féministe estime que l'éducation, la sensibilisation et l'autonomie financière des femmes aidera à éliminer les violences visant les femmes. Il existe en effet un fossé entre l'égalité des sexes promue par la constitution et la réalité.

Les résultats de notre recherche effectuée sur « l'importance d'être femme aujourd'hui en Haïti ». Sur un échantillon de 120 personnes ayant répondu au questionnaire qui avait été préparé dans le cadre de ce travail, démontre les faits suivants :

- À la première question qui est la suivante : est-ce difficile d'être femme aujourd'hui en Haïti ? 74.2% ont répondu : « oui » et 25.8% non. Ce qui nous permet de conclure que le combat pour arriver à l'égalité des sexes en Haïti est encore loin. La majorité des réponses obtenues ne diffèrent nullement de ce que nous avons évoqué plus haut, les difficultés qu'ont les femmes à intégrer le marché du travail, les obligent souvent à taire le harcèlement constant de leurs patrons, à subir des violences verbales, domestiques et/ou conjugales etc.

- 91.7% disent qu'être femme en Haïti est différent d'être homme. Pour appuyer leurs réponses certains prennent l'exemple de l'inégalité salariale qui existe entre un homme et une femme occupant un même poste avec les mêmes compétences, d'autres enchainent avec le milieu politique haïtien qui est occupé en majorité par des hommes, le système patriarcal qui sous-entend que la femme est le sexe faible, qui la réduit a un foyer, que leur place est a la cuisine etc.

- En ce qui a trait à la question sur les politiques d'Haïti concernant les femmes 50.8% estiment qu'ils ne suffisent pas, 16.2% ont répondu qu'ils ne savent pas, 13.3% estiment que les politiques du pays en faveur les femmes sont justes, 10% pensent qu'il n'existe pas de politique concernant les femmes et 9.2% estiment que les politiques du pays en faveur les femmes sont faux.

- A la question, par rapport à 10 ans, est ce que les conditions des femmes ont changé en Haïti

18 personnes, soit 15% estiment que rien n'a changé, 31 personnes soit 25.8% pensent qu'il y'a un tout petit peu de changement, 52 personnes soit 43.3% estiment qu'il y'a eu assez de changement et 19 personnes soit 15.8% ont répondu qu'il y'a eu beaucoup de changement. Et comme argument la majorité a répondu qu'avec l'aide des organisations féministes, le quota de 30% des femmes dans les administration de l'état, même si c'est pas facile mais le Ministère à la condition féminine et aux droits de la femme essaie de jouer son rôle tant bien que mal, certaines femmes commencent à réclamer ce qui leur revient de droit, les femmes cherchent leurs places ailleurs que dans la cuisine, on retrouve beaucoup plus de femmes qui militent que ce soit sur le plan social, culturel et politique, les femmes essaient de tracer leur propres voies, elles sont beaucoup a diriger leurs propres entreprise donc la situation a vraiment évolué durant ces 10 dernières années même s'il reste beaucoup plus à faire.

Coté technologie comme l'indique 75% des personnes, j'estime qu'une femme autant qu'un homme ont le même accès à la technologie et les mêmes opportunités qu'avec l'émergence des téléphones intelligents presque tout le monde ont accès à internet, 8 personnes sur 10 ont un compte sur les réseaux sociaux. Cependant tout le monde n'utilise pas internet à cet effet, sinon les opportunités peuvent être les mêmes pour tous.

Conclusion. Mise à part les difficultés auxquels font face les femmes haïtiennes, elles constituent la force motrice de cette société, elles sont des héroïnes à travers les réponses obtenues sur la question « est-ce qu'une femme peut mener une carrière réussie en Haïti tout comme le font les hommes » 85.5% des réponses sont plutôt positive ce qui explique que nos femmes Haïtiennes ne s'avouent jamais vaincu, et les preuves sont là, elles croient qu'autant qu'un homme, elles ont aussi le droit de mener la carrière qui lui fait plaisir et ceci dignement sans qu'on lui fasse de faveur, d'ailleurs on les voient plus présentes de nos jours, elles tracent leurs propres chemins, elles défiaient le tabou disant que leur place se trouve dans la cuisine. Et côté politique malgré le fait que c'est un milieu dominé par les hommes, mais les femmes se fraient leur chemin dans la politique. Et pour y parvenir, elles ont compris que tout ceci doit se faire en se formant. Haïti n'a malheureusement aucun soutien pour les femmes voulant concilier travail et famille. Les plus aisées des familles font souvent appel à des « nounous » et/ou à une femme de ménage pour s'occuper de leurs enfants et de la maison, mais certaines sont obligées de sacrifier l'un ou l'autre, au mépris de leur épanouissement personnel. Toutefois, ceci n'empêche pas que certaines femmes arrivent à réussir dans les trois domaines : travail, études et familles mais y laissent souvent leur santé.

Être femme c'est important aujourd'hui, et le sera toujours tant que le monde continuera d'exister, les femmes sont l'alpha de la naissance, elles sont sensibles et protectrices, elles incarnent l'humanité et la douceur. Mais l'importance des femmes ne doit pas être réduite à son corps ou aux travaux ménagers mais plutôt comme une entité complémentaire de sa vis à vis masculin. Dans la société moderne que nous prônons et travaillons activement à construire, nous ne voudrions pas de rôles préétablis qui enferment homme ou femme dans un carcan coercitif, les obligeant à sur jouer un scenario qui, reconnaissons-le, est contreproductif, mais nous rêvons d'un monde, ou il n'y aurait plus de genre mais des humains, libres de choisir leur destinée[15].

---

15   *Source de documentation:* Le droit des femmes de vivre libre de violence et de discrimination (commission Interaméricaine des droits de l'homme); ASF-Canada (le féministe haïtien, portrait d'un mouvement fort); L'histoire du mouvement féministe haïtien (Ayibopost).

1.7 *La importancia de ser Mujer hoy en Venezuela (Jesús Álvarez, Miguel Ángel Altuve, Juan Pedro Pereira Medina[16])*

"Puedes cerrar todas las bibliotecas si quieres/Pero no hay barrera, ni cerradura ni cerrojo que puedas imponer/A la libertad de mi mente" (Virginia Woolf).

Nacer mujer en la actualidad y con las características propias de la realidad existente que se está viviendo podría decirse que es más difícil a diferencia de la realidad que viven los hombres. Sin embargo, es importante señalar, que en estos momentos es más aceptable que hace 50 años atrás, después de haber pasado por toda una serie de actualizaciones legales (que todavía siguen en estudio), donde se busca desde instituciones tan prestigiosas como la ONU y la Agenda 2030 la llamada "igualdad de género" (ODS No. 5), el cual solo se refiere a mayores oportunidades para las mujeres en los distintos campos sociales donde se desenvuelve, entendiendo que la equidad de género va mucho más allá.

Este estudio se realiza gracias a los aportes que, desde la Universidad Yacambú, ubicada en Cabudare, edo. Lara (Venezuela), juntamente con la Pontificia Universitá de la Santa Croce de Roma, siempre en la búsqueda del crecimiento científico en diferentes áreas, con un tema tan susceptible para la sociedad como es el ser mujer y su posición en términos sociales, económicos, políticos, culturales, demográficos, entre otros.

Según un estudio de Rausell (2015) "garantizar educación, protección e igualdad de oportunidades para las niñas es fundamental para solucionar algunos de los problemas más acuciantes del mundo, desde la expansión del sida hasta el ciclo de la pobreza" (p.23). Es importante recalcar la importancia de la educación para generar las condiciones necesarias que permitan que la sociedad entienda la igualdad de género como uno de los objetivos fundamentales a conseguir, el acceso a las distintas oportunidades que ofrece el entorno para la mujer y su participación directa en los procesos de enseñanza aprendizaje con el propósito de generar condiciones favorables en pro de su desarrollo integral como ser humano y ciudadana.

Continuando con el aporte de Rausell (ob. cit) "pese a los avances en el acceso a la educación, atención sanitaria y empleo, aún queda mucho por hacer para lograr la igualdad de género" (p.29). En efecto,

---

16 Lcdo. Jesús Álvarez, Enlace de Atención Comunitaria del Departamento de Vinculación y Proyección Comunitaria; Lcdo. Miguel Ángel Altuve, Decano de Extensión, Cultura y Deportes de la Universidad Yacambú, Barquisimeto, Edo Lara, Venezuela, bajo la coordinación y supervisión del ciudadano Rector, Dr. Juan Pedro Pereira Medina.

las estrategias que se han implementado para brindar un trato y una vida digna no han sido suficientes, lo que evidencia en el siguiente dato: "una de cada 10 mujeres menores de 20 años ha sido obligada a tener relaciones sexuales" (National Geographic, 2020); casos de matrimonio infantil que aumentan considerablemente el riesgo de contraer VIH-Sida; casos de mutilación genital, todavía en pleno siglo XXI, lo cual genera una serie de consecuencias irreparables en el transcurso de sus vidas; limitaciones para ascender en puestos claves en empresas o transnacionales; inequidad en cuanto a la remuneración laboral, tasas mundiales de abandono escolar de hasta 2 veces mayor con respecto a los hombres; la pobreza de los países en general se traduce en un aumento drástico del embarazo precoz (o embarazo en adolescentes), lo cual trae consigo más pobreza; incluso aún cuando su nivel de participación en puestos de gobierno para la generación de políticas públicas sobre la igualdad de género ha aumentado en los últimos años, sigue siendo insuficiente.

Como se puede observar, no es un camino fácil nacer mujer en este mundo, en términos generales. Sin embargo, los indicadores para América Latina son bastante aceptables, ya que incluso superan la media mundial de participación de la mujer en procesos claves de producción de bienes y servicios. Podemos considerar que esta situación es un gran adelanto para la sociedad latinoamericana, producto de los avances y decisiones que se han tomado en los últimos 25 años, a partir de la implementación de políticas inclusivas en algunos de sus gobiernos, con el propósito de disminuir la pobreza y la generación de mayores oportunidades para toda la población. Pero, aun así, sigue siendo insuficiente.

"Para combatir el antisemitismo no hace falta ser judío,
como para luchar contra el racismo no hace falta ser negro.
Lamentablemente, a veces parece que para combatir
la discriminación de la mujer, hace falta ser mujer"
(Soledad Gallego-Díaz, periodista)

Para América Latina no ha sido fácil entender el rol de la mujer. Hablar de ello en la actual sociedad es tan profundo como el amor que siente ella por su hijo al nacer, pero igualmente complejo como los dolores de parto. Esa representación de una guerrera con grandes rasgos de empoderamiento que se encuentra alojado en el imaginario social latinoamericano, y que no es nuevo en el quehacer histórico. Se cuentan siglos y centenares de batallas en las que participó o se vio de una u otra manera vinculada con la toma de decisiones para la liberación de los pueblos.

Tomando en cuenta dicha información, y a pesar de que en los últimos 20 años América Latina y el Caribe han progresado considerablemente hacia el empoderamiento de las mujeres en distintas áreas tanto sociales como económicas, estos logros no han sido suficientes en función de la ampliación de oportunidades para el acceso a los recursos de la misma manera que los hombres. Según el informe ONU Mujeres (2017) los índices de participación de las mujeres en Latinoamérica supera el promedio mundial; sin embargo "todavía se ubican 26 puntos porcentuales por debajo de los de los hombres en la región" (p.2).

Como señala el informe ONU Mujeres (2017) "Latinoamérica ha hecho su mejor esfuerzo, sin embargo, las brechas de género persisten y la pobreza se ha feminizado" (p.12). Al analizar cualquier informe a nivel mundial, es relevante al observar y tomar conciencia de como algunos sectores de la sociedad y sobre todo los actores políticos en sus acciones dejan a un lado a la figura de la mujer, como madre, como esposa, como hija, fuente dinamizadora de todo proceso que necesite entender que sensibilizar para canalizar soluciones también es otra alternativa ante el mapa de problemas que se presentan en la globalidad, y en este sentido las mujeres han permitido resolver problemas históricos al permitírsele participar en los procesos. No es por casualidad que hoy en día, según un estudio de ONU Mujeres (2021) señala que "en promedio, hasta un 4% ha avanzado la participación femenina en la toma de decisiones a nivel mundial". Y parece un avance luego de la batalla que se viene dando para permitir su inclusión y participación en todos los procesos sociales de envergadura. Pero una vez más, es insuficiente en función de las estadísticas que se obtienen.

Para Venezuela, El Troudi (2021) explica que "la figura femenina es una constante en la historia". Y así puede confirmarse en todos los procesos históricos que se han vivido en nuestro país. En tal sentido, el autor señala que, durante las luchas del movimiento emancipador, se rompieron los estrictos cánones de la organización de genero de la época colonial para abrazar la causa de la libertad, en un lapso extraordinario en el que se llegó a dibujar la igualdad entre los géneros; siendo sin duda, un grupo de mujeres notables y heterogéneas el que jugó un rol trascendental, con arrojo y valentía y, sobre todo, convicción libertaria. Provenían de todos los sectores sociales las féminas que, con diferentes niveles de compromiso, estuvieron presentes desde el inicio del movimiento independentista.

Igualmente, recuerda El Troudi (ob. cit) en su artículo que, a pesar de que "parte de la historiografía tradicional minimiza la figura femenina en la escritura de los hechos", pretendiendo mostrarlas como simples acompañantes, hasta la actualidad llegan las extraordinarias historias de heroínas independistas; tales como a, Juana Ramírez, Josefa Camejo, Luisa Cáceres de Arismendi, Ana María Campos, entre muchas otras, quienes dejaron un legado de fortaleza, convicción libertaria y espíritu de lucha que hoy no solo se reconoce sino, además, evidencia en la voluntad con que la mujer venezolana enfrenta los retos actuales, asume las coyunturas que lamentablemente los procesos políticos internos no han podido resolver, y de manera individual cada una ha dado la cara ante la sociedad y el mundo para salir adelante.

Desde esta perspectiva histórica en Venezuela, nos trasladamos a la actualidad, donde Maribel Gil (2017), en su artículo "La mujer y su rol en el desarrollo de las sociedades" nos señala que, el tema ha sido suficientemente estudiando y analizado en cuanto al ámbito del desarrollo en todos los países del mundo, éste ha sido sin duda el del género y concretamente el rol que desempeñan las mujeres en la mejora de las condiciones socioeconómicas y políticas de las sociedades.

Sobre ello, Gil (ob. cit) hace mención importante sobre un aspecto dinamizador, donde señala "la lucha de las mujeres de los países desarrollados se originó gracias al acceso progresivo de la mujer a la educación formal, plataforma fundamental que les proporcionó un arma muy poderosa de formación e información a través de la cual canalizaron sus aspiraciones y reivindicaciones sociales y políticas, así como su integración en el mercado laboral".

Según una encuesta realizada en el país, sólo el 29% de las mujeres encuestadas indican estar estudiando, tomando en cuenta que el acceso a la educación en Venezuela además de ser gratuito posee un sistema de inclusión particular, que se ha puesto en revisión en los últimos años y ha mejorado al menos sus procesos internos; en este caso, para las mujeres sigue siendo limitado, no precisamente por cuestiones de género, ya que hombres y mujeres tienen igualdad oportunidades de acceso, puedan sufrir, según datos de la Cepal.

En este mismo orden de ideas, cabe destacar que, para la respuesta sobre las condiciones necesarias para el desarrollo profesional de una mujer, el 92% de las mujeres encuestadas señalaron que era la educación el medio que les permitía conseguir el desenvolvimiento en términos profesionales, señalando abiertamente estar claras con respecto a los elementos necesarios para poder trascender y liberarse financieramente. La educación o la formación continua es trascendental para el ser humano, pero en este caso particular, a pesar de que en el país el acceso a la educación es gratuito hasta pregrado o nivel universitario, es importante generar las condiciones para que esa población de mujeres pueda acceder de manera masiva.

En tal sentido, se reafirma que la realidad de la mujer es diferente dependiendo del lugar geográfico en el que esté ubicada. La gran variedad de países que conforman el planeta provoca que nos hallemos con múltiples modelos aplicables a la situación en la que se encuentra una determinada mujer. Cada país regula el tema de género de forma distinta, de tal manera que las mujeres se ven integradas o apartadas de la sociedad en mayor o menor medida y dependiendo de la estructura sociocultural de cada sociedad.

Como podemos observar en la respuesta con respecto al "apoyo de las diferentes instituciones públicas y privadas para que la mujer equilibre familia y trabajo", se puede observar que casi el 50% de los encuestados señalaron que existe el apoyo para que éste equilibro entre familia y sociedad se pueda materializar. En un alto porcentaje de países a nivel mundial, la mujer que decide ser madre y tener familia, indirectamente pareciera que hace un "stop" en su vida, y le corresponde sólo cumplir sus labores de madre. En Venezuela, como lo indica la encuesta, se han realizado numerosos cambios en los últimos años, juntamente con la "Ley Orgánica sobre el Derecho de las Mujeres a una Vida Libre de Violencia", para que la mujer, luego de pasado el llamado período post parto, pueda nuevamente entrar en el proceso laboral e integrarse a la sociedad, entendiendo que existen instituciones para el cuidado diario de los bebés en apoyo a esas madres que por una u otra razón ameritan de dicho servicio.

Es importante destacar, así como lo señala Gil (ob. cit) donde expone que hay "una relación de corresponsabilidad directa entre una mejor situación de la mujer en países desarrollados frente a una situación de mayor discriminación en los países en vías de desarrollo", por lo que podemos ver cuál es el rol de la mujer en cada una de las sociedades, el cual depende de muchos factores que condicionan su vida, como son la cultura, las tradiciones, la religión, y en la mayoría de los casos los aspectos y decisiones políticas.

En tal sentido, la concepción de la mujer como una persona destinadas muy puntuales el rol de jefe de hogar no es exclusivo del hombre, puesto que la responsabilidades y aceptaciones sociales se han diversificado exponencialmente, teniendo en cuenta que podemos encontrar en cualquier profesión u oficio a presencia, accionar y prospectiva femenina, permitiendo de esta manera conquistar espacios que años atrás eran impensables, por lo cual, se ha avanzado en el desarrollo de la fuerza y empoderamiento de reivindicaciones que van más allá de lo económico.

Actualmente en Venezuela, las mujeres han variado en su proceso de empoderamiento y accionar en pro del desarrollo familiar y personal, pues han asumido de roles, tales como, madre, trabajadora, sostén de hogar, líder, estudiante, hija, esposa, entre otras, que en décadas anteriores no eran ni bien vistas o aceptadas, ya sea por razones religiosas, económicas e incluso socioculturales, dejando la mayor carga de codependencia hacia el hombre.

Finalmente, como se ha dejado ver en la investigación realizada en este artículo, se tomó en cuenta la encuesta realizada a un grupo de 132 mujeres en diversas ciudades de Venezuela, cerrando dicho instrumento con la pregunta central de esta disertación, ¿Es importante ser mujer hoy?, lo que para ello en su gran mayoría dejaron ver palabras claves en sus respuestas, como "espiritualidad, virtud, fortaleza, equipadas, emprendedoras, luchadoras, constancia, dedicación, vitalidad, respeto, amor, educación", entre muchas otras. Siempre será un honor poder ser parte de los procesos que dinamizan las mujeres día a día, en un país tan diverso y tan complejo al mismo tiempo, donde efectivamente se ha visto un gran avance en los últimos años en asuntos legales, tomando en cuenta que poseen una Ley Orgánica sobre el Derecha a las Mujeres de una vida libre de Violencia (2007), en donde el Estado se compromete a salvaguardar los derechos de las mujeres, indistintamente de raza, credo o posición económica, dejando bien en claro su objeto en el artículo no. 1:

> La presente Ley tiene por objeto garantizar y promover el derecho de las mujeres a una vida libre de violencia, creando condiciones para prevenir, atender, sancionar y erradicar la violencia contra las mujeres en cualquiera de sus manifestaciones y ámbitos, impulsando cambios en los patrones socioculturales que sostienen la desigualdad de género y las relaciones de poder sobre las mujeres, para favorecer la construcción de una sociedad justa democrática, participativa, paritaria y protagónica.

También, tanto el Estado como la población en general deben promover un ambiente de paz y convivencia donde se respete el derecho a la vida, pero en este caso en particular a potenciar la cultura de paz en función de la igualdad de género, como lo señalan los objetivos de desarrollo sostenibles (ODS, 2016) en su quinto (5to.) objetivo "La Agenda 2030 para el Desarrollo Sostenible impulsa el compromiso para el logro de la igualdad de género y el empoderamiento de todas las mujeres y niñas de forma transversal con otros objetivos". Se hace mención del mismo ya que desde la Universidad Yacambú, y el nuevo Modelo Educativo por competencias, es inherente al proceso de internacionalización que está viviendo la Universidad, al vincularnos con los Objetivos de Desarrollo Sostenible y, en consecuencia, próximamente pasaremos a ser parte del grupo de Universidades del país Pro-ODS, en trabajo conjunto con el Fondo de Población para las Naciones Unidas.

Como último aspecto a destacar, agradecemos muy gentilmente al Profesor Francesco Petricone, titular de la cátedra de Sociología de la Universidad de la Santa Cruz de Roma, por habernos permitido participar en tan importante trabajo, que plasma un trozo de la realidad existente en el país, en este caso particular, cuán importante es para nosotros entender la importancia de la mujer en el contexto actual[17].

1.8 Investigación "La importancia de ser mujer hoy" en Venezuela (Dra Yalitza Therly Ramos Gil[18])

En Venezuela «ser mujer» no es difícil, aunque si, complejo. En mi caso, soy una venezolana de 48 años de edad, que emigró de forma forzada por cuestiones de inseguridad hacia la insegurida fisica y emocional, por la inestiabilidad política y el deseo de cambio. Desde hace seis años, estoy residenciada en Ecuador. En Venezuela fui profesora universitaria y luego tras la llegada a Ecuador, continué dando clases como profesora universitaria. Actualmente, alterno actividades lúdicas y científicas. Soy madre soltera, con una hija de 21 años. Decendiente de una familia numerosa, mayoritariamente de mujeres, que han estado al frente de sus hogares, encabezando todos los procesos familiares.

La importancia de ser mujer en Venezuela conlleva a varias reflexiones. La mujer venezolana en su papel de migrante, lleva consigo valores como la voluntad, la herencia de país y el deseo de paz en las diferentes etapas o dificultades que le trae configurar una nueva vida. La mujer venezolana ha ganado un liderazgo de entre los grupos desplazados de migrantes. Esta

---

17 Referencias Bibliográficas:
National Geographic (2020). Los datos que demuestran lo difícil que es ser mujer en el mundo. Redacción. Disponible en https://www.nationalgeographic.com.es/mundo-ng/los-datos-que-demuestran-dificil-que-ser-mujer-mundo_11268/8
ONU Mujeres (2017). El Progreso de las Mujeres en América Latina y el Caribe 2017. Transformar las economías para realizar los derechos. Ciudad de Panamá, Panamá.
El Troudi, Haiman (2021). La independencia venezolana se forjó con fuerza de mujer. Revista Gentilicio, lo afirmativo. Caracas, Venezuela. Disponible en https://haimaneltroudi.com/etiqueta/participacion-de-la-mujer-en-la-independencia/
Gil, Marisol (2016). La mujer y su rol en el desarrollo de las sociedades. Revista virtual Ágora, inteligencia colectiva para la sostenibilidad. Disponible en https://www.agorarsc.org/la-mujer-y-su-rol-en-el-desarrollo-de-las-sociedades/
Rausell G., Helena (2016). El papel de las mujeres en la sociedad actual. Editorial Santillana Educación. Tres Cantos, Madrid – España.
18   Directora de la ECOMS, Docente, Periodista, Miembro del Grupo de Investigación METACOM y DEHUCS.

situación es producto de la tenacidad cultural de hacer frente los momentos difíciles. Busca mejorar sus condiciones con sentimientos de esperanza y valentía, aspectos claves que le permiten no dejar atrás la posibilidad de conformar su presente, su pasado y su futuro. En su individualidad y en su colectividad, se prepara un hogar para el hogar, anhela ser madre, y vivir en paz. También recrea escenarios de libertad. Creo que, a diferencia de la mujer europea, ser madre venezolana va inmerso en el papel de la mayoría de las mujeres. La familia es, por tanto, sinónimo de ser mamá. Ella responde a los nuevos escenarios, se adapta a los cambios, trata de innovar su adaptación y no pierde su esencia.

Tiene consciencia ante su historia. Sus aportes hacen frente a las nuevas generaciones cuidando de ellas con ímpetu y da crédito a sus propios esfuerzos. Cuenta consigo misma, empero da espacio a otros. Los cambios visionarios y la preparación frente a los nuevos escenarios lo hacen parte de ella, de allí la larga lista de mujeres en puestos claves a nivel nacional e internacional, en la ciencia, la tecnología, el deporte, la economía, el arte, la música y la política. Hay un grado de madurez en la mujer venezolana, único, porque va acompañado naturalmente del humor, dando lugar al humor, como una herramienta de deconstrucción de infelicidad para crear su propio humor en contra de la desdicha personal. Ella, se ha visibilizado en reproducir un país en la distancia, adhiriendo a su corazón, la salud mental necesaria.

Las familias que han quedado en Venezuela, se han recreado en favor del otro. Gracias a la fuerza del papel de la mujer venezolana, se han creado fundaciones, organizaciones y ONG. La labor se orienta en la bùsqueda de donaciones. Velando la virtuosidad de madre de familia, esposa y empresaria. Es emprendedora por naturaleza. Tratando temas y hechos tan diversos como la solidaridad y la posición firme de su papel ante la vida. De ahí la conquista a su derecho.

Es importante aclarar que el papel de la mujer de la venezolana ha cambiado mucho, y parte de ese papel es enigmático. La risa y la lucha son paradojas que van de su lado. Porque su lucha por ganar espacios, asumiendo multiplicidad de funciones, les ha permitido el acceso a campos laborales, generar oportunidades y combatir visiones exclusivas para hombres.

Sin embargo, este alcance dista mucho de la realidad ganada con referencia a la estadística y la cantidad de los espacios ocupados por los hombres. Al hombre venezolano, le ha costado asumir su papel equitativo frente a la mujer venezolana. El reconocimiento de los hombres de confiar y abrir más espacios a favor de la mujer ha sido dado por la dejadez del Estado venezolano y las responsabilidades gubernamentales de los hombres. Muchos de los valores que se han perdido en el sentimiento de unidad se debe a una cultura de irresponsabilidad en cada función personal, tanto del derecho de ser mujer como del propio género.

La complejidad de ser mujer venezolana además se entiende en la transferencia de funciones sobre las responsabilidades compartidas entre el Estado, los hombres y otros actores sociales. En otras palabras, la mujer asume dentro de un discurso de paz y silencioso, las cargas de la familia frente a la conquista de los espacios educativos, sociales, políticos, económicos y personales.

La mujer asume los retos aceptando un liderazgo sin reglas de pares. Implica la desconstrucción de una imagen que fue acuñada por mucho tiempo en el imaginario social a través del símbolo de la belleza venezolana, desarrollada en concursos nacionales e internacionales de belleza física y en la búsqueda de ese tratamiento igualitario a favor de sus derechos humanos. Dice Peranza (2013) que la cultura nos hace aprender a ceder. Ahora, esta experiencia de la belleza a nivel de concurso es para la mujer venezolana un trampolín de surgimiento y de conquista de espacios, trasciende màs allà de la belleza, utiliza el canon de la hermosura femenina como un atributo intelectual de su capacidad de generar nuevos logros.

Por otro lado del relato, encontramos otros elementos. La fuerza política en Venezuela empujó a cambiar estereotipos de múltiples formas, entre ellas, las protestas políticas. Las mujeres marcharon junto a los hombres, en las protestas estudiantiles, las estudiantes fueron y son guerreras del campo de batalla, se alzaron contra los militares y emprendieron rutas migratorias como escape de subsistencia en la toma de decisiones.

Ser mujer también implica una percepción de caracter matriarcal que nclusive, está representada en la cosmovisión indígena venezolana. Sin embargo, podríamos decir, que fuera de la cosmovisión indígena, en el ámbito socio-cultural del contexto venezolano, esta percepción traslada a la mujer de forma no armoniosa la responsabilidad del hogar y el trabajo como un desequilibrio en relación a las responsabilidades que debemos tener de manera equitativa frente al hombre. Dejando al hombre sin cuotas o algunas cuotas de participación.

De alguna manera este desequilibrio ejercido en el entorno socio-cultural venezolano estigmatiza de forma sexista el imaginario cultural patriarcal donde el papel de la mujer denota ser padre y madre a la vez, o en su defecto, asumir el rol de madre soltera. Cumpliendo ella sola, multiplicidad de funciones como madre, hija, hermana, líder, ama de casa, cuidadora, trabajadora, y varios etcétéras...El Estado y el hombre, sea venezolano o no, le trasladaron a la mujer su responsabilidad a través de un otorgamiento ilegítimo de poderes "aparentemete legal".

Esta desigualdad en la mujer venezolana, creada a través de una indiosincracia de su caracter de independencia, muchas veces es asumida por la propia mujer como el deseo de salir adelante y poder llevar las cargas sin dependencia del contrario. Este contexto, ha sido consecuencia del incumplimiento de los derechos del hombre con los hijos y del incumplimiento del hombre con otras responsabilidades laborales, profesionales y ciudadanas. Esta omisión en el cumplimiento de la leyes venezolanas dista mucho del acompañamiento legal y legítimo en materia de corresponsabilidad.

Para entender el conocimiento de la invisibilidad de la mujer en los espacios de las diferentes esferas económicas, sociales, culturales, intelectuales y políticas, es necesario separar conceptos claves que marcan la indiferencia entre el reconocimiento de los derechos humanos con relación a ellas y el sistema patriarcal que rige las capacidades, oportunidades y retos, en la vida diaria de las mujeres.

Algunos de los conceptos a los que las mujeres venezolanas reemplazan desde su experiencia son: sexo, mujer, género, hegemonía, ciencia, desigualdad, errores sistemáticos e invisibilidad. Consideramos que algunas de esas definiciones representan paradigmas y dualidades discriminatorias y que no se ajustan a la realidad de la mujer venezolana intelectual y luchadora, la mujer que traslada atributos de espontaneidad.

Para contextualizar un poco esta distorción de la realidad que se ha vivido en contra de la mujer veneolona como política de Estado, veamos por ejemplo, las políticas públicas llevadas a cabo durante los últimos vintiún años. Por decreto presidencial, la Misión Madres del Barrio, fue creada en el ano 2006 en Venezuela, tenía en sus inicios, el objetivo general asistencialista de, por una parte, la superación de las situaciones de pobreza extrema, y por la otra, la de la inclusión. No obstante, mediante una intervención dirigida a las mujeres madres de familia de los estratos más pobres, el Estado recargó con dinero, esta política, subsidiando con bonos mensuales, el papel de "ama de casa". Quizás, esta trayectoria, ha dado lugar que el hombre que ha dejado a la mujer venezolana, juega también una complicida implìcita de ser su ex-amigo. Son muy pocos los casos de enemistad entre las partes.

Según esta política pública, el papel de liderazgo que tuvo la mujer en la familia venezolana era clave para "empoderar" los programas sociales. Si miramos desde una perspectiva paradójica, el liderazgo de la mujer fue una consecuencia del incumplimiento de las leyes con relación a la pareja, que respondía a lógicas dominantes como sujeto femenino. De allí que es importante que indiquemos reflexiones con relación a las desigualdades de la mujer.

En esta política pública, el contexto histórico del liderazgo de la mujer venezolana promovió las formas de la participación de las mujeres bajo una visión limitada en su rol familiar de madre y cuidadora. Evidentemente, la integración de todos estos aspectos condujo a exacerbar un populismo denigrante debido a que representó la feminización de las mujeres pobres como instrumentos de la política social. Pues por cada hijo, recibía una ayuda económica que no la obligara a trabajar por ser "ella" quien estuviera al cuidado de los niños en su hogar, propiciando la procreación no planificada y populista.

Ciertamente, no se puede negar el surgimiento de las venezolanas en espacios ocupados en las universidades y el mundo laboral en general, incluyendo el campo gerencial con un nuevo paradigma caracterizado por la libertad y la flexibilidad en las estructuras sociales, acompañadas por la voluntad de los gobiernos. En especial, aquellos que alcanzaron el poder político, legislativo, judicial, electoral y moral. El costo político de las decisiones de inclusión de la mujer, se basó en un reconocimiento del trabajo doméstico de las mujeres como trabajo productivo, que no apeló a garantías de equidad y escenarios de libertad, liberando a otros actores y sectores sus propias responsabilidades.

En el contexto sociopolítico, muchos proyectos incorporaron en sus discursos expectativas en materia de inclusión. Sin embargo, en temas de violencia física, la impunidad siguió de manera desigual. Prácticamente, en el ámbito socio histórico, podemos decir que ha correspondido a las mujeres asumir y aceptar realidades desiguales frente a los otros. Un ejemplo más, es que las mujeres venezolanas tienen la responsabilidad 'asumida' como jefa de hogar, cuidadoras de niños, ancianos, animales, enfermos, rol que muchas veces deben compaginar con su trabajo y deseo de equidad social.

Evidentemente, la diferencia ha demostrado los errores sistemáticos, que son mucho más peligrosos que los errores estadísticos a favor del hombre venezolano comparado con el de la mujer. Esto se observa en los cargos de decisiones militares, políticos y deportivos, como el fútbol y el carácter machista de muchos. Hoy se siguen negando los espacios a las mujeres en aspectos claves. Es por ello, que las mujeres, todavía, están menos presentes en las áreas científicas, políticas, militares y económicas que los hombres.

La invisibilidad de las mujeres venezolanas puede notarse en ideas unilaterales desde la perspectiva masculina, únicamente. Los errores sistemáticos también persisten en materia educativa, en estudios y proyectos de investigación en el ámbito científico. Las disconformidades refrendan que pocas mujeres ocupan el sector de las tecnologías de la información y la industria petrolera con relación, digo a la estadística. La eminente estadística desborda los estudios de invisibilidad.

Cada mujer venezolana tiene su propia historia, su propio mundo y su manera de narrar los triunfos. Su voz está acariciando los lugares que recorre. Con silencio y sin él, va tomando de la mano el ingenio de las palabras que descubren los horizontes con diferentes miradas, con la autoría firme de ser mujer venezolana.

La mujer venezolana no busca un patrón de igualdad, lo construye. Aunque las autorías, las patentes, la producción de conocimiento y la consolidación de inventos y obras, están fuertemente marcadas por los hombres, las mujeres venezolanas se acreditan doblemente, el desmontaje de los mitos exclusivos de la investigación masculina.

1.9 *Las mujeres en Perú: hacia la conquista de espacios y derechos. En el marco del bicentenario de la independencia del país, el dizque sexo débil en la tierra de los Incas lucha por superar las barreras culturales (Iris Teresa Obispo Tejada[19])*

Perú está ubicado al oeste de Sudamérica. Entre otras cosas, es mundialmente conocido, por poseer una de las maravillas del mundo como lo es Machu Picchu, ciudad construida por el Imperio Inca, civilización milenaria ampliamente expandida en América del sur durante el período precolombino. En el marco de la celebración de sus doscientos años de independencia, este país constituye uno de los lugares donde la mujer permanece en la lucha constante por el respeto a su dignidad, derechos y por conquistar nuevos espacios y reconocimientos.

A lo largo de la historia de esta nación andina, la mujer ha jugado roles significativos en el ámbito social, político y económico. Salles y Noejovich (2006) consideran que la transferencia del mundo prehispánico al mundo colonial implicó ciertas modificaciones en cuanto al papel de la mujer. Según ellos el rol de las féminas fue adecuándose al nuevo sistema, pero mantuvo las pautas ancestrales, principalmente en lo concerniente a las estructuras de autoridad y toma de decisiones.

Del poder a la sumisión. Los citados autores refieren la existencia de una "jefatura étnica femenina", y explican que la "jefatura étnica" se encargaba

---

19 Venezolana. Comunicadora Social Institucional egresada de la Pontificia Universidad de la Santa Cruz, Roma, Italia. Actualmente Profesora de Educación Secundaria en el área de razonamiento verbal y comprensión lectora. I.E.A.C. "Apóstol San Pedro", Mala, Perú.

de administrar los recursos de la comunidad, pero sin disponer de los mismos. Salles y Neojovich deducen que la "jefatura étnica femenina" coexistía con la "jefatura étnica masculina". Concluyen que la mujer indígena desempeñó una función significativa en los órganos de poder, como estrategas, luchadoras y otros roles.

Sin embargo, Rostorowski (1988) asegura que, en la época prehispánica, la poliginia era una muestra de autoridad y de prestigio, más aún si la fémina era entregada por el Inca. La subordinación de la mujer y su imbricación en el ámbito de una sexualidad, donde el varón es el dominante, constituirá un factor influyente en el desarrollo de una cultura machista dentro la sociedad peruana cuyos efectos permearán varios períodos históricos.

En la época colonial el modelo patriarcal de corte occidental se implanta en la región, en este, la figura del hombre tiene mayor relevancia y el papel de la mujer se ve reducido a las labores del hogar, centrándose en el cuidado de los hijos y del esposo, por supuesto que en este escenario se diferencian aún más los roles de las mujeres según su pertenencia a una determina clase social y a aquellas de carácter étnico. En esta fase se distingue la participación de mujeres en las celebraciones religiosas católicas.

Durante el período independentistas las mujeres también batallaron por conquistar la libertad. Algunos historiadores reconocen la presencia de mujeres espías, conspiradoras, informantes y guerreras que dieron su vida por tal empresa. La historiadora Ana Belén García López menciona el papel de Micaela Bastidas (1745-1781), esposa de Túpac Amaru II, como co-dirigente del movimiento independentista más importante del siglo XVIII conocido como la rebelión de Túpac Amaru, destacando el papel de esta como guerrera y estratega del mismo. Entre otras figuras femeninas relevantes nombra a María Andrea Parado de Bellido (1777-1822) y a Francisca de Zubiaga de Gamarra, conocida como la Mariscala (1803-1835). No obstante, son muchas las crónicas independentistas que relegan por completo la figura femenina.

En la sociedad republicana la sumisión de la mujer al varón sea el padre o el esposo prevaleció, quedándose profundamente anclada en el seno de las familias peruanas y sirviendo como germen que daría lugar al fortalecimiento de la denominada cultura machista. Giraldo (1972) precisa que el machismo consiste fundamentalmente en la exageración o énfasis en los rasgos masculinos y en la percepción de superioridad del hombre sobre lo que se consideran débil. Erich Fromm por su parte dice que, el machismo "es una consecuencia de la desadaptación neurótica de los impulsos instintivos del individuo", además lo presenta como "consecuencia de las sociedades patricéntricas, donde se manifiesta una autoridad paterna y una sensación de placer por el dominio de los débiles".

Una mirada al contexto contemporáneo. Actualmente, la apreciación que la sociedad peruana tiene acerca del estatus de la mujer está dividida, algunos asumen que, más allá de lo establecido en las leyes, aún mujeres y hombres no gozan de los mismos derechos. Aunque las mujeres han ganado mayor visualización en la vida social, política y económica, el machismo es considerado como la causa principal de las desigualdades entre ambos géneros, en diversos ámbitos. Según el informe "Estado de la Población peruana 2020" del Instituto Nacional de Estadística e Informática (INEI) de Perú, la nación se ubica en el séptimo puesto entre los países más poblados del continente americano, con una población estimada en 32 millones 625 mil 948 habitantes; las féminas representan el 50,37%, es decir, 16 millones 435 mil 53 mujeres, para una correspondencia de 99 hombres por cada 100 mujeres. De allí que las políticas y acciones del Estado no deben ignorar a quienes representan poco más de la mitad de sus residentes.

En este artículo se presentan algunos datos relevantes en torno a la "Importancia de la mujer hoy" en Perú, estudio virtual efectuado a través de la plataforma Forms, aplicado entre marzo y abril de 2021 y que contó con la participación de 229 personas. De ese estudio 67 de cada 100 peruanos cree que ser mujer en Perú aún presenta marcadas diferencias en comparación con los hombres. El 42% de los encuestados considera que sí es difícil ser mujer en Perú. El acoso sexual en el ámbito laboral y comunitario de que son objeto las mujeres, así como la violencia doméstica, los bajos sueldos, entre otros actos discriminatorios fueron algunos de los argumentos expuestos. Expresaron que todavía en el contexto familiar es común que la mujer al iniciar una vida conyugal deba someterse al marido y dejar de estudiar o trabajar para dedicarse exclusivamente al hogar. Socialmente sigue siendo mal visto el acceso de las mujeres a ciertos lugares, así como el desempeño de algunas labores. "El machismo y las creencias ancestrales erradas dificultan el ser mujer en Perú", es una respuesta frecuente en la encuesta. No obstante, en comparación con el papel de la mujer hace 10 años atrás, más del 47% de los consultados cree que se han registrados algunos cambios, mientras que el 18% estima que es mucho, circunscribiéndolo al campo de trabajo y doméstico. Indicaron que la accesibilidad a internet y las redes sociales han facilitado dichos logros.

Políticas públicas en favor de la mujer. Respecto a las políticas públicas en beneficio de las mujeres, los consultados admitieron que sí existen, pero el 59% estima que son insuficientes y otro 11% que son incorrectas. Comentaron que, en el campo laboral aún se subestima a las féminas, pues existen trabajos donde solamente permiten hombres, presuntamente porque las labores son muy pesadas y difíciles desde el punto de vista físico, como para ser ejecutados por féminas. Los bajos sueldos, los abusos contra las mujeres en etapas de gravidez o lactancia, fueron otros de los puntos mencionados por muchos encuestados. Del sondeo se desprende que, 56 de cada 100 peruanos creen que el Estado no ofrece suficiente apoyo a las mujeres para que puedan equilibrar sus roles en el seno de la familia, cuidado de la prole, estudio y trabajo.

Siguiendo con las apreciaciones expresadas en el tema laboral, hubo encuestados que refirieron la existencia de cargos importantes al mando de mujeres, estos creen que en la actualidad hay más ofertas laborales para mujeres que para hombres. Consideran que, las mujeres debidamente capacitadas sí pueden alcanzar plazas importantes tanto en instituciones públicas como privadas. Mencionaron el emprendimiento propio como una vía en la cual las peruanas logran cierto desarrollo.

El informe del INEI arriba mencionado indica que, en 2019, la tasa de actividad de la población en edad de trabajar se ubicó en 71.6%, presentando diferencias por razones de género. El índice para la población femenina se ubicó en 64%, 15.8 puntos porcentuales por debajo de los hombres que fue de 79.8%, evidenciando que las féminas tuvieron menos posibilidades de participar en el mercado laboral. En cuanto a la tasa de desocupación, el estudio del INEI muestra que las más afectadas fueron las mujeres y los jóvenes. El índice para las mujeres fue del 5.1% mientras que en los hombres 4.2%. Además, el estudio expresa que la desaceleración económica del país a causa de la pandemia precarizó aún más a las mujeres en el contexto laboral.

Las peruanas ante la violencia y el feminicidio. En materia de seguridad los encuestados asumen que las mujeres siguen siendo más vulnerable que los hombres en Perú. Ante la pregunta de si alguna vez ha sufrido o conoce a alguien que haya sufrido violencia doméstica, más del 66% de los encuestados respondió que sí sabe de casos. Carhuavilca Dante, jefe del INEI, en el informe "Violencia Familiar en el Perú: Mitos y Realidades" del 2020 mostró que, en 2019, el 57.7% de las mujeres en edades comprendidas entre los 15 y 49 años han sufrido violencia familiar por parte de la pareja, y el 67.7% fue víctima de algún tipo de violencia – psicológica, sexual, física, económica u otra. El informe muestra que en Perú durante el 2019 la tasa más baja de violencia psicológica y/o física contra la mujer fue del 49.4% y se observó en el estrato socioeconómico más alto, mientras que en sectores más populares 60 de cada 100 féminas sufrió algún tipo de violencia. Igualmente, dentro del sector social con nivel educativo superior el índice porcentual fue de 51.4%.

Según estimaciones extraoficiales se cree que en 2020 las cifras aumentaron, debido a las condiciones de confinamiento social producto de la pandemia generada por la Covid-19. La "cartilla estadística" N° 06-2020 publicada por el Programa Nacional AURORA del Ministerio de la mujer y poblaciones vulnerables (MIMP) difundió que, entre marzo y setiembre de 2020 a través de los Equipos Itinerantes de Urgencia (EIU) atendieron 15.924 casos de violencia contra la mujer, cifra que representó el 86% del total de casos atendidos. Desde los Centros de Emergencia Mujer (CEM) otros 15.284 casos fueron registrados lo que equivale al 84.5%.

El informe detalla que entre julio y septiembre del mismo año atendieron 10,728 casos de violencia contra personas adultas, entre los 18 y 59 años, de los cuales 10,289 (95.9%) casos corresponden a mujeres y 439 (4.1%) casos a hombres. Con respecto a las tasas de feminicidio/femicidio, en esta nación andina, del 16 de marzo al 30 de setiembre de 2020, el Programa AURORA reportó unos 60 casos con características de femicidio y otros 129 casos de tentativa de feminicidio. Vale destacar que Perú es uno de los países latinos con una ley que penaliza el feminicidio/femicidio, además posee una serie de programas e instancias en favor de la mujer como el MIMP, defensorías, ONG's u otros, sin embargo, la población cree que es insuficiente. Estiman necesario acabar con la impunidad y educar más a la ciudadanía en la formulación de denuncias y mejorar la administración de justicia.

Papel protagónico de la mujer peruana. Pese a los escollos antes mencionados que deben enfrentar las féminas en Perú, muchas logran alcanzar sus metas y el éxito profesional, así lo cree el 88.6% de los participantes del sondeo "Importancia de la mujer en hoy", algunos opinan que, dependiendo del estrato social de pertenencia de la mujer y el hombre en Perú, estos pueden tener las mismas probabilidades de éxito en sus carreras profesionales. En lo relativo a la participación en la vida pública, especialmente en la política, 70 de cada 100 personas creen que una mujer bien formada puede tener éxito en dicho sector. Al consultarles acerca de las condiciones necesarias para lograr el desarrollo profesional de la mujer el 91.7% apunta a la educación de calidad, un 62.9% piensa que las habilidades personales también son de gran ayuda, entre otras cualidades. La capacidad relacional de la mujer, sus valores y el respaldo familiar fueron mencionados.

No faltó quien acotara que aún en el mundo de la política, es muy difícil el avance de las mujeres, aunque desde unos años para acá existen varias mujeres ejerciendo altos cargos públicos, en el congreso, ministerios, alcaldías, u otros. Conviene resaltar que para el momento del desarrollo de este artículo Keiko Sofía Fujimori disputaba la presidencia de Perú representando al partido de derecha Fuerza Popular y confrontando en la segunda vuelta al candidato Pedro Castillo, del partido de izquierda Perú

Libre. La hija del expresidente del Perú, Alberto Fujimori, fue primera dama de Perú de 1994 al 2000 durante el gobierno de su padre y congresista por Lima Metropolitana de 2006 a 2011. Actualmente es investigada por el Ministerio Público y se encuentra en libertad bajo fianza.

Keiko Fujimori fundadora y presidenta de Fuerza Popular por tercera vez pasó a la segunda vuelta, pero por una diferencia mínima de votos tampoco logró la presidencia de Perú. Pasado un mes de los comicios y tras semanas de disputa e impugnación de resultados el Jurado Nacional de Elecciones proclamó a Castillo como presidente, postergando la posibilidad de que una mujer se convierta en mandataria nacional.

Importancia de ser mujer hoy. Al finalizar la encuesta, la muestra estudiada mencionó diversos aspectos que reiteran la importancia de ser mujer en la actualidad. Recalcaron algunos rasgos antropológicos como su capacidad para el cuidado de las relaciones interpersonales, el equilibrio y fortaleza que brindan a la familia y otras instancias sociales, su talante emprendedor, incansable entre otros. También fue referido el don de la maternidad con el cual fueron premiadas por Dios, y que les permite acoger y dar vida, asumiendo la misión coceadora. La complementariedad con el hombre como forma ideal de conformar e impulsar a la familia, pilar fundamental para el buen desarrollo de los pueblos, fue igualmente nombrada. Perú tiene tanto que agradecer a sus mujeres, desde las más sencillas e invisibilizadas hasta las que han destacado en la esfera pública en diversos ámbitos y épocas. Isabel Flores de Oliva, mejor conocida como Santa Rosa de Lima, es una de las más importantes figuras de la historia religiosa del país que vivió entre los siglos XVI y XVII, su testimonio de servicio y entrega a los demás ha irradiado a través del tiempo a muchos en el mundo.

Otro ejemplo más reciente de peruanas sencillas con vidas trascendentes es Sor María Agustina Rivas López, popular y cariñosamente llamada como "Sor Aguchita". Vivió en el siglo XX, se caracterizó por poseer un espíritu de entrega y compromiso en la defensa de los pueblos asháninca y de los más vulnerables de su tiempo, fue la primera monja asesinada por el grupo guerrillero Sendero Luminoso, sin embargo, su vida y legado siguen brillando en Perú. Vale recordar que, el 22 de mayo de 2021, el Papa Francisco autorizó promulgar el decreto que reconoce el martirio de esa Sierva de Dios. Pronto se elevará a los altares a otra digna representante de la mujer peruana[20].

---

20 Referencias bibliográficas: Carhuavilca, Dante, (2020). Informe "Violencia Familiar en el Perú: Mitos y Realidades". García, Ana. (S/A). Las heroínas calladas de la Independencia Hispanoamericana. Publicado en: Https://cvc.

2. Africa

The experience in two African countries - Tunisia for North Africa and Ivory Coast for Western Africa - has been examined by the IWT research. It is about different geographical and political realities, but very similar in some aspects of gender inequality.

Below are the comments of our correspondents on the territories in relation to the two French-speaking countries.

2.1 *Etre une femme en Tunisie aujourd'hui (Silvia Finzi*[21]*)*

Quelques mois après la déclaration d'indépendance du pays (20 mars 1956), l'État tunisien a promulgué le 13 août 1956 un « Code du statut personnel » (CSP) qui n'entrera effectivement en vigueur que le 1er janvier 1957. Le CSP sera perçu comme une véritable révolution dans le monde arabe notamment pour les droits acquis par les femmes en matière de divorce, pour rendre illégale la polygamie, pour empêcher la célébration d'un mariage sans le consentement de la femme et pas avant l'accomplissement de ses dix-huit ans sauf obtention d'une dérogation spéciale.

Autrement dit, la répudiation est interdite, pratique toujours en vigueur, une femme peut demander le divorce, peut se marier sans le consentement de la famille si les deux conjoints sont majeurs et la polygamie est interdite : à ce jour et quoiqu'avec la libéralisation progressive de la condition de la femme dans divers pays musulmans, aucun code de la famille dans le

cervantes.es/literatura/mujer_independencias/garcia.htm; Giraldo, O (1872). El machismo como fenómeno psicocultural. Revista latinoamericana de psicología. Publicado en: http://www.redalyc.org/pdf/805/80540302.pdf; Instituto Nacional de Estadística e Informática de Perú (INEI) (2020). Estado de la Población peruana 2020. Publicado en: www.inei.gob.pe/media/MenuRecursivo/publicaciones_digitales/Est/Libbro.pdf; IWT (2021); Ministerio de la mujer y poblaciones vulnerables (MIMP). (2020). La "cartilla estadística" N° 06-2020 Estado de emergencia nacional, Cifras de violencia durante el aislamiento social. Programa Nacional AURORA. Publicado en: https://portalestadistico.pe/wp-content/uploads/2020/10/Cartilla-; Estadistica-AURORA-16-de-marzo-al-30-de-setiembre-2020.pdf; Salles, Estela y Noejovich, Héctor. (2006). La herencia femenina andina prehispánica y su transformación en el mundo colonial, Bulletin de l'Institut français d'études andines. Publicado en: https://doi.org/10.4000/bifea.4758. Rostorowski, María (1988). La mujer en la época prehispánica. IEP Ediciones. Tercera edición. Lima, Perú.

21   Professeur chez Faculté des Lettres des Arts et des Humanités Université La Manouba, Tunis, Tunisia.

monde arabe n'a adopté ces mesures, permettant ainsi à la Tunisie d'être considérée comme «une exception». Cette exception identifiée a été identifié au premier président de la République tunisienne Habib Bourguiba même si les mouvements féministes tunisiens ont toujours contesté cette liberté octroyée en affirmant que dès les années 30 du vingtième siècle un mouvement moderniste prônant l'égalité des genres était déjà actif en Tunisie et que Bourguiba a appliqué juridiquement ce que les femmes et certains intellectuels revendiquaient déjà.

Néanmoins ce code de la famille, aussi révolutionnaire soit-il et même s'il a eu le mérite de rompre avec la tradition et d'inaugurer un lent processus de modernisation du pays, n'a cependant pas abordé la question de la parité d'une manière globale de telle sorte qu'il est un texte tronqué dans la mesure où en voulant satisfaire modernistes et conservateurs à la fois, il reste encore aujourd'hui des inégalités encore actées par la loi qui empêche la femme d'avoir les mêmes droits que les hommes. En effet la question de la parité s'est heurtée au texte religieux qui empêche par exemple que la femme puisse hériter au même titre que les hommes. La peur de déroger à la lettre du texte religieux mais aussi dans une société basée sur les privilèges acquis par les hommes celle de compromettre leurs avantages certains a créé une sorte d'immobilisme sociétal qui sert les intérêts des hommes et qu'ils masquent sous couvert religieux. Ainsi l'égalité des sexes est considérée préjudiciable dans certains domaines car elle toucherait le texte religieux qui est perçu comme intouchable (comme par exemple la question de l'héritage dans laquelle les hommes héritent aujourd'hui deux fois plus que les femmes). Autrement dit, on peut parler d'interprétation du texte religieux dans plusieurs domaines mais étonnamment cette capacité interprétative ne s'applique pas aux droits des femmes. Nous assistons donc à une étrange coexistence du droit civil et du droit coranique grâce à laquelle une loi peut être appliquée différemment selon la nature du texte servant de référence en matière juridique. La révolution de janvier 2011, bien qu'elle ait permis des avancées en matière de parité, cogne encore contre ce double langage.

Il est intéressant en ce sens de noter qu'à la suite de l'adoption du nouveau texte constitutionnel de 2014 qui établit l'égalité des droits et des devoirs et ce à partir du 14 septembre 2017, les Tunisiens peuvent également épouser un non-musulman sans exiger un acte de conversion à l'islam, ce qui était auparavant impossible. Mais le conservatisme de certains maires a exclu la célébration de ce type d'union dans leur circonscription alors que dans d'autres, c'est devenu une pratique fréquente. Cette dichotomie visant à satisfaire les modernistes d'un côté et les conservateurs de l'autre a trouvé son épicentre sur la question de la femme et qui s'est transposé en devenant l'objet d'un débat plus large qui est celui posé par les prétendants de la sécularisation de la société ou pas. Avec l'affirmation du parti islamiste au pouvoir après 2011, la question du sacré et de la liberté sont devenus à nouveau au centre du débat politique en Tunisie et après une tentative ratée de ces derniers de remplacer le terme d'égalité par celui de complémentarité dans la nouvelle constitution, la société civile et en particulier les associations féministes ont réussi à imposer que dans l'article 21 de la Constitution soit transcrit que «les citoyens et les citoyennes sont égaux en droits et en devoirs. Ils sont égaux devant la loi sans aucune discrimination ». La question de l'égalité est également évoquée dans le préambule de la constitution.

L'État tunisien jusqu'à la chute du président Ben Ali (1987-2011) et dans le sillage de Bourguiba (1956-1987) a institutionnalisé la question des femmes en en faisant le miroir de sa modernité et en l'utilisant comme carte de visite dans ses relations internationales, surtout avec l'Occident, occultant de par la même l'action et les revendications des mouvements féministes et de la Ligue pour les droits des hommes, considérés comme abusifs et en opposition à l'État.

Ce n'est pas un hasard si le statut juridique de la femme en Tunisie a toujours été conditionné et piégé par le débat entre modernité et tradition qui, selon les majorités politiques ou les gouvernements passés (Bourguiba, Ben Ali) jusqu'à la révolution de 2011, l'ont utilisé comme porte-drapeau d'un pays respectant les droits dans un pays où ces derniers n'ont jamais été respectés. En cela l'institutionnalisation de la question féminine a été très utile aux régimes précédents car elle leur a servi pour démontrer qu'ils étaient politiquement corrects et fiables en particulier aux yeux des démocraties occidentales. De 2011 à nos jours, les partis d'inspiration religieuse ont à nouveau posé la question de l'égalité des genres et de sa concordance ou pas avec la loi islamique, en voulant tout d'abord remplacer le terme d'égalité par celui de complémentarité (qui n'a pourtant pas réussi à passer face à la forte mobilisation des femmes et à certains partis laïcs) et s'opposant à la promulgation d'une loi qui aurait pu consacrer l'égalité dans l'héritage (à ce jour la femme hérite la moitié que l'homme et dans le cas de l'épouse beaucoup moins).

Il y eu une tentative de consacrer la parité avec la création d'un Collectif Civil pour les Libertés Individuelles (Colibe) qui a publié en 2019 un rapport dénonçant les violations de ces droits et dans lequel il revendiquait, entre autres, l'égalité en matière de succession, la liberté de genre, la lutte contre toutes les formes de discrimination et de violence.

"Cinq ans après la promulgation de la Constitution le 27 janvier 2014 et l'adoption de nombreux textes juridiques révolutionnaires et progressistes, des violations flagrantes d'un caractère hautement alarmant continuent de se produire. En effet, la consécration constitutionnelle claire de la liberté de conscience (article 6), l'égalité de tous devant la loi sans aucune discrimination (article 21), la garantie par l'État des droits et libertés individuels et publics (article 21), la garantie de la dignité humaine et l'intégrité physique (article 23), la protection de la vie privée, l'inviolabilité du domicile, la confidentialité des correspondances, des communications et des données personnelles (article 24) et autres, ne seront véritablement efficaces que si les mentalités et les comportements sociaux sont modifiés, si les pratiques policières et judiciaires sont maîtrisées, fortement influencées par de longues années de dictature, et si les textes juridiques inconstitutionnels et liberticides sont abrogés. Après cinq ans, les autorités continuent de bafouer les droits les plus *élémentaires* des Tunisiens et des non-Tunisiens sur la base de pratiques policières et judiciaires et de textes juridiques dépassés qui empêchent encore le droit au libre choix au sens strict : choisir son propre style de vie, son comportement et son apparence.

Ces libertés fondamentales se heurtent encore *à* des notions et considérations issues de la dictature qui s'infiltrent dans la vie privée des individus, notamment *à* travers la mise en examen d'actes indéfinis tels que la pudeur, l'indécence ou l'homosexualité, rendant ainsi tout accusé potentiellement un criminel. Ces ingérences permettent la violation de la dignité humaine et de l'intégrité physique des individus, ouvrant la voie *à* des perquisitions, *à* la saisie des médias et *à* la pratique d'examens honteux: tests anaux, tests de virginité, analyses d'urine ... Violences physiques et morales *à* l'encontre des personnes dont le seul crime est de revendiquer leur droit *à* la différence, menaçant les libertés individuelles ainsi que la cohésion du corps social et l'effectivité du pacte social récemment conclu. Dans ce contexte, et depuis sa création le 19 janvier 2016, le Collectif Civil des Libertés Individuelles (CCLI), qui regroupe 40 associations de défense des droits humains et notamment des libertés individuelles, n'a cessé d'observer, d'alerter et d'agir, de dénoncer ces graves atteintes et violations des droits des individus. Au cours de l'année 2018, le Collectif a mené des campagnes et actions visant *à* faire des libertés individuelles et du libre choix des principes fondamentaux qui structurent la vie en commun : campagne pour la liberté de jeûner ou de ne pas jeûner pendant le mois de Ramadan, campagne de soutien *à* la relation COLIBE, actions pour interdire le recours aux tests anaux et de virginité, mobilisation pour *établir* l'égalité successorale... La Colibe a documenté ses argumentations

pour mener des actions pour l'année 2019 auprès de l'Assemblée des
Représentants du Peuple, du Gouvernement et notamment, des Ministères
de l'Intérieur et de la Justice, des partis politiques, auprès des candidats aux
élections législatives et présidentielles et des médias... et ce, dans le but de
faire de 2019 l'année *électorale* des libertés individuelles»[22].

Les résultats des élections de 2019 ont été gagnés par les partis les
plus conservateurs et au lendemain du décès de l'ancien président de
la République Caïd Essebsi qui avait fortement soutenu la création du
collectif, les conclusions du rapport Colibe ont été définitivement écartées
et enterrées.

Sur le plan juridico-législatif, il faut toutefois noter que la Tunisie a ratifié
la Convention sur l'élimination de toutes les formes de discrimination à
l'égard des femmes (CEDAW) en 1985, mais avec quelques réserves, qui ont
cependant été abrogées par décret-loi en août 2011. En avril 2014, la levée
des réserves de la Tunisie a été officiellement notifiée au Secrétaire général
de l'ONU. La nouvelle Constitution tunisienne (janvier 2014) montre
donc des signes positifs en matière de défense des droits des femmes, avec
notamment deux articles (les articles 21 et 46) qui réglementent la question
des discriminations, de l'égalité des chances et des violences basées sur le
genre. Cependant, force est de constater que le cadre juridique favorable
initialement mis en place par Bourguiba est parfois resté méconnu à la
plupart des Tunisiens en restant dans un cadre élitiste ne touchant qu'un
nombre restreint de personnes et parmi ces derniers les plus éduqués, les
intellectuels les progressistes et des membres de la société civile[23].

L'ouverture des femmes à l'éducation a eu un rôle moteur dans
l'accès des femmes au monde du travail et l'égalité avec les hommes est
au moins formellement assurée même s'il existe encore des formes de
ségrégation et d'exploitation, notamment dans le monde rural avec un
très faible pourcentage d'accès à la propriété pour les femmes[24], avec peu
de garanties sur leur travail, un salaire moindre par rapport aux hommes,
un pourcentage de scolarisation beaucoup plus faible que dans les villes.
Le pourcentage d'élèves du primaire au baccalauréat montre une légère

22   Le collectif civil pour les Libertés individuelles, *Rapport sur les Principales Violations des Libertés Individuelles, 2019.*

23   Boutheina Gribaa, Giorgia Depaoli, *Profil genre de la Tunisie*, Document élaboré dans le cadre de la « mission d'identification d'un programme de promotion de l'égalité entre les hommes et les femmes en Tunisie » financée par l'UE, 2014.

24   Seuls 4,07% de la population des porteurs de projets agricoles sont des femmes, 6,4% sont des agricultrices et seulement 4% des entrepreneurs agricoles possèdent des titres de propriété (Boutheina Gribaa, Giorgia Depaoli p.8)

supériorité de la présence féminine sur celle masculine et le phénomène de décrochage scolaire, surtout ces dernières années, se reflète davantage sur les garçons que sur les filles. Néanmoins et malgré un taux de réussite féminine supérieure par rapport aux hommes en matière scolaire et universitaire, l'accès aux postes de direction est réduit pour les femmes dans l'administration publique et privée et aux postes politiques[25].

Le questionnaire qui a porté sur 132 personnes, dont 56,1% de femmes et 39,4% d'hommes, le reste n'ayant pas voulu se prononcer sur leur appartenance, s'il ne permet pas vraiment d'établir une radiographie de la société tunisienne (par régions, entre le monde rural et le monde urbain) est cependant intéressant car il révèle les nombreuses contradictions de la société tunisienne qui sont aussi le miroir des contradictions juridico-politiques que traverse la société depuis l'Indépendance jusqu'à nos jours.

En effet, à la première question «Est-ce difficile d'être une femme dans votre pays aujourd'hui ?», 55,3% des personnes ont répondu non, affirmant que la loi protège les femmes, que les femmes sont libres et qu'elles ont des chances égales notamment dans le milieu du travail, considèrent la Tunisie est un pays moderne qui respecte les droits des femmes et qui, compte tenu du niveau d'éducation atteint, donne la possibilité au genre féminin de s'imposer dans la société. Au contraire, 44,7% ont répondu que la femme est dans l'ensemble discriminée, «considérée comme un être imparfait», en permanence jugée, qui ne jouit d'aucune liberté individuelle ni dans la société ni dans la famille car elles sont soumises à un harcèlement et à une oppression continue et même sont victimes de violences à la fois dans l'espace public que privé.

Le problème de la violence revient souvent et beaucoup en ont souffert directement ou indirectement. 66,7% des personnes interrogées ont répondu oui à la dix-neuvième question « Avez-vous déjà subi ou connaissez-vous quelqu'un qui a subi des violences conjugales ? ». Tandis que 8,3% ont préféré ne pas répondre à la question. Ces réponses contrastent fortement avec celles données à la première question et montrent que la femme est

---

25   L'activité politique et civique reste l'apanage des hommes, ce qui reflète la division traditionnelle du travail social dans la société. En ce sens, la présence des femmes aux postes de décision dans l'administration publique devrait également être renforcée. Les données mises à disposition par le SEFF (et mises à jour en janvier 2014) montrent que le pourcentage de femmes occupant des postes à responsabilité par rapport au nombre de femmes travaillant dans l'administration publique n'est que de 2,03% et que le pourcentage de femmes occupant des postes à responsabilité par rapport au nombre total de fonctionnaires n'est que de 0,76%. Idem p.11

confrontée à un réel problème de violence au sein de la famille mais pas seulement.

Comme le dit la juriste et féministe Sanaa Ben Achour :

> «Rappelez-vous simplement que la loi 2017-58 se heurte toujours aux catégories de genre immuables du code pénal qui pénalisent les personnes non pas pour leurs actes criminels mais pour leur statut et leur position sociale de» subordonnés «et discriminés dans une société patriarcale ordonnée sur la différentielle valeur des sexes et des classes. Comment la loi 2017-58 peut-elle *être* appliquée correctement lorsque les idées de prostitution féminine (art. 236), d'infanticide des mères (art. 211), de « pauvre mauvais mendiant » (art. genre 230), de l'enlèvement de la fiancée (art. 239) continue-t-il d'être officiellement transmis ? A ces survivances d'une autre *époque,* il faut ajouter celles, sacro-saints, du statut personnel. Comment appliquer correctement la loi 2017-58 sur les violences conjugales et intrafamiliales face *à* un code du statut personnel qui reproduit les privilèges masculins, le pouvoir des agnats et organise la servitude des femmes ? Ce code contient encore le modèle du mari chef de famille, le double héritage pour les hommes, le devoir conjugal, la dot des femmes, le domicile conjugal, l'obligation de consommer le mariage, la filiation paternelle, le délai de carence de la femme, la tutelle du père, la religion du père, l'enfant trouvé, etc. La lutte contre les violences basées sur le genre n'est pas une mince affaire qui peut *être* abordée par une loi, aussi courageuse soit-elle, sans un environnement législatif et réglementaire adéquat. Il s'agit d'une question grave et urgente qui appelle une révision générale d'une loi anormale qui est clairement en conflit avec les valeurs fondamentales d'égalité, de non-discrimination et de dignité humaine»[26].

Le problème de la violence à l'égard des femmes, bien que puni, continue d'être considéré comme normal par la société masculine mais est également excusé par certains religieux qui la considèrent comme un épiphénomène naturel de l'obéissance. C'est pourquoi le nombre de celles qui ont subi ou subissent des violences à l'égard des femmes est si élevé.

Il est également intéressant de noter qu'aucune personne interrogée n'a évoqué la liberté de disposer de son corps comme s'il s'agissait encore d'un tabou qu'on ne peut briser.

Si la femme a du mal à trouver une place dans la sphère publique mais aussi dans la sphère familiale, la réponse à la question « Pensez-vous que les femmes trouvent un travail dans votre pays comme les hommes ? » 78,8 ont répondu oui à la question et seulement 21,2% non, sachant que 56,1% des répondants sont des femmes et 39,4% des hommes mais ces réponses

---

26   Sanaa Ben Achour, *Féminicide: Une justice pénale blottie dans ses stéréotypes de genre Refka, Rahma et toutes les autres*, Leaders.com, 22/5/2021.

ne peuvent qu'apparemment contredire l'idée d'une discrimination effective. La présence des femmes a en effet fortement augmenté en vingt ans mais surtout dans les emplois peu qualifiés et sous-payés alors que les postes à responsabilité restent aux mains des hommes dans la majorité des cas. S'il est vrai qu'aujourd'hui l'éducation des femmes est supérieure à celle des hommes, en fait les femmes ont moins d'opportunité de carrière que les hommes. Les personnes interrogées considèrent que les études sont un facteur de promotion sociale comme elles l'étaient d'ailleurs depuis l'Indépendance mais aujourd'hui les chômeurs de l'enseignement supérieur constituent le groupe le plus important de personnes qui n'arrivent pas à trouver un emploi. Le risque est aussi d'assister à la dévalorisation progressive de ceux qui poursuivent des études.

Les personnes interrogées dans leur ensemble font partie de la classe moyenne qui a un certain niveau d'éducation mais l'on note qu'elles se contredisent souvent: en effet, entre la première question déjà évoquée et la cinquième «est-ce qu'être une femme dans son pays est différent d'un homme ? » 67,4% ont répondu oui et 32,6% non, invoquant la question de la non-liberté des femmes, de se considérer ou d'être considérées comme le maillon faible de la société, d'avoir la double charge du travail à la maison et à l'extérieur du foyer, d'élever seuls les enfants et aussi de devoir plaire au mari par peur d'être remplacée. Pour beaucoup, il n'y a pas d'équité et l'autorité masculine prévaut. La femme peut sortir plus difficilement, surtout le soir par peur d'être agressée ou violée mais aussi d'être mal jugée par son entourage.

Pour conclure, je cite quelques-unes des réponses qui me semblent exemplaires « *L'homme* fait tout ce qu'il aime simplement parce qu'il est un homme. La femme est toujours contrôlée si ce n'est par la famille, par la société. Ce n'est jamais gratuit. Il y a des lois qui protègent les femmes mais les mentalités sont plus fortes que les lois. On trouve aussi des gens qui sont en faveur des lois sur l'égalité, qui sont pour la démocratie, mais eux-mêmes ne les appliquent pas dans leur vie privée, comme le droit d'épouser une personne d'une foi différente qu'il refuse *à* leurs filles ».

La religion est souvent citée comme un frein à la liberté des femmes et par religion il faut comprendre les traditions, la mentalité, la culture.

La réponse d'un homme parmi les interviewés clôturera cette brève réflexion avec une certaine autodérision « Dieu soit loué, je suis né mâle ! ».

2.2 L'importance d'être femme aujourd'hui en Côte d'Ivoire (Kouadio Kouassi Hubert[27] - Manzan Kouame Jean[28])

En Afrique, avec l'avènement de la colonisation et celui de la religion comme le christianisme, nous assistons à un développement social, technique et économique de nos peuples en d'autres expressions, il s'agit de la reconfiguration sociale de cette société dans son ensemble. Ce développement est le spectacle sur le plan social de l'introduction de nouveaux concepts comme la promotion du genre, le relèvement du statut social de la femme dans certaines actions sociales, voire l'égalité entre homme et femme dans les sociétés actuelles africaines qui jadis était des situations et des questions impossibles à aborder. Cette innovation sociale dans nos sociétés africaines noires constitue un enjeu majeur pour de nombreux organismes qui militent en faveur de la femme.

« Depuis la nuit des temps, la femme a toujours eu un rôle important dans nos sociétés, et cela n'est pas près de s'arrêter aujourd'hui. Elles ont des rôles tous aussi importants au même titre que les hommes ». Extrait d'entretien d'enquête.

En Côte d'Ivoire, une panoplie d'institutions sont consacrées à la promotion de la femme : Le ministère de la femme, de la solidarité et de l'enfance, ONU femme, etc. Ainsi, le paysage est très coloré avec une kyrielle d'organisation non gouvernementales (ONG) qui assurent le relai de cette bataille. Toutes ces institutions ont pour but de relever le niveau de vie et le statut social de la femme. C'est dans cette dynamique que nous analysons le thème : L'importance d'être femme aujourd'hui en Côte d'Ivoire.

Ce développement social peut être caractérisé d'innovation sociale dans la mesure où ce sont de nouvelles manières de faire, de concevoir et de reconfigurer le système social. Ces pratiques sont par exemple dans ce contexte actuel comme le changement social de la femme à avoir accès certains espaces sociaux comme le marché de l'emploi, à être reconsidérée dans la définition des politiques sociales et de décisions dont sa fonction première de femme dans la société africaine était de s'occuper du foyer. En dépit de toutes ces actions visant à reconstruire le statut social de la femme, cette étude sur l'importance d'être femme aujourd'hui en Côte

---

27   Doctorant en sociologie de l'économie et de l'emploi Université Félix Houphouët-Boigny, Abidjan, Côte d'Ivoire.
28   Ingénieur en management des Ressources Humaines, Director of the Niéré Cultural Centre, Abidjan, Côte d'Ivoire.

d'ivoire permet d'analyser les différents aspects sociaux qui favorisent le climat social de ce statut. De nombreuses ressources sociales contribuent à l'importance d'être femme aujourd'hui en Côte d'Ivoire.

Il faut d'un premier point de vue, souligner la valorisation de la femme dans le contexte social ivoirien comme un structurant de la perception de l'importance d'être femme aujourd'hui dans cette société. En effet, cette valorisation de la femme s'explique à travers la multiplicité des institutions de nature diverses (nationales et internationales) à l'égard de la femme. Ainsi, il faut citer certaines institutions nationales et ses reformes publiques, les ONG et le département de ONU femme qui militent en faveur de l'épanouissement de la femme et de son statut social. Sur cette base, la multiplication des actions émancipatrices de la femme dans son insertion socioprofessionnelle, dans tous les secteurs d'activités avec certains comités de veilles aux droits des femmes fait de celles-ci des actrices et non des agents dans le tissu socio-économique ivoirien. Les cadres sociaux normatifs sont perçus ici, comme ceux qui entretiennent cet adjectif d'importance eu égard à la femme.

Toujours au niveau national, le gouvernement ivoirien conjugue des actions en faveur de l'émancipation et de l'autonomie de la femme. Ces actions entre autres ont donné le jour au ministère de la femme dans ce pays. Avec la nomination de nombreuses femmes au rang de ministre, de directrices et autres, l'accès des femmes à certains espaces socioprofessionnels qui étaient classiquement monopolisés par les hommes comme l'école de gendarmerie, ainsi que le privilège donné aux femmes d'accès à certains ministères et entreprises sont autant d'éléments non exhaustifs de cette litanie qui illustre l'importance d'être femme et de leur épanouissement ainsi qu'à leur autonomie en Côte d'Ivoire. Ces fonctions assumées par ces dernières avec plus de responsabilité et de succès constituent des ressources sociales à la reconstruction de l'image de la femme et de leur position sociale comme une innovation sociale.

Les 68,8% de cette population qui ont participé à cette enquête et qui postulent qu'il est facile d'être femme en Côte d'Ivoire illustrent bien les propos ci-dessus. Voir le diagramme circulaire

- 76,6% de notre population d'étude sont dans l'intervalle d'âge de 18 à 30 : cela peut s'expliquer par le fait que la population ivoirienne[29] est très jeune, dont la majorité populaire est de 18 ans.

---

29   C'est avoir la nationalité ivoirienne.

- Quant aux 23, 4% se situant entre 31 et 56 ans, nous pouvons les justifier par le fait que l'espérance de vie des Ivoiriens se situent entre 45ans et 50 ans.
- Aussi, il faut noter cette question d'âge faisant partie de l'intimité de l'africain ce qui l'empêche réellement de donner son âge ni de situer son âge dans une tranche quelconque soit pour des causes de marginalisation ou soit de garder toujours son statut positif.

En outre, être femme est différent d'être hommes en Côte d'Ivoire. Cela ne se traduit non pas seulement par leur aspect morphologique mais par cette faveur sociale positive faite à l'égard de la femme. Elle leur donne droit et accès au marché de l'emploi qui facilite leur insertion socioprofessionnelle voire à un certain degré de favoritisme. Ainsi de nombreuses structures ont vu le jour et promeuvent l'employabilité de la femme. Les 67, 4% du sondage soutiennent qu'être femme est différent d'être homme. Ce privilège accordé particulièrement aux femmes leur donne plus de chance dans de nombreux domaines d'activités. Il faut aussi mentionner cette différence d'une part sur le plan sociojuridique. Le pouvoir législatif et exécutif décrète et votent un ensemble de lois et de normes sociales qui favorisent les femmes dans plusieurs domaines. Sur ce plan juridique de nombreux organismes ont vu le jour pour secourir et favoriser leur droit dans cette société ivoirienne.

D'autre part, les politiques nationales et internationales sont favorables dans la construction sociale de l'importance d'être femme en CI. 31,2% de cette population enquêtée estiment que ces politiques sont justes. Ces politiques sont la promotion de la gent féminine avec la journée nationale de la femme qui est célébrée en Côte d'Ivoire, la journée de la fête des mères célébrée au dernier dimanche du mois de mai et de leur accès à certains espaces sociaux et de leur redéfinition sociale.

"Parce que les femmes peuvent maintenant s'exprimer librement".

La condition sociale de la femme a connu une grande amélioration. D'un point de vue de la main-d'œuvre, elle est aujourd'hui présente dans tous les secteurs d'activités et détiennent très souvent les rennes de certaines institutions.

"Les quotas obligatoires pour l'insertion des femmes dans les entreprises sont une avancée assez remarquable".

D'un point de vue académique, il faut noter que l'école pour tous, initiée par le gouvernement ivoirien depuis près de 5 ans maintenant est aussi l'un des processus d'amélioration des conditions de vie de la femme.

"Il y a eu plusieurs politiques de sensibilisation sur la scolarisation de la jeune fille. Intégration des femmes dans les différents gouvernements et la lutte contre les mutilations génitales".

De plus en plus, l'on constate une correction de la perception sociale négative faite à la femme, et le sens de responsabilité incarné dans la société et dans son foyer comme décideur ou sa coparticipation décisionnelle dans de nombreuses situations sociales.

"Les conditions des femmes ont changé pas seulement au sein de la main d'œuvre parce que de plus en plus dans les ménages, les femmes sont respectées et vues même comme les hommes".

Par ailleurs, il faut postuler que l'accès des femmes à la technologie est un élément qui privilégie sa construction sociale. Ce faisant, il faut noter que tout le monde a accès à la technologie. Et il n'existe pas des règles et normes qui régissent ce domaine.

84,4% des acteurs enquêtés ont répondu favorablement à l'accès à la technologie sans distinction de sexe. Effet, il faut noter que l'accès à l'internet s'inscrit dans des dimensions socialement variées. Très souvent, l'accès à internet relève d'une capacité individuelle. Cette capacité individuelle est tributaire du pouvoir d'achat de l'acteur à se doter d'une connexion internet personnelle. En outre très souvent aussi, l'accès à l'internet dépend de la capacité de certaines familles à fournir l'internet à tous les membres de la famille via une connexion wifi.

Cet accès à l'internet garantit la chance entre homme et femme sur le marché de l'emploi. Il n'existe pas encore dans ce contexte ivoirien des sites destinés à des femmes et d'autres aux hommes.

Cependant tous les postes de secrétariat sont dotés de machines dont les femmes se servent pour faire leurs travaux quotidiens sans pour autant être des informaticiennes. Elles arrivent à naviguer sur internet avec les moteurs de recherche. Elles profitent aussi de l'internet pour celles qui sont entrepreneuses de faire la publicité de leurs produits à travers leur smart phone par le biais de leur page Facebook, WhatsApp, Imo...

D'un troisième point de vue, le marché de l'emploi dans le contexte ivoirien est ouvert à tous. La femme trouve de l'emploi comme l'homme dans ce pays dans l'optique que l'homme et femme ont les mêmes avantages en termes de formation. Les politiques nationales par ailleurs ne font pas de discrimination sociale quant aux femmes et aux hommes dans le spectre ou dans le champ social des recrutements et des concours en termes de quota homme/femme. Ici, le seul dividende qui prévaut est le capital humain c'est-à-dire la compétence. Or on trouve dans cette catégorie sociale de la gent féminine un capital humain à même de dépasser celui des hommes et qui rend le marché de l'emploi plus compétitif. Les politiques nationales permettent même d'avancer que les femmes sont plus favorisées dans ce rapport à l'emploi.

Dans cette même veine, l'homme est égal à la femme dans la mesure où tous deux possèdent les mêmes chances concernant le marché de l'emploi. Femme et homme assument les mêmes responsabilités et parviennent tous deux différents à un meilleur rendement. Le statut juridique et le libre accès du marché de l'emploi range les deux acteurs dans la même pièce et ne représentant tous deux la même face de la même pièce. Il faut définir de ce fait la position égalitaire entre femme et homme comme une relation sociale à l'accès à certaines ressources sociales dans leur système de fonctionnement de la vie sociale. De plus, cette importance d'être femme en CI peut s'illustrer par le canal de nombreuses conditions d'évolutions mises en place favorables à leur autonomie et à leur épanouissement social. A cet effet 96,52% des participants à l'étude avancent que la femme peut mener une carrière réussie en CI comme le font certains hommes. Il faut également signifier certains parcours socio-professionnels de certaines femmes en CI comme des preuves illustratives. Il existe de nombreuses femmes ministres, directrices et responsables de certaines institutions fortes de l'État, qui ont prouvé par les différentes missions et fonctions qui leurs sont assignées. Aujourd'hui, l'on constate en CI l'omniprésence des femmes dans presque tous les secteurs d'activités. Ces carrières que ces dernières épousent continuent de soigner l'image social de la femme ainsi qu'à son repositionnement social.

> "Car il y a des femmes ministres, juges avocates et elles peuvent mener une carrière réussie car il y a des associations qui sont créées pour soutenir les femmes travailleuses en difficulté dans le domaine du travail".

Le monde ayant été révolutionné d'une façon ou d'une autre, on constate un peu partout que la scène politique ou le champ politique, qui autrefois socialement disqualifiait les femmes n'épargne personne aujourd'hui en CI. De ce fait, parlant du champ social politique de notre pays, il n'y a aucun inconvénient que celle-ci s'y intéresse. En plus, elle a les mêmes chances que les hommes d'être élue. La preuve en est qu'en CI le taux de femme exerçant dans le gouvernement est maintenant considérable par rapport aux années 60.

"En effet de nos jours, nous observons un taux quand même élevé de la participation des femmes à plusieurs domaines tels que la politique notamment à l'assemblée nationale. Cela est due au fait que les femmes sont en majorité éduquées et donc connaissent leurs droits et leur capacité à développer leur pays ; et ces femmes sont soutenues par des personnes qui prennent conscience de leur importance et lutte avec elles pour le changement"; "De nombreuses femmes ont une carrière bien réussie aujourd'hui et son dans le domaine de la politique du fait de leurs compétences, leur intelligence comme les hommes".

Enfin, le capital humain ou l'éducation serait le meilleur domaine pour qu'une femme évolue convenablement. En effet, en matière d'éducation, les femmes sont de plus en plus nombreuses dans les établissements secondaires et dans les universités. Elles arrivent à faire de longues études qui participent à leur présence sur de nombreuses scènes sociales. On ne peut rien reprocher à la femme car nous le savons tous, elle incarne certaines vertus et le pouvoir d'inculquer des valeurs aux enfants. C'est pourquoi depuis plusieurs années maintenant, la CI n'a pour ministre de l'éducation nationale que des femmes qui mènent à bien leur responsabilité. Au regard de tout ce qui précède, il convient de retenir que de nombreuses ressources participent à la reconstruction du statut social de la femme et de son importance dans la société ivoirienne. Toutefois, certaines perspectives sont à explorer.

En dépit de toutes ces actions qui concourent à refaire la place importante de la femme en CI d'aujourd'hui, de nombreux défis restent à relever à plusieurs niveaux. Les perceptions diverses associées à la femme sont celles qui consolident la notion difficile d'être femme en Côte d'Ivoire. Avec une mesure statistique de 31,2%, les Ivoiriens construisent la perception selon laquelle, il est difficile d'être femme en Côte d'Ivoire. En effet, cette étude fait ressortir des perceptions et représentations multivariées de la notion de « femme ». L'objet de sexualité, la place de la femme se trouve au foyer, l'inégalité sociale sur le marché de l'emploi, le statut social de la femme dévalorisé dans certains contextes sociaux, ainsi que la perception de la femme dans un contexte social africain, sont ces représentations et perceptions sociales qui répondent à la difficulté d'être femme en Côte d'Ivoire. Ceci peut être illustré par ce verbatim suivant :

« Pour ma part être une femme est difficile du fait qu'elle ne puisse prendre de décision sans l'accord d'un homme, en général, elle est minimisée, du fait qu'en société, on juge bon que ce soit les hommes qui restent au-devant de la scène, elle n'a donc pas son mot à dire».

Cela peut s'expliquer par le fait qu'en Afrique généralement et en Côte d'Ivoire en particulier, la femme dans un contexte culturel ne peut se permettre de prendre des décisions ou vaquer à certaines occupations sans le consentement de son conjoint. Ce système de fonctionnement des couples africains est perçu socialement comme une forme de domination de l'homme (mari) et d'affaiblissement de la femme (mariée). Aussi, l'on peut qualifier le cadre relationnel entre l'homme et la femme dans ce contexte social ivoirien comme aboutissant à des formes de violences symboliques. Cette consultation décisionnelle qui n'aboutit toujours pas à une réponse favorable et qui détruit le projet en question illustre bien la posture de cette catégorie d'acteurs pour qui, il est difficile d'être femme.

Toujours dans cette même dynamique, nous pouvons rappeler les perceptions négatives faites aux femmes pour qui la place se trouve dans les foyers. Le marché de l'emploi dans les années des indépendances était en quasi-totalité saturé par des hommes. Dans ce contexte socioculturel africain, il faut mentionner que les travaux ménagers étaient assignés aux femmes et les autres champs d'activités aux hommes. La femme n'avait pas le droit d'exercer dans certains champs d'activités. Cette répartition des activités caractérisait la femme comme étant physiquement et socialement faible dans l'exercice de certaines activités. Et les hommes avaient des attributs de guerriers, de braves, de vaillants... Cette idéologie est réinvestie sur le marché de l'emploi faisant des femmes des victimes sociales. Donc cette propension à vouloir favoriser l'employabilité des hommes par rapport aux femmes est liée à cette socialité primaire de la répartition du travail et ainsi que tous les attributs que l'on lui conférait. Cet extrait d'entretien affirme :

"La discrimination sur le terrain de l'emploi, les employeurs préfèrent les hommes que les femmes (les congés de maternité, les permissions pour les enfants malades et aussi la pression sociale en termes de statut matrimonial, les enfants ; Les femmes sont considérées comme des êtres faibles incapables de faire de longues études".

Donc, il faut loger toutes ces perceptions d'ordre anthropologique qui affectent le caractère de la femme dans tous ces aspects. Les seules différences que l'on n'établit pas ici entre l'homme et la femme se situe sur le plan juridique de jouir des mêmes droits et sur le plan du marché du travail. Sur le plan juridique, l'homme et la femme sont tous égaux devant les lois qui régissent cette société. Aussi, il faut comprendre ce manque de différence par le législateur ivoirien qui prône l'égalité entre l'homme et la femme. A cet effet, jouissant des mêmes droits à l'arbitrage pour tous, l'homme n'est pas différent de la femme qu'au sens juridique qui donne de leur nature différente un dénominateur commun qui est l'égalité devant les normes sociales. Les 32,6% qui n'établissent pas de différence entre homme et femme dans cette enquête sont corroboratifs.

43,3% des acteurs estiment que les politiques nationales relatives aux femmes sont insuffisantes. Cela peut s'expliquer par les bornes sociales qui caractérisent ces politiques à l'égard des femmes. De ce fait, ces politiques se limitent pour la plupart au niveau des grands espaces socio-urbains c'est-à-dire les grandes villes. Ces politiques en question qui n'atteignent pas les villages, dont la représentation sociale classique faite à la femme demeure, met en marge la plus grande partie de la population féminine et fait de ces politiques des politiques citadines et limitées socialement dans leur plan d'action. Ces politiques sont perçues pour la plupart comme étant des politiques destinées à certaines franges sociales, comme les femmes lettrées ou celles qui sont citadines. Aussi, ces dites politiques riment avec des formes d'exclusions sociales du fait de leur système de fonctionnement et selon leur manière d'être diffusées. Il faut noter que ces politiques sont en contradictions avec le système de fonctionnement social et culturel de la quasi-totalité des communautés africaines donc une idéologie qui n'est pas épousée dans cette communauté africaine. Il faut relever la concentration de tous les organismes de promotion du genre féminin dans les grandes villes.

"Il y a une politique, mais beaucoup reste surtout à faire dans les zones rurales, ou les mentalités n'ont pas très évolué".

Donc cette innovation sociale attribuée aux femmes est socialement perçue par cette société ivoirienne comme un effet d'imitation du fonctionnement socio-culturel du monde européen. Ces politiques dans leur application restent de façon formelle et superficielle vu l'aspect culturel qui définit le système social de fonctionnement de toutes les instances sociales des différentes communautés. Cependant, les métiers comme l'informatique sont plus réservés aux hommes dans ce contexte social. Cela se traduit par le fait que dans le début de l'introduction de ces outils en Côte d'Ivoire, c'étaient particulièrement les hommes qui étaient privilégiés de par leur pouvoir d'achat comme un pouvoir d'accès et était jonchée de perceptions sociales rangées dans cette catégorie sociale d'homme. La femme avec sa position sociale améliorée, ne peut surtout s'adonner à l'informatique qui nécessite d'ailleurs plus de temps à consacrer devant l'écran. La femme s'occupe du foyer, après le travail et ce qui ne lui permet pas de se donner plus de temps vis-à-vis de ses devoirs familiaux. Ce pouvoir d'accès peut être analysé d'un point de vue de la vulnérabilité de la femme car seul l'homme était privilégié à l'accès à l'emploi.

Toutefois, les employeurs ont une préférence à recruter plus d'hommes que de femmes compte tenu à certaines réalités liées au statut social de la femme. Ces réalités sont liées à sa moindre disponibilité par rapport aux hommes, les préjugés sur sa faiblesse intellectuelle ou physique. Ce sont autant de motifs qui poussent certains employeurs à limiter le quota de femmes dans leurs effectifs du personnel. Pour certaines aussi, leur employabilité dépend de certains facteurs sociaux péjoratifs en termes de pouvoir et de conditionnalité à l'accès au travail comme le cuissage lié à leurs instincts personnels. Il existe encore des violences à l'égard de la femme dans le milieu domestique. 39,7% montre qu'il existe des femmes qui ont subi des violences domestiques. Ces violences proviennent de l'autorité de chef de famille des hommes à infliger certaines formes de violences sociales et physiques pour donner suite à des incompréhensions.

Au terme de cette étude, il apparait que de nombreuses réalités africaines d'ordre social, juridique, politique favorisent une ascension de la femme dans la société, mais que le poids encore très lourd de la traditions cause par moment un frein. De nombreux défis restent à relever pour une innovation sociale et totale de la femme, pour qu'elle contribue pleinement au développement de nos pays.

3. *Europe*

In the Old Continent, two nations have been considered, Italy and Poland, different but similar somehow. Below, the experience commented by academics and scholars from these countries.

3.1 *An outsider's reactions to the results of the Research Questionnaire "The Importance of Being Woman Today" in Italy (Maria Galli Stampino)*

It is stimulating to compare one's perception of life, events, and customs against survey results. For full disclosure, I was born and educated in Italy and left after my *laurea* to pursue additional educational and, later, career opportunities in the United States. I return often, sometimes multiple times a year, and I did spend a whole academic year in Rome two years ago. I also read newspapers and newsmagazines daily and, as much as I can, from a variety of ideological positions. Yet I have never been part of the Italian workforce and my life experience as a woman is very different because of this facet.

When I read the survey results from Italy, there are several elements that stand out. For starters, there is an emphasis on Italy being a "democracy" or a "democratic country" (the term and phrase recur a total of seven times; it is not included in the results from the United States). Gender equality seems to be a consequence of democracy; one respondent directly states as much in answer to question 2: "È una paese democratico con parità di sesso." Interestingly, this respondent utilizes "sex" rather than "gender," arguably indicating a rather simplistic knowledge of these terms. Compared with the results from the United States, where a belief in the legal and political system is coupled in many responses with a desire to see further protection, this recurring terminology is salient.

Another, perhaps stereotypical, Italian element that surfaces from the survey answers is the excessive attention paid to personal (physical) appearance, which is skewed against women. This aspect emerges in the references to cat calling (in answers to questions 2 and 9) and to comments to physicality (in an answer to question 6: "they always ALWAYS say something about my body. I never heard appreciates [sic] men appearance in the work world"). Underscoring physical standards of beauty of course is reductive and demeaning, but it also subtly reminds a woman of her embodied experience, including her lack of bodily strength. In other words, it is a way to keep a woman "in her place," fearful and cowering. The issue of violence is also present in the survey answers; the first time a respondent brings it up, it is in answer to question 2, in a highly strained statement: "I don't feel to [sic] much difference. Except for the fear for a woman to walk alone in the dark." Another respondent is more open in answering question 6: "some basic actions can be risky for a woman, not for a man, like going home late on my own, or going out and drinking a lot, or running on my own in a park without paying attention to my surroundings or travelling through the country on my own". Lastly, one brings up *femminicidio*, murders of women, also in answer to question 2. This topic has been heavily present in media recently and it is clearly on at least one responder's mind.

As compared with the responses gathered in the United States, family is a much more pervasive topic in Italy, again, perhaps stereotypically. The term occurs thirty times in English-language responses and twenty-eight in Italian-language ones. There are several references to the possibility or the reality of job discrimination because "motherhood scares companies" (in answer to question 11) and because "everybody also thinks that pregnancy is a money loss. So, nobody wants [to] give us work." The onus of making a decision is on a woman (in answer to question 16, we read "La donna ancora deve fare una scelta tra famiglia e lavoro per fare carriera. Se sceglie il lavoro può avere le stesse opportunità di un uomo nella partecipazione alla vita pubblica"). Family dynamics are presented as traditional and even old-fashioned: respondents talk about "wrong standards," "concezione maschilista," "tanto maschilismo" (in answers to question 2), "stereotipi," "society expectations (have a family, take care of the home)," "visione arcaica," "L'uomo [...] All'interno della famiglia ancora troppo spesso esercita prepotenza e pressione psicologica" (in answers to question 6), "Italy's culture is very sciovinist [= chauvinisistic]" and "A man who focus on his career is a successful person, a woman in the same position is always thought to be one who sacrificed family and children, a kind of less than a woman" (in answer to question 16). One more family-related and perhaps Italy-specific elements of note is the need to take care of elderly parents, which puts further pressure on women: "Difficile perché è sempre necessario conciliare lavoro, famiglia, gestione della casa, spesso anche dei genitori anziani e questo può essere frustrante perché talvolta non si arriva a fare tutto nel migliore dei modi: si può scontentare qualcuno e/o fare qualcosa nel modo non corretto" (in answer to question 2), "Men aren't required generally to take care of children and old parents and do all homeworks [sic]" (in answer to question 6), "we are the ones Who care about children, parents and family" and "Le necessità di un genitore anziano non possono essere posticipate dj [sic] mesi dalla burocrazia" (in answer to question 9). Some respondents clearly identify a vise-like situation, in which women have to tend to both the younger and the older generations, leaving very little time and energy for pursuing their own interests and careers.

This is borne out by the different percentages in the responses to questions having to do with the work sphere:

Question	Yes%	No%
11. Do you think women find a job in your country as men do?	48.1	51.9
13. Do you think women are able to have a successful career in your country as men do?	68.1	31.9

14. Do you think women are allowed to participate in public life, especially politics, in your country as men do?	73.1	26.9
17. In your country, is there support for women to balance family and job?	46.5	53.3

The questions based on belief and pertaining to general sentiments (13 and 14) see a prevalence of Yes responses; those that specifically have to do with finding jobs and balancing work and personal life (11 and 17) see a slim majority of No, which is nevertheless interesting when juxtaposed to the clear prevalence of Yes in the other two. It is almost as if things look OK in the abstract, and not so OK in practice. A response to question 6 (explaining if "being Woman in your country is different from being man," where 57.4% say Yes and 42.6 say No) puts it pithily: "In apparenza no. Ma in sostanza si [*sic*]." Appearances of equality are deceiving, this respondent indicates.

One final observation: some discursive answers indicate that respondents are unaware of their own patriarchal notions, to the point that they do not see the irony in replying to a survey about women with statements that clearly betray them. It is not an issue of self-censure or of politically correct speech; it is one of self-awareness. For example, in answer to question 9, a respondent wrote that things are improving for women: "Fortunatamente non esistono più le famiglie patriarcali, ad oggi, nel maggior [*sic*] dei casi, nella famiglia anche la volontà di una donna è presa in considerazione." A woman's opinion is also taken into consideration, which means that it potentially is an also-ran, not the expression of an integral member of a family. Even more blatantly, in response to question 12 someone stated that "Le donne sono più portate ad essere delle brave educatrici" and another one opined that "[Women] Non sono all'altezza per certi ruoli, come molti dicono." Or my favourite (in response to question 20: Is it important being woman today? Why?): "La donna è stata creata per completare l'uomo, oggi come in ogni tempo è importante e di grande valore la sua presenza nella società." This is a rehashing of clichés that go back to the Bible and that women at least since Christine de Pizan have fought against. This indicates that there is more work to be done to share the awareness that gender is socially constructed; or, as Lucrezia Marinella states in her 1635 epic poem *L'Enrico, ovvero, Bisanzio acquistato*, that "l'uso e non natura ha messo / Timor ne l'un, valor ne l'altro sesso" (canto 2, stanza 29, lines 7-8).

3.2 *The importance of being woman in Italy (Gianpiero Gamaleri[30])*

It is interesting to note that almost two out of three women in Italy, having to express a summary opinion on the difficulties they encounter, despite the difficulties, show an overall positive evaluation. And they also give the motivation, centered on freedom of speech and thought superior to that recognized in other countries and in other cultures.

1) Is it difficult being woman today in your country?
216 responses

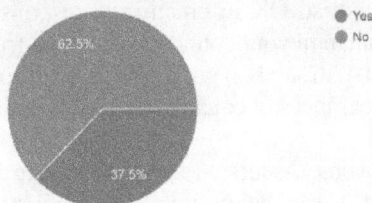

62.5%

37.5%

● Yes
● No

According to this majority, this also corresponds to a widespread gender equality, in social life, in the family and in work. In the face of this positive evaluation, just over a third of the interviewees, however, noted various types of difficulties that make the woman remain in a subordinate position and social, cultural, professional suffering for which she "is not treated on a par with men". A recurring word is "discrimination", which results in the need to "fight" to obtain the right conditions, accepting many "compromises". This occurs in various areas, which affect both social and family structures.

Above all, however, there is a gradation of the difficulties that women must overcome, ranging from ethical, professional and human relationship aspects to the point of resulting in forms of material conditions. A revealing phrase is the one indicated by the "fear of walking alone at night" which is very disturbing because it discriminates against women solely for her greater physical weakness, which on average is an unavoidable structural datum.

---

30   Uninettuno, Rome, Italy

This introduces us to the very delicate theme of "violence against women", highlighted by the answers that reveal "so much machismo", to the point of recalling "the cases of femicide", still too numerous. The summary that can be drawn from the answers to this fundamental question is that the majority of interviewees recognize a much-improved female condition in Italy, on the basis of rights acquired by the democratic system ("the situation of women has evolved"), but it is emphasized at the same time the need for vigilance to maintain them and make them increasingly effective, removing the not indifferent areas of pathology that still exist.

3) Which is your age?
216 responses

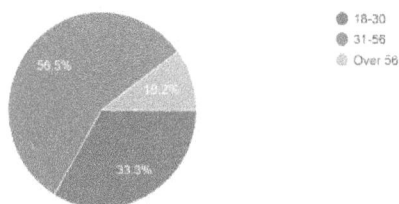

- 18-30
- 31-56
- Over 56

4) Which is your main activity? You can answer one or more of the following options
216 responses

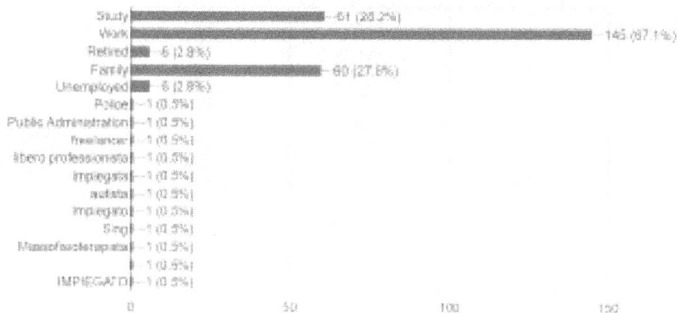

The composition of the sample notes that the survey covered all age groups of women and covered the various activities.

There is some correspondence with the statistical data concerning the general composition by age group in Italy. In fact, in the graph below regarding age and civil status, the "belly" of the drawing coincides, in the part concerning women, with the age from 45 to 59 years, adequately represented also in our survey, while it also maintains a considerable consistency up to the age of 29 represented by predominantly celibate women, also in consideration of the older age with which they enter marriage or stable and procreative relationships today. And this class is also well represented in the research, referring to exactly one third of the interviewees.

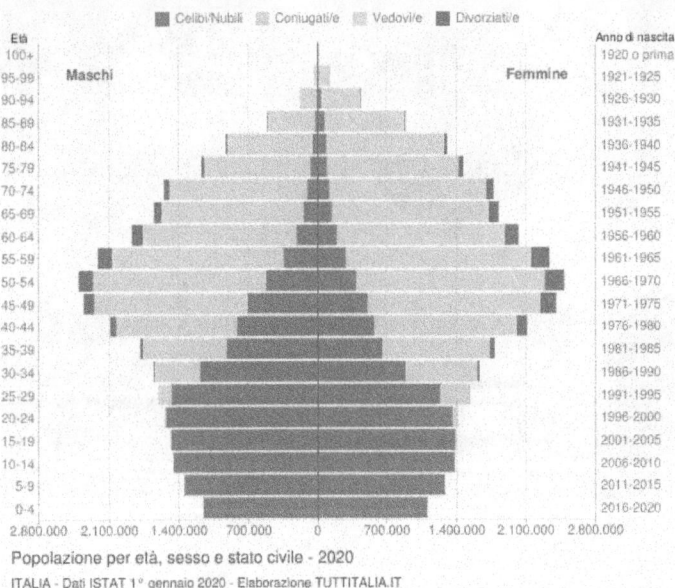

Popolazione per età, sesso e stato civile - 2020
ITALIA - Dati ISTAT 1° gennaio 2020 - Elaborazione TUTTITALIA.IT

Also, with reference to the activities, the sample is sufficiently representative, with 28 per cent of female students and 67 working in various sectors. This wide representation of the "working woman" (to recall the title of a classic television investigation by Mario Soldati and Ugo Zatterin from the 1960s) has allowed us to have first-hand voices on the issue of the relationship between women and employment. Recurring is the expression "Whatever he does will be less and less paid", although many other testimonies emphasize equal pay. But what often persists is the discrimination in career progression: "Men occupy the best work positions". This is attributed to the persistence of a lack of cultural evolution, by virtue of which "man is always seen in a superior way than woman".

In this regard, however, it should be noted that with reference to the most prestigious roles, the affirmation of women in top positions is increasingly frequent as in the case of the president of CERN in Geneva.

The "quadrilateral of female excellence". In recent press articles there has been talk of the quadrilateral of female excellences. About the relationship between women and scientific culture, an interview with Fabiola Gianotti, director of CERN in Geneva, the largest laboratory in the world for particle physics, spoke recently (in *la Repubblica* May 30th, 2021). An interview released shortly after she was called by the British government to join the G7 Advisory Council for Gender Equality. In Gianotti's words, an "Italian quadrilateral of scientific excellence for women" is outlined, with the names of Samantha Cristoforetti, destined to be the first European woman in command of the International Space Station, Cristina Messa at the helm of the Ministry for universities and scientific research, Maria Chiara Carrozza president with the National Research Council. But, Gianotti immediately adds, these very visible female presences must not deceive us. The access of young women to scientific faculties and professions is still insufficient. Their presence in the STEM sector - Science, Technology, Engineering, Mathematics - is still scarce, around 20 percent.

Also interesting is the observation of the recent appointment of a woman as editor of the weekly "7" of *Corriere della Sera*, flanked by two other women as vicar and head of the editorial staff.

However, the fact remains that in normal conditions women still must "fight too much" against an "archaic vision" that disadvantages them especially in the family-work relationship: "although men are nowadays devoted to family and home, the commitment is never comparable ".

7) Generally speaking, according to you, the policies of your country about women are:
216 responses

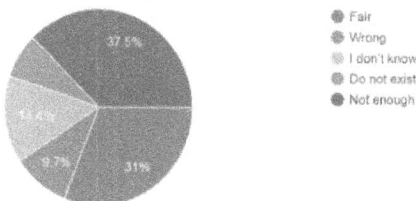

- Fair
- Wrong
- I don't know
- Do not exist
- Not enough

8) From 1=nothing to 5=a lot, according to you, compared to 10 years ago, women's conditions in
your country have changed, not only within the worforce?
216 responses

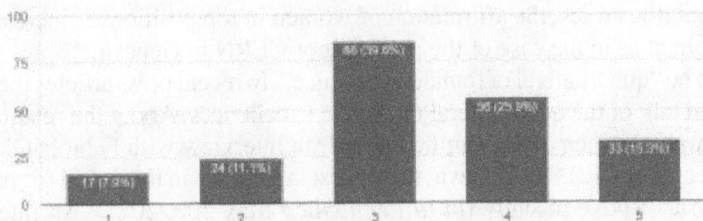

These questions concern policies towards women and their change over the last decade. And here it is striking that a high percentage (37 and a half percent) consider them wrong and that there is no significant improvement in the recent period. Faced with progress, some denounce a "false parity", up to the point of saying: "Italy is a male-dominated people". And in any case, the change does not appear adequate.

The more moderate positions admit that "the role of women is more valued, even if many objectives have not yet been achieved", especially since the pandemic has contributed to worsening the situation of women, both in the family by burdening women with new tasks, such as assistance to children in distance learning, both at work, as women are in a more precarious position.

10) Do you think men and women have the same access to technology - such as internet - and the same opportunities thanks to technologies in your country, also in the labor force?
216 responses

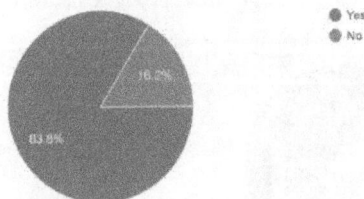

11) Do you think women find a job in your country as men do?
216 responses

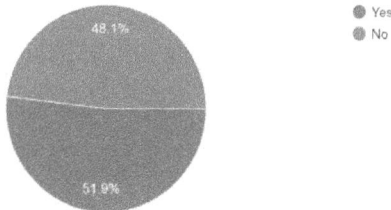

The interviewees admit: "By now, I think access to technologies is the same for both sexes, especially in the context of school education, given the prevalence of women in primary schools. On the other hand, I think that for some professional figures it is still more complex to employ women because for some roles the male figure is preferred or for the workload or because they cannot be absent due to pregnancy ". Although women are often more valued for their preparation and commitment, they also tap into higher jobs. There are also those who say: "Man or woman it doesn't matter. What matters are the skills".

Regarding the relationship with the world of work, some answers say that there is no distinction, while others note significant differences or even discrimination. They relate not only to salary or career elements, but also to ethical aspects such as relationships of trust. The difficulties connected with pregnancy and the maternal role are once again highlighted. Some answers refer not only to discrimination in the workplace, but also to the renunciation of work by women involved with children. However, it should be added that the situation of women is like that of men in a market that mortifies all employment opportunities, offering scarce job opportunities. A recurring distinction is that which refers to the difference between the public sector and the private sector. On average, in the former, equal opportunities are more respected, while the latter sometimes suffers from an archaic employer or paternalistic management that disadvantages the female component. Drastic albeit rare remain some statements such as: "Power belongs to men."

Finally, it is necessary to point out some measures adopted by the Council of Ministers regarding the adoption of "pink quotas" in terms of employment in projects related to the Recovery Found. It has been repeatedly said that the pandemic has hit three sectors in Italy. Women, young people and the South. The project for the Recovery Found - better known as Next Generation EU - aims to "compensate" these disadvantaged areas. And in this sense, attention to women is an absolutely priority objective.

The subsequent questions of questions 13, 14, 15 and 16 concern career opportunities, participation in public life and the conditions for success in the workplace.

13) Do you think women are able to have a successfull career in your country as men do?
216 responses

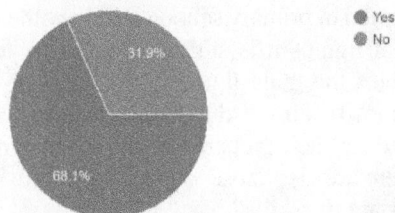

- Yes
- No

31.9%

68.1%

14) Do you think women are allowed to participate in public life, especially politics, in your country as men do?
216 responses

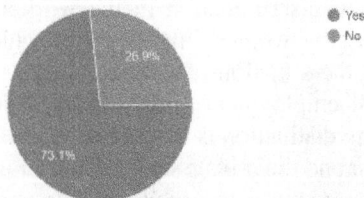

- Yes
- No

26.9%

73.1%

5) According to you, which are the conditions for a woman for a career development? Please choose one or more of the following answers

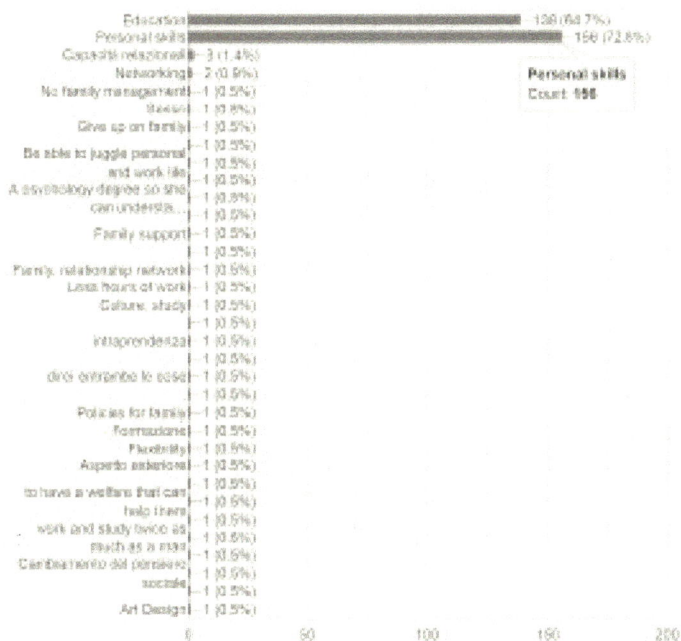

215 responses

Answer	Count
Education	129 (60.7%)
Personal skills	155 (72.8%)
Capacità relazionali	3 (1.4%)
Networking	2 (0.9%)
No family management	1 (0.5%)
Stress	1 (0.5%)
Give up on family	1 (0.5%)
Be able to juggle personal and work life	1 (0.5%)
A psychology degree so she can understa...	1 (0.5%)
Family support	1 (0.5%)
	1 (0.5%)
Family relationship network	1 (0.5%)
Less hours of work	1 (0.5%)
Culture, study	1 (0.5%)
	1 (0.5%)
intraprendeza	1 (0.5%)
	1 (0.5%)
dire entrambe le cose	1 (0.5%)
	1 (0.5%)
Policies for family	1 (0.5%)
Formazione	1 (0.5%)
Flexibility	1 (0.5%)
Asperto aziendale	1 (0.5%)
to have a welfare that can help them	1 (0.5%)
work and study twice as much as a man	1 (0.5%)
Cambiamento del pensiero sociale	1 (0.5%)
	1 (0.5%)
Art Design	1 (0.5%)

Personal skills
Count 155

A fundamental question concerned the issue of women's participation in public life, with reference to politics, always in comparison with the male gender. There are also two key positions on this topic. On the one hand, there is a broad affirmation of the progressive recognition of women's rights, within the broader framework of the development of democracy. Naturally, the survey lends itself to subsequent investigations, in relation to the situation of different countries in the context of very varied socio-cultural areas. On the other hand, there are not a few answers that underline the persistence of generalized difficulties in the path of equality.

Let's take a closer look at the most significant statements of the two orientations. In some cases, there is a clear answer, from which unequivocal positive consequences derive: "We live in a democratic country". Corresponding to it is the conviction regarding the "woman's ability to evolve at the working and political level". In relation to the other sex, women can "have the same success as men", based on certain elements, such as respect, honesty, dignity, education and professionalism.

There is also an element that acts as a glue between all these prerogatives and is made explicit in some answers: the will, the capacity for commitment and application in which many women excel more than their companions. The statement is explicit especially in the workplace: "A woman can make a career if she wants to". According to many responses, this is not an explicit hostility or discrimination, but what is called "a social opinion", a widespread preconception that risks relegating many to subordinate conditions. It follows that the recognition of the female function does not depend only on an act of honest recognition of quality in individual cases, but on the promotion of a wider diffused cultural climate, in which its function is not discriminated against prejudice.

The second group of responses, mentioned above, identifies, less optimistically, the various obstacles that female emancipation encounters. The most common one concerns the difficulty of reconciling work or political commitment with family responsibilities. Many responses refer to the need to look after not only children but often also parents. Obviously, these answers indicate that in many cases gender equality has not been achieved because parity of family responsibilities has not been implemented. And it is not worth pointing to the greater "practical sense" of women as a justification for forcing her into domestic roles from which the man shuns.

17) In your country, is there support for women to balance family and job?
215 responses

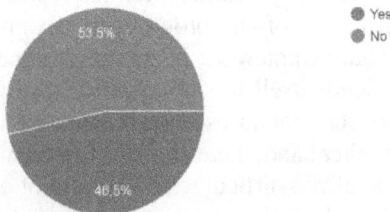

18) What is your gender
215 responses

- Female
- Male
- Other
- Prefer not to answer

23.7%

70.7%

19) Have you ever suffered or know someone who suffered for domestic violence?
215 responses

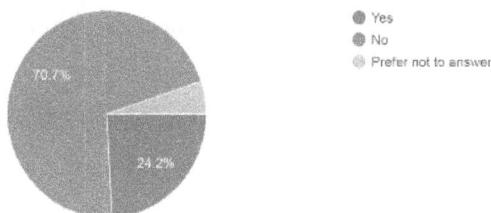

- Yes
- No
- Prefer not to answer

70.7%

24.2%

20) Thank you for your collaboration just a finally question: Is it important being woman today? Why?

The last question ("is it important to be a woman today and why?) Allowed the interviewees to express a summary judgment on the condition of women today. Here there is a general appreciation of his condition. In no response there is a rejection of the female condition or a situation of unbearable suffering. On the contrary, there is a general positive acceptance of one's gender condition, revealing a broad recognition of the rights and function of women today, at least in the Western world. In this general positive sharing, however, very different positions are recorded, even diametrically opposed.

On the one hand, there are categorical and absolute statements. "Woman is everything", "woman is future", on the other hand the definition of woman as a factor of balance in the family and in society and therefore of her mission of complementarity is recurrent. In both cases, the conclusion is unanimous: the interviewees are satisfied and sometimes proud of their female condition in this evolutionary phase of society. But this element of satisfaction is not without the awareness of the effort to be made. The verb "demonstrate" often recurs: "we must demonstrate our abilities in every area". This is associated with the recurring consideration of the multitasking function of women compared to men. The areas of work and the family to be reconciled dominate, but there are also references to the excellence of female activity in the most advanced fields of research. But all this is frequently associated with the request for more effective intervention by the public authorities, the State, both to speed up professional paths and above all to ensure the services that allow women to enhance their skills and their "independence", word which often occurs in the answers. With a view to recognizing their rights.

In conclusion, the document "The digital Community of the women, for the women" about women in Italy, with references to the international framework, in order to establish a comparison with the data collected by the research, is considered as a coherent comparison with the data considered

3.3 *The Importance of Being Woman Today in Poland (Stefan Bielański*[31]*, Joanna Podgórska-Rykała*[32]*)*

There were 176 people who took part in the survey, of which 83% were female, 15.3% were male and the remainder did not wish to respond (Q18). The majority were between 18 and 30 years old (64.2%), more than a third of the respondents were between 31 and 56 years old (33.5%), while the rest were over 56 years old (Q3).

Respondents were asked (Q4) what their main life activity was. It was possible to indicate more than one answer. Most respondents are students (as many as 63.1%), furthermore 47.4% of respondents work. Family is taken care of by 15.3 people, 2.3% are retired. Unemployed people constituted 3.4% of respondents. Other activities (such as hobbies, others) were chosen by less than 1% of respondents.

On the question of whether it is difficult to be a woman in Poland (Q1), more than 1/3 of the respondents (33.5%) answered that it is not difficult.

---

31   Professor in the Institute of Political Science of Pedagogical University (Up), in Kraków, Poland.
32   PhD in Political Science, Assistant professor at the Department of Public Policies, Institute of Law and Economics, Pedagogical University of Krakow, Poland.

However, most respondents (66.5%) indicated that it is hard to be a woman in Poland.

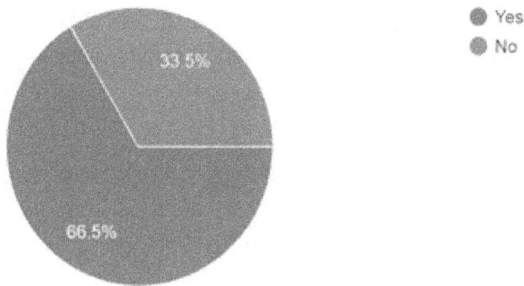

The next question (Q2) asked respondents to explain their reasons for giving these answers. A smaller part of respondents (1/3), who consider that being a woman in Poland is not difficult, supported their answer by the fact that in Poland we have equal rights, women can perform the same professions as men, they have the right to decide about their lives, they achieve similar professional and scientific success.

Among the reasons listed by respondents convinced that it is not easy to be a woman in Poland, the most frequently indicated were:
- discrimination and violation of women's rights,
- lack of structural support for mothers e.g., on the labor market,
- restriction of reproductive rights of women and limited access to health care (abortion, assisted reproduction, prenatal care, childbirth), lack of access to contraception,
- endemic and structural gender-based violence, including domestic violence,
- unequal pay (average pay for women is lower than for men),
- discrimination in the labor market (e.g. women +50),
- the strong influence of the Catholic Church on society, the emphasis of the conservative part of society on the traditional role of women as homemakers and mothers,
- the ruling right-wing political party, which does not respect human rights and defends the traditional role of women by promoting the idea of patriarchy,
- lack of sufficient representation both politically and in business,

- the objectification of women (promoting a culture of perfect appearance),
- the need to reconcile work and family life, this results in higher demands being placed on women,
- gender stereotypes (e.g., Polish Mother), the belief that women are weaker, inferior, less intelligent, less efficient at work,
- insecurity in the evenings, at night, in public places.

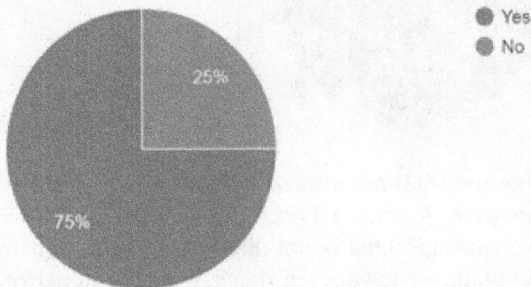

Respondents were asked whether, in their opinion, being a man in Poland is different from being a woman (Q5). 75% of respondents believe that gender matters and being a woman is different from being a man in Poland. The remaining people (25%) disagree with this perception. Respondents were asked to explain the reasons for their answer choices (Q6). The opinions of respondents indicated that there are many things that only men can do. Men can develop themselves in many areas, they are paid more for the same work. Moreover, they are not affected by the problems women face (lack of reproductive rights, sexual harassment and gender-based violence). Gender stereotypes mean that a man's opinion is often considered more important, and in politics in particular, views promoted by men predominate. Despite equal rights, women are more often discriminated and unfairly treated. They have more responsibilities and are expected to do more (e.g., rigid family roles, household duties, child and elderly care). Women are more often treated as objects than men. Men are much more likely to hold senior positions. This is related to the ever-present belief that they are more powerful, both physically and mentally, and the stereotypical perception of women's role as those who take care of the home. It is believed that certain professions are not suitable for women. There is also a tendency to expect women to choose and pursue less prestigious occupations. Many employers, especially in private companies, still ask personal questions about private and family life - only to women - during job interviews.

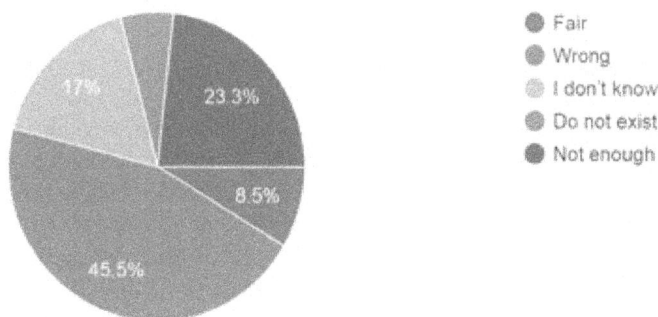

On the next question (Q7), concerning policies towards women in Poland, the majority (45,5%) of respondents said that they are wrongly conducted. Only 8.5% of respondents felt that Polish policy towards women is fair. 17% of respondents could not answer this question. As many as 23% of respondents consider that public policy in Poland pays too little attention to the problems experienced by women.

In the next question (Q8), respondents were asked to rate (on a scale of 1 to 5) how the living conditions of women in Poland have changed over the past 10 years. Almost half of the respondents (47.7%) rated the change at 3 – they chose an answer between "not at all" and "very much". A total of 34.7% of respondents rated the changes as 4 and 5, which allows us to conclude that in general, most respondents agree with the opinion that changes are taking place, although there are not very dynamic. Respondents were then asked (Q9) to explain their reasons for choosing such answers in question 8.

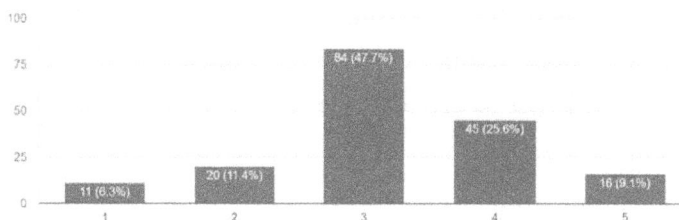

The analysis of the answers given allows for the identification of three trends, basically balanced in terms of the number of answers given for each of the trends.

Some respondents believe that changes are taking place, but in the wrong direction. The reasons for this are mainly attributed to the government policy towards women and their reproductive rights (the abortion ban), strengthened by the Catholic Church and right-wing political parties, which are currently stronger than they have been in the last ten years. Respondents believe that women still must fight for their rights. The second group of respondents indicates the opposite trend, that changes, although slow, are taking place and that they are moving in an equal direction. The respondents underline in this context the importance of changing gender stereotypes regarding traditional roles of women and men in families. Respondents recognise that the labour market is becoming more flexible and that it is easier for women to find high-paid jobs, but that salaries are still not equal. A third group of respondents believes that women's living conditions are the same as they have been in recent years and that the changes that are taking place are not sustainable and do not affect the gender position in a long-term, structural way. The part of respondents who do not perceive changes also believe that the position and role of both genders is identical. In conclusion, the answer to this question depends largely on the perspective taken. The situation of women has improved over 10 years, but in recent years, or even months, it has started to change drastically, and women and their reproductive rights have become the subject of a lively social debate. First and foremost, there is the abortion law, which, according to many women's groups, is too restrictive in Poland, leading to the creation of a huge abortion underground. In addition, an important issue is domestic violence, which politicians continue to fail to deal with.

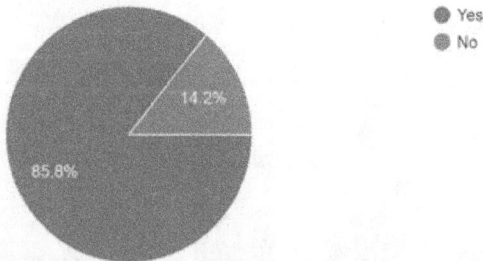

Another question (Q10) asked to the respondents was whether women and men have the same access to technology (e.g., the Internet) and consequently the same opportunities thanks to technology in accessing e.g., the labour market. In response to this question, 85.8% of people said yes - women and men have the same access and the same technological possibilities. The rest (14.2%) disagreed.

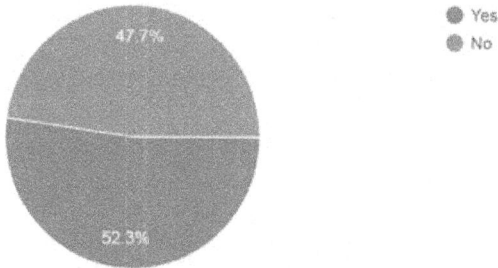

To the question (Q11) of whether women find a job in Poland as men do, more than half (52.3%) of the respondents answered yes. In contrast, 47.7% of those asked disagreed with this statement.

Then (Q12) respondents were asked to explain their answers chosen in questions 10 and 11. First, many of the respondents expressed the conviction that being a specialist (also in new technologies) is not related to gender. Many people also pointed to the fact that in Poland women are better educated and both genders have equal access to technology. In addition, it was emphasised that finding a job is available regardless of gender, but that subsequent earnings differ precisely because of gender. Fewer women work in specialised sectors - IT, High-Tech - because they choose science-related career paths less rarely than men and prefer humanities more often. It is still believed that women should not do "men's work", such as electricians, professional drivers, construction workers - so it is more difficult for women to find a job in these industries.

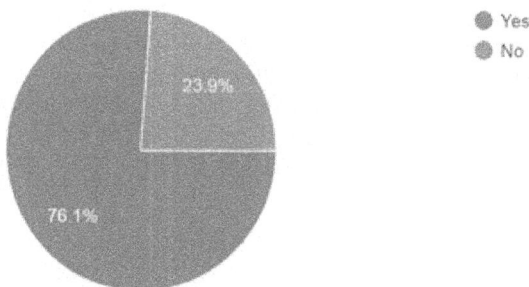

In response (Q13) to the question of whether women in Poland can have as successful a career as men do, as many as 76.1% said yes. Only 23.9% of respondents disagreed with this statement.

When asked whether women can participate in public life (especially politics) in the same way as men (Q14), 65.3% of respondents said yes. The remaining people think that women do not have the same opportunities in this area.

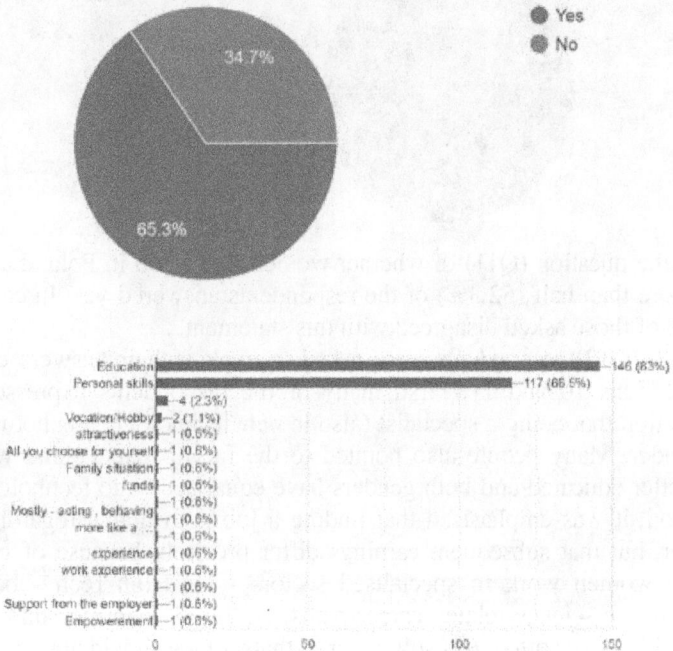

The next question (Q15) asked what the most important conditions for women's career development are. Respondents could indicate more than one answer. Most chose 'education' (83%), followed by 'personal skills' (66.5%). Other factors, such as family situation, experience or support, according to the respondents are of little importance.

Respondents were asked (Q16) to explain why they chose the indicated answers in questions 13, 14 and 15. Here again, respondents raised similar arguments as in relation to the questions asked earlier. There were allegations of gender-based discrimination in the workplace, strong stereotypes related to opportunities for both genders, sexism in society and the workplace. It was also noted that there are far fewer women than men in politics. Some interviewees made women's ability to succeed dependent on living in a large city. In addition, many people are concerned that for women to advance their careers they must sacrifice their family life. Despite many expressed fears, most respondents believe that women can make a successful career in Poland, both in the professional and political sphere. However, it is more difficult for them, even though they are generally better educated, have more soft skills and can organise their time more efficiently. However, the problem often lies in low self-esteem, in the subjective belief of women that they are inferior to men.

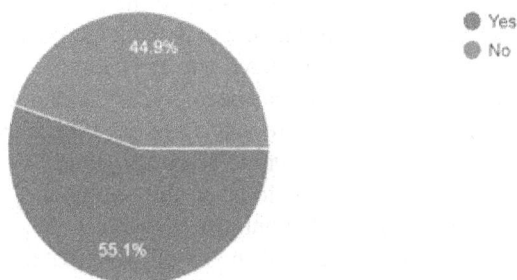

Question 17 asked whether women are supported to balance work and family life. 55.1% of respondents believe that women have support to balance work and family life, which is slightly more than half of the respondents. The other half does not agree with this statement.

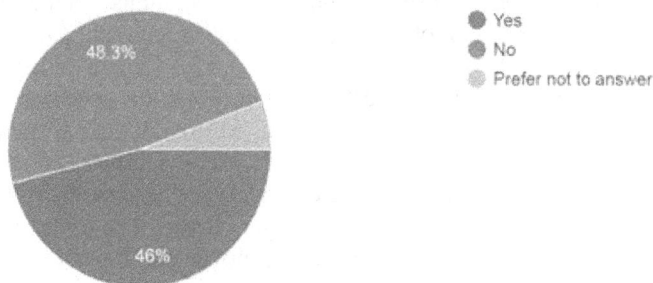

The next question (Q19) asked if you have ever suffered or someone you know has suffered from domestic violence. As many as 46% of respondents answered this question in the affirmative. 48.3% had never experienced domestic violence and the rest preferred not to answer.

The last question (Q20) posed to respondents was: is it important to be a woman these days? Why? Respondents answered overwhelmingly that yes - being a woman is important. Above all, arguing that without women the world could not exist at all. Diversity is a value. It is good to be different and inspire each other.

It was also pointed out that women:
- must fight for the rights and well-being of future generations,
- should change the world and try to improve it,
- should prove that they are mentally strong and can succeed,
- are the basis for the development of society and the world,
- should develop and fulfil their dreams just like men,
- must fight with different problems and difficulties,
- are more responsible and sensible in making many decisions,
- more and more often maintain a home and a family.

The "women's issue" in Poland has been of specific character since the beginning of the 19th century. There was a pre-existing religious context related to the Marian cult; in the 19th century a myth of "Polish-mother" has emerged especially in the periods of the struggles for the state's independence (a "Polish-mother" would sacrifice personal aspirations and needs for the benefit of the Fatherland and Family). At that time the women were frequently required to replace men in the structures of social and family life (replacing fathers, brothers, and sons) as the men were directly involved in military struggle (mainly against the Russian forces in the 19th century and German forces in the 20th century), and in consequence died, or they were being sentenced to labor camps (and in the mid-20th century also to the German concentration camps, and Soviet gulags; then a peaceful and eventually victorious struggle against the communist regime was led by "Solidarity" movement of the 1980s, and the women did participate in the movement).

On the edge of the 19th and 20th century on the Polish territories (divided by three invaders: tsarists Russia, Austria-Hungarian monarchy of the Hapsburg family, and united Prussia – German empire) the movement for women's suffrage and emancipation has emerged, however its participants drew from middle and upper classes. The movement was politically related to the independence left movement, represented by the Polish Socialist Party (Polska Partia Socjalistyczna, PPS). Emancipatory postulates addressed not only equal participation in the politics but also (if not above all) they claimed a right for autonomous participation in culture, arts, education, and science. Among the model figures of the period active in fields of arts and science one finds Gabriela Zapolska (playwright who unveiled hypocrisy of the petty-bourgeois livelihood in the city of Krakow), Helena Modrzejewska (a world-famous theater actress who performed in the USA), or Maria Curie-Skłodowska (a twice-receiver of the Nobel Prize, and perhaps the most talented Polish scientist). It is worth mentioning that the life history of Maria Curie-Skłodowska reflects academic conventions of the period (compared with the results of the presented survey, several of them are still maintained today), among them a conviction that the independent research may be conducted only by men researchers. Thus Curie-Skłodowska worked in Paris instead of Warsaw or Krakow. *Notabene*, such prejudices of traditionalist approach towards female scientists and women working independently (outside of "men's care") were quite similar in both "progressive" France and "regressive" Poland (which did not constitute its own state's institutions at that time).

Polish women's role was appreciated by the political leaders (especially by Józef Piłsudski) at the time of Poland's gaining independence in 1918. In fact, already in 1919 in the first parliamentary elections in free Poland, the women (as one of the first in Europe) fully exercised their civic rights. Paradoxically the majority of women supported traditional, national direction in politics which demonstrated a limited support for women's independence in politics, social and economic life. One finds women's situation in the times of Polish People's Republic (Polska Rzeczpospolita Ludowa, PRL) similarly paradoxical. PRL was a state subject to USSR domination, and it executed a communist model of women's emancipation. On the one hand, under the system of so-called real socialism the women were granted (not only declaratively) a wide range of social and health care rights, but on the other hand, no thorough changes in the social structure were implemented. In the consequence women did not have a chance to advance to prominent, managing positions even in the highly feminized sectors of labor. Similar conditions prevailed in the spheres of mono-party rule or within the state's institutional structures. Paradoxes maintained also in the sphere of personal and moral choices, and life-conduct.

The 1960s cultural changes emerged also in Eastern Europe, and legal regulations facilitated forms of social transformation, e g. providing women with a right to abortion. Simultaneously – specifically since the end of 1970s (coinciding in time with John Paul II's pontificate, and reinforcement of the Catholic Church's authority) – a significant part of the Polish society returned to traditional social and national values as they were motivated by the will to politically defy communist regime. The communists' fall and transformation (or rather return) to the capitalist system made evaluation of the women's situation more complex. Undoubtedly some groups of women benefited from the 1990s new economic opportunities (a figure of a "businesswoman" emerged) or from the changing media environment (a figure of "celebrities known by the fact that they are known" emerged). However, for the majority of women, the turbulent transformation in consequence led to significant social stratification (reinforced in regard to geographical territories: big urban centers benefited from the transformation while smaller provincial towns and villages *de facto* became its victims).

Such divides are reflected in political life: liberal (Democratic Union/ Unia Demokratyczna, UD, Civic Platform/ Platforma Obywatelska, PO) and left (Democratic Left Alliance/ Sojusz Lewicy Demokratycznej, SLD) parties enjoyed the support of urban women (and generally the support of the big cities' population), while the women's constituency supporting the biggest conservative group that governs in Poland since 2015, Law and Justice (Prawo i Sprawiedliwość, PiS) lives in small towns and villages. "Women's issue" understood mostly in terms of personal choices and life-conduct, and related to the radical feminism movement, became a subject of a heated social discussion in the times of pandemic 2020/2021 in the result of tightening up anti-abortion regulations (at that time being already a highly restrictive law) what led protesters to the streets. This aspect is observable in the answers of the survey respondents, especially given the fact that it was mostly answered among the representatives of the academic environment, a group quite active in the above-mentioned events. It is significant (given the respondents' background) that the majority (66,5%) identified "being woman in Poland" as "difficult", but a significant minority (33,5%) presented completely contrary views. It is also worth noticing that the survey shows that the prevailing and most important problems faced by Polish women are related to the labor, social and health care, and that the economic and social concerns interweave with preoccupation with the living conditions of the individual and their families. This proves that the "women's issues" should not be examined only through the ideological and political prism.

4. *Western and Southern Asia*

Finally, proceeding in the analysis, the experiences of two regions of the East of the world have been considered in Western and South Asia. It is about historically, culturally and politically diverse and contrasting countries, chosen for their differences: Iraq and Iran, in Western Asia, and

India and Pakistan in the Southern part of this Continent. Below are the comments of academics and scholars on these territories.

4.1 *The Importance of being Woman Today : Iran Chapter (Raana Malik[33])*

Background. The Iranian constitution grantees human rights and political freedom to everyone, irrespective of their gender, age and race. Moreover, Iran has also signed human rights agreements pledging no discrimination based on sex. However, these promises, and agreements are not adequately implemented until the law enforcement is gender sensitive and strong. The Islamic Republic of Iran ranks 150 in Global Gender Gap Index among the 156 countries in the world (World Economic Forum, 2021). However, Iranian women have experienced substantial social change and progress over recent decades linked to improvements in their educational and occupational status. A study conducted in Iran reported that women, in general, are more educated than men, and the percentage of university educated women is twice that of men (Salehi-Isfhani & Egel, 2007). Education is now an essential part of women's rights, due to its valuable role in enabling women to be active members of their society, enhancing individuals' welfare (e.g., women as mothers to raise a better generation), improving economic and social conditions overall (Islam, 2019) . Educated women understand their own rights, and are likely to protect themselves against inequity and discrimination (Islam, 2019). Improving the socio-economic status of Iranian women (e.g. education and work), has a high impact on self-efficacy, and self-esteem which are indicators of wellbeing and quality of life (Azar & Vasudeva, 2006).

In this survey, total 100 respondents participated, among which mostly were females.

Findings. Q. 1. Is it difficult being women today in your country? The survey shows that more than two-third of the respondents (85%) perceived that being woman, it is difficult to live in Iran whilst only 15% respondents thought that women can manage. It's noteworthy to mention that 88% respondents were females, participating in the survey:

---

33 Chairperson at Department of Gender Studies University of the Punjab, Lahore, Pakistan.

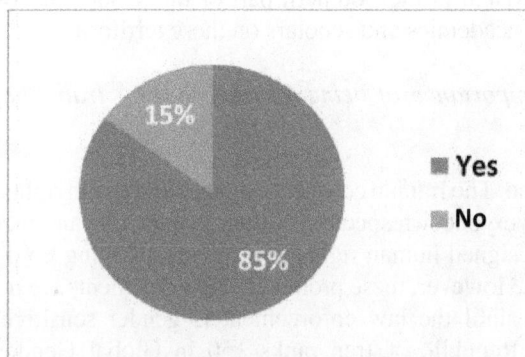

Q. 2. Can you explain the reasons for your answer to Question No. 1

Majority of the respondents mentioned that Iran is a patriarchal and strict country. Women are given very space to exercise freedom. Women in Iran are facing discriminations in most aspects of life. Women have no legal protection against domestic violence or sexual harassment. Women's participation in the work force is very low. Women lack decision-making power and suffer from low confidence and self-esteem. They are not allowed to hold leadership offices like the Presidency or the Supreme Leadership. Social barriers continue to restrict women in the four walls of the home. They are ideally seen as in the roles as mothers and wives. Males are mostly thought to be head of the household with complete control over his wife's choices. For example, a husband can prevent his wife from working (some employers even ask for the husband's written consent) and can even not allow her from traveling abroad and from obtaining a passport. *"For even a simple surgery, she is supposed to take permission from his father, husband or brother"*.

The respondents further shared that gender equality is just a term in their country as most of women do not get equal wages for equal work. Moreover, there are wide gender wage gaps. Women are being judged in so many things and men always want women to act according to their wishes. There are a lot of inequalities in so many things. A respondent mentioned, *"Women are treated as servants. Even if they have an income and contribute in living expenses, the man is still the master of the house and the woman is responsible for raising and caring of children. And protect her husband and children, but no one feel responsibility towards her."*

In the recent years, Iran has made notable progress in women's education and health, including an increased ratio of literate women and girls. Women make up more than half of all university students and they can now participate in sports as well. The respondents agreed that Hijab or Purdah is not a hurdle for Iranian women to grow or empower themselves. They can do anything by wearing Hijab as per Shariyah of Islam. It's actually our socio-cultural values creating gender inequality in our country.

Q. 3. What is your age?

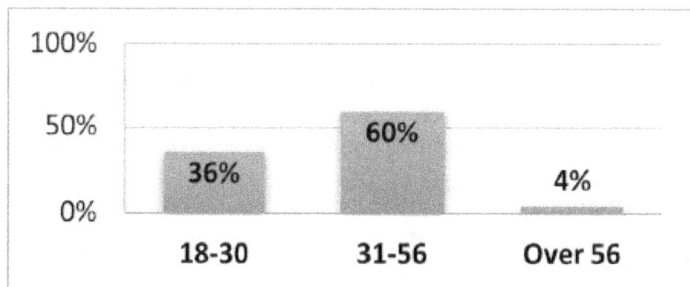

More than half of the respondents (60%) fall in the age bracket of 31-56 years which means most the sample is mature and have faced realities of life. About 36% respondents are young; however, very few respondents (4%) are in the late age group.

Q. 4. Which is your main activity?

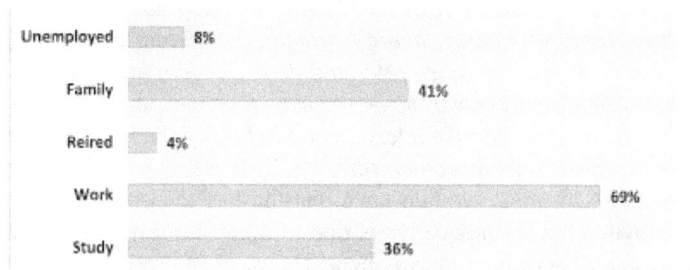

The survey found that 69% respondents have working status and are working in different capacities. 'Family' means staying at home and doing household chores, 41% respondents (females) are staying at home and doing housework. Another 36% respondents are students, studying at different levels of education.

Q. 5. Being woman in your country is different from being man?

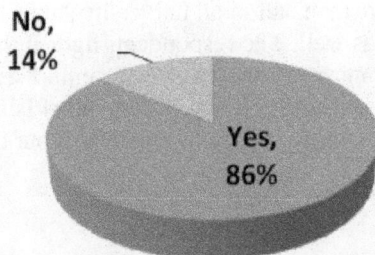

It was found that more three-fourth of the participants agreed that men and women are enjoying different status in the Iranian society, whilst only 14% disagreed and believed that men and women have equal status in Islamic Republic of Iran.

Q. 6. Please explain the reasons of your answer at Q5?

Iran is still going through a tough time and both men and women are suffering from the last four decades. However, in comparison, men are enjoying more rights and freedom than women. Women are facing discrimination both in the public and personal domains like matters related to marriage, divorce, inheritance, child custody, jobs, harassment etc. A married woman cannot get a passport or travel outside the country without the written permission of her husband. There is discrimination in almost every aspect of life either it an employment opportunity or mobility. A respondent said, *"Of course, being a woman is different from being man in my country. Excessive patriarchy and their freedom have caused more problems. Women will never have security that men experience. Many men allow themselves to take decisions on behalf of their women, but the situation is upturned from women side."*

Compared with men, women have one-third of the chances of getting any employment. This inequality is due to domestic laws discriminating against women's access to employment. The types of professions available to women are restricted and benefits are often denied. Husbands have the right to prevent wives from working in particular occupations and some positions require husband's written consent. Moreover, the superstitious thoughts are also hindering women economic empowerment as people believe that if a woman works, she will neglect his husband and house.

Iran is a patriarchal society, where men have freedom whereas women are answerable to their men for their actions. Men have right to choose their jobs, their careers whereas women do not enjoy such liberties. Women are not allowed to join key positions in any sector. Women are working at low positions with less pays without any job securities. Women are facing gender pay gap and glass ceiling in the country, Men is considered the head of the family, he will decide the fate of his women in every aspect of life and holds the position of decision maker in the households as well as in the society. Another respondent added *"because men are valued more than a woman, although in our current society, both men and women work side by side, but still women have more restrictions."*

Q. 7. Generally speaking, according to you, how are the policies of your country about women?

The results of the survey found that half of the respondents 50% believed that policies related to women are discriminatory, whereas one-fourth respondents did not have enough knowledge about pro-women and remained salient. Another (18%) respondents thought that there must be more legislation and policies for women. Only 2% respondents viewed policies for women as fair in the country. This clearly shows that more policies and reforms are needed to raise the status of women in the country.

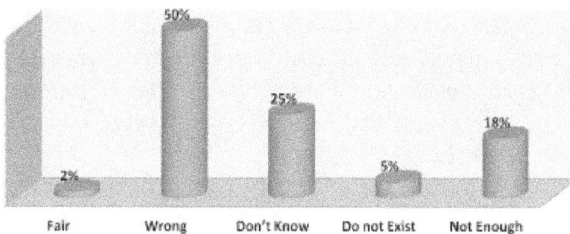

Q. 8. From 1=nothing to 5=a lot, according to you, compared to 10 years ago, women's conditions in your country have changed, not only within the work force?

The participants were asked to rate the changes in the condition of women in the last 10 years in their country. The results show that overall, more responses were towards slight change in the condition of women in the country. Only 13% respondents perceived that the changes have occurred in the status of women in Iran. This is very much evident from the data that change in government did not have much impact on the condition of women; rather, the rules stick to the policies designed years ago.

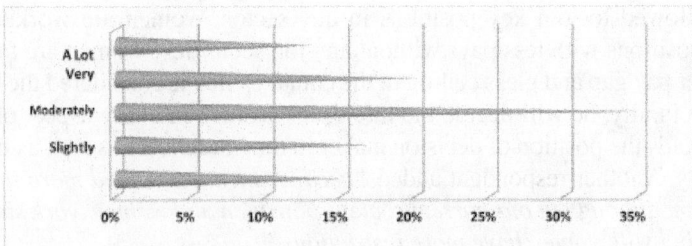

	Nothing	Slightly	Modertely	Very	A Lot
Series1	15%	17%	35%	20%	13%

Q. 9. Please can you explain the reasons of your answer at question number 8?

The responses of the interviewees revels that in the past decades, the women's condition in Iran was worse but with the passage of time, it has improved a lot. In past women were not allowed to get education and work. They were bound to homes and not even allowed to go out for recreational purposes. However, today women are getting education and the enrolment of girls is increasing in school, colleges and universities. A participant says, *"In the past, women had more problems with recreation, education and even work. In recent years, I see positive changes in terms of women becoming more independent"*.

The respondents mostly agreed that the rulers/people in Iran believe that social evils (rape, sexual harassment) from the society can be minimized by restricting women's mobility and keeping them to homes. Majority of the respondents were hopeful that condition of women will be improved gradually because the literacy rate is increasing, and people are getting awareness. One of the respondents added, *"Families have become more aware due to increase in education, women's expectations from themselves and becoming part of the community have increased."* Respondents reported some change in the mindset of people. *"Women are working alongside with men in the factories, which can't even be even imagined few years back"*.

Some of the respondents don't find any improvement in the status of women in the recent years. The laws remain the same. However, their percentage is very in the data.

Q.10. Do you think men and women have the same access to technology such as Internet and the same opportunities in your country, also in the labor force? The data concludes that more than half of the respondents (57%) thought that men and women have equal access to technology and labor force. However, 43.3% respondents saw gender imbalance in access to technological facilities and labor force participation in Iran. The labor participation rate for women in Iran is about 18%, which is among the lowest in the world.

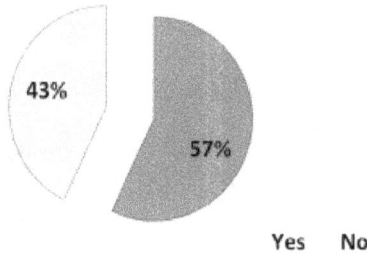

Yes   No

Q. 11. Do you think women find a job in your country as men do?

The survey found that 70% respondents thought that a woman can't find a job as a man can find in our Iran. This means that job opportunities for women are less than for men.

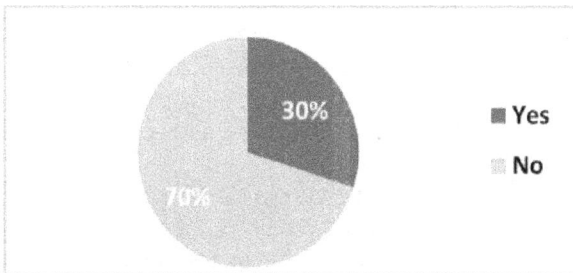

Can you explain the reasons for your answers at Questions No. 10 and No. 11?

In Iran, there is a lot of difference in the nature of jobs for men and women. The data presents that it is hard for women to get a job as compared to men. Respondents shared that for most of the jobs only men can apply i.e. they are reserved for men and women are ineligible for such jobs. These jobs mostly relate to upper management jobs. Most of the women respondents articulated that our society has specified fields for women and they are not allowed to enter in the technological, mechanical, industrial, engineering discipline and sport fields. Masculine jobs like electrician and technical are also specified for men. Even high ranks jobs like president and judge are for men. According to the respondents, there are specific rights and regulations for women, they have fewer opportunities and benefits. *"Men are supposed to do work as compared to women because they have responsibilities to run household. Only if women are allowed by their men, they can work outside, otherwise in our society only men do work".*

The respondents also stated that there are wide gender gaps in salaries and wages. Women get lower wages. *"In our society, women are deprived of so many things because of their sex"*. Another respondent stated, *"firstly there is no women in our society ever in the same rank or position as men because she has no right to choose and no right to move freely as that position requires, and secondly no organization created a safe and healthy environment for women"*.

Although few in numbers, but some respondents had the viewpoint that equality of job depends on skills and attitude. If women have desirable skills, they can also get similar job as men. *"Yes! one hundred percent, women find jobs as equal to men because of education, emerging new thoughts and development of new technologies. Time has changed the mind of our parents and society"*.

One of the woman respondents stated, *"In our country accessibility to internet is controlled by the government"*. Another respondent shared, *"access to technology is available to both males and females. But females have limited opportunities; therefore, their access to technology is also low"*.

Do you think women are able to have a success full career in your country as men do?

The survey indicates that about (70%) respondents believed that women could have a successful career as men, if given opportunities. However, 30% respondents found it difficult for women to have a successful career in Iran. This is mainly due to patriarchal nature of society prevalent in the country:

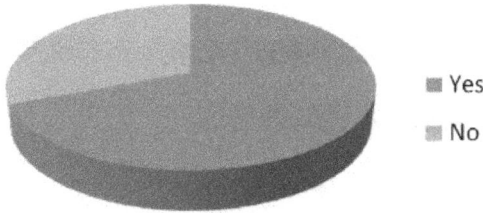

Q. 14. Do you think women are allowed to participate in public life, especially politics, in your country as men do?

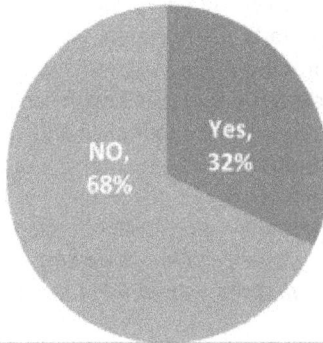

The data shows most (32%) respondents believed that women can equally participate in public life and can have political participation as men in our country. However, most of the respondents (68%) reported that women are not allowed to participate equally as men in the public and political places.

Q. 15. According to you, which are the conditions for a woman for a career development? Please choose one or more of the following answers.

Most (61%) respondents mentioned Personal Skills are foremost needed for having a good career, whereas 32.6% believed that the most important factor for the career development of women is Education.

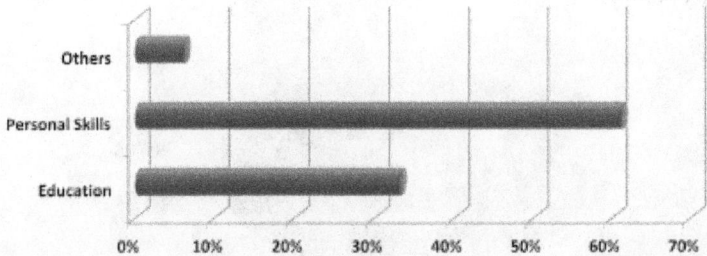

16) Can you explain the reasons for your answers at Questions No. 13, 14, and No. 15?

The respondents stressed the need for the acceptance of women in every field of life, equal wages, and give healthy work environment for their career development. Moreover, increased quota for women in public and private institutions, especially in technical departments can create job opportunities for women. One of the respondents shared, *"in my area no woman is allowed to go gym. It's our basic health need"*. Most of the women stated that quality education, work experience and skills are important for successful career development. Unfortunately, women lack in technical skills required for getting a good job; government of Iran should take steps to create technical institution to take women in mainstream.

Most of the respondents stated, *"Our community environment should be supportive for women so that they should feel themselves secure and safe to move freely"*.

It's very difficult for women to become part of political system of the country. There are very few women who have joined politics. *"It's not possible for women to join politics in our country"*. Another respondent added, *"Career of the women in politics is not easy because of the acceptance issue by the society. The more acceptances of women, the more progress, this country can do"*.

Q. 17. In your country, is there support for women to balance family and job?

Most of the respondents (65%) reported negatively that women can balance work and family with help of any support. However, 35% respondents that women got support to balance work-life situation.

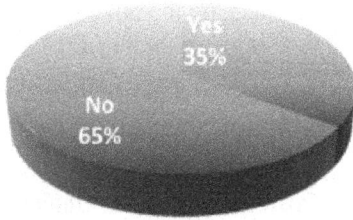

Q. 18. What is your gender?
The data mainly consists of female respondents (88%). Therefore, the findings of the survey must be seen with a female eye more than male.

Female

Male

Q.19. Have you ever suffered or know someone who suffered for domestic violence? Majority of the respondents (78%) had themselves experienced domestic violence or was witness of women facing violence. This shows a very alarming situation in Iran. A high percentage of violence against women exists in the country.

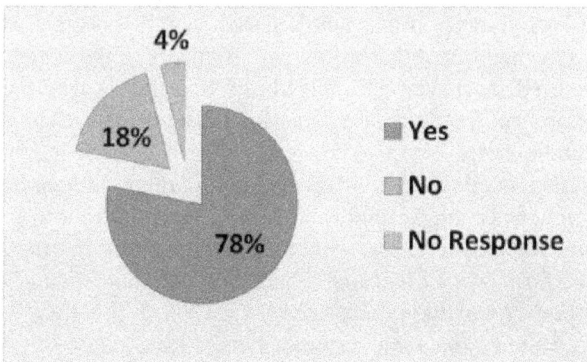

Q.20. Is it important to be a woman today? Why?

Most of the respondents articulated in their views, *"........Yes, I am proud to be a woman...."* Women are the pillar of the family and can bring happiness to everyone in their families. Some of the respondents also stated that women are important but the discrimination in career development, socio-cultural barriers, and lack of women representation in politics and also   cultural discrimination makes women weak.

Some of respondents mentioned that limited mobility and lack of personal freedom makes women's position down in the Iranian society. *"........in our society, even if we are considered human not women then our life would be easier than what is today"*. One of the respondents shared, *"women have different roles as mother, daughter, and wife and also as mother in-law, but some roles are powerful, and some roles are faced discrimination. So, the situation of women varies"*. Another woman stated, *"being a woman, it is the most beautiful thing in my life"*. Some of the women stated that *"women are very important factor of the society because they are more influential than men. They are flourishing the society and are not only precious for our society but also for world"*.

According to different views of respondents explained that the women have the power to change to the society and also the future of the nation. Women bear the burden of society, share the equal responsibility as men, and support their families in different and difficult situations.

One of the women expressed their feeling in different way, *"it is important, it is very important as being a woman.... As a woman I enjoyed lot but unfortunately, I am living in such a society where women have no value. Patriarchal society and our culture are using women only to give birth a child and a source of enjoyment for a man"*.

Women are most important pillar of society, if the pillar is educated and have full confidence in her abilities then it will bring a great change. Some of the women stated that women are founders of the society, actually men are terrified from women, their ability and that is way they control women's mobility, freedom of expression, discriminate their rights and bond them in houses.

Another respondent stated, *"from the beginning of the human existence women till now has been an important component of the society; women is the half part of the society. As a woman is key factor for the successful life of men in the form of a mother, sister, wife and daughter then definitely for themselves they can bring a great change"*.

The survey shows that some respondent expressed that it is not important to be a woman or man; the important is that what the role and responsibilities they perform for the betterment of society, and the world. *"Our backward minds should be changed so that the society will change"*. Men and women are the basic pillars of the society. The gender inequality is because of the societal norms, their acceptance and behaviors toward women.

Conclusion. The sample of the survey mainly consists of women. Thus, the findings present the opinion and perceptions of women in Iran. The women have very openly criticized the lower status of women in Iran. Gender inequality prevails in the society. People follow the patriarchal norms and values and perceive women ideally as mothers, daughters and wives confined in the homes. The pro- women legislation is much needed to provide women safe and conducive work environment and fearless mobility. Although the situation in education for women in the country is improving, but there is a long way to go to overall status of women in Iran.

4.2 *The Importance of Being Woman Today in Iraq (Ameera Abdul Kareem Marran[34])*

Keywords: Percentages and answers analysed according to the sample's point of view, and results interpreted according to the evidence sample. Search sample: 155; responders; 93.5% of women of percentage; 6.5% of men of percentage

First question: "Is it hard to be a woman in Iraq?". Table 1 shows the percentage of responses answers:

Table 1 - percentage of women who have difficulty being women in society

No.	Answer	The percentage
	Yes	67.1%
	No	32.9%

As shown in table No. (1) proportion of the sample (67.1%) are faced that is difficult, the change for the better and the acquisition of rights must come from the social environment, the power of the State, the laws, a major change in society, customs, traditions and the abandonment of a legacy that is hundreds of years old. The main reasons are:

---

34 Lecturer Master of mental health at the University of Basra, College of women for education, Department of psychological & educational sciences and Director of Bahjat Al-Fuad rehabilitation centre for torture victims (NGO).

1. Ignorance, religious, societal constraints, customs and traditions, such as the man has all the rights, criticism of women specifically.
2. An inferior view of certain professions, such as nursing, because they require staying out of the house with patients while the doctor is respected.
3. Denial of education, especially at the university level, on the grounds of gender mixing.
4. Power of the State, no laws protecting women, and most existing laws do not do justice to them.
5. Inferiority, women only body, easy prey to hunt and exposure harassed, for that, her role is limited only at the home care.

The answer (no) is 32.9%, it shows that the societal and family constraints imposed are social contexts that differ because of cultures and the nature of the formation of societies. These are mechanisms for controlling individual human behaviour, aims is to control society, in other words, how an individual responds to the laws of the community, whether is opposed to them or not, but can identify positive and negative from it.

These restrictions are not imposed to limit freedom of thought, action or movement, but rather to protect and strengthen women, and the main reason for their point of view. The source of women's power stems from within them. They believe that women are strong enough to face difficulties and contribute to building their lives and future, their families and society. Because they are half of society, raise, and care for the other half, this category sees them, as being more powerful to reach the goals, are exactly the opposite of the category that responded (Yes) did not directly or indirectly mention her internal strength.

Table 2 explains the repeated views of the sample as to how difficult.

Yes, it is hard.	NO, NO HARD
A society that restricts women in everything, and its tools are customs, traditions, and misperceptions of religious. Inequality of rights, ignorance. masculine society that gives all opportunities to men The difficulty of dealing with men because women are perceived as easy prey to hunt Discrimination in education, choice of specialization and certain professions are examples: Women are denied college education. They have no right to be a nurse or a lawyer	Societal constraints are means of protecting women Women are part of society and can contribute to the building of the country, as well as they have equal rights, many families, husbands that support women, especially in education and work. Women's employment opportunities have become greater than men's have, have the right for election and participating political life. According to some laws and religious beliefs, women have their rights and there is respect and appreciation for women.

Questions 2, 3 and 4: How old are you, and what is your activity now and the difference between men and women, respectively, will be ranked in the following table:

Table 3

Answers to 2, 3 and 4 questions

Age group	Percentage	Activity	Percentage	Difference	Percentage
18-30 years	74.8%	Student	32.2%	Yes	87.1%
31-56 years	23.2%	Housewife	13.5%	No	12.9%
+ 56 years	2%	Employee	12.9%		
		Without work	10.3%		
		Other	9%		
		Retired	1.3%		

1) The highest age group (18-30 years) is in the largest group (74.8%), which is very large, we are talking about 3/4 sample. This age group can be divided into two parts: (18-24) years, other (25-30), we explain why they feel it is difficult: First category (18-24 years): A. Education: Some of them are at university and the family pays to them for completing of study, and some of them are married and have children, as well as the difficulty of making certain decisions relating to their lives. B. Socialization (methods of education): some of families gives men very freedom. Second category (25-30 years): women faced from Unemployment and lack of employment opportunities, Women in this group subjected to psychological, family and community stress.

2) The age group 31-56 in second place with 23.2% participation (1/3) of sample, women have:

- Completed education or at the completion stage of education, have jobs, family, children and grandchildren.
- Different roles women play at this age, the diversity of goals, different life experiences, difficulties and ability to manage family life, career, hobbies or work within civil society, some of them have leadership tendencies and political life, all of which have given them a leadership dimension. It is well known that the severe societal constraints here have been significantly reduced.
- The corner of life gives - work, education and family formation - powerful factors that contribute to the empowerment of women and make them stronger.

From the above, the 18-30 age group has difficulty life. Because the most of these families come from the countryside, and their lifestyle is predominantly tribal and clan-based, which severely limits women's; the last 10 years have seen changes in the fabric of society, because of the reverse migration from the countryside to the city, the emigration of the population outside the city to other governorates or countries. In fact, with all the development in the city, the Iraq's rural composition have preserved their customs and traditions and even imposed them on the remaining people of the city, so many of women suffering the difficulty of adjustment with life of city, on the one hand, and the demands of family and tribal social life, on the other.

The rest of the percentages, which different greatly, and this explains the answer to the fourth question: Is being a woman in your country different from being a man? The answer came with (yes) 87.1%, which is a very large percentage, and this difference was determined in difference in body structure, strength and the level of absolute freedoms given to a man, family and community support him, customs, traditions, a misconception of religious.

The main reason is the nature of the family's composition, social pattern, and clan affiliation. The other group (12.9%), which sees this difference gradually fading away and the family, becomes more supportive of women, reflecting positively on the whole society. According to table (4)

Table No. (4)

The difference between men and women in Iraqi society

Yes, there's a difference	No Difference
At 87.1%, answer yes, and the reasons are: 1. Customs and traditions gives to the man all freedoms in the work, study, marriage, and the role of woman just at home 2. Additional responsibilities: between home and work family management and a working (difficulty balancing work and family requirements)	With 12.9%, answers (no) for the reasons: 1. Raising society's awareness about: Equality in Employment opportunities, for women are higher than for men, choice of type of study and right of participating in political field 2. Difference power: Women have a special role in society, she is stronger and braver to face difficulties, the source of affection, love and energy and she is half the community, raised and care the other half.

Question 5 and 6: How do you see the politics of your country? Have the country's situations changed? Because changes in societies are closely related to the policies Government, the views on the assessment of government policy are very close together with their assessment of the extent of changes in the country,

The percentage (21.3%) finds that government policy is very wrong, so changes in the country in various areas of life, specifically in the improving the status of women, is bad, which had a negative impact on their lives and future, and the large percentage shows 36,8% that there have been good

changes in the situation of women; the country's conditions have changed
for the better through:
- Raising awareness for women's rights, in study, work, marriage,
  participating in political life and entry into military services.
- Technological helps to increases awareness of women's rights
  because of learning about the experiences of other countries.
- Legislation of the laws for the protection of women.

As for the other of the percentages and their total (63.20%), they came
much less than the first percentage and indicated that there was no change
in the status of women, because:
- A backward society does not respect women and there is no law that
  does justice to women.
- Increase the phenomenon of harassment of women

Table No. (6) - The answers of seventh and eighth questions

Are job opportunities for men and women equal?		Equal access to modern technologies between men and women	
Yes	35.5%	Yes	50.3%
No	64.5%	No	49.7%

The table shows that get to modern technologies has become available
to all, and equally according to (50.3%) of sample. because the technology
in all its shapes has become a necessity of life, but the other half (49.7%)
shows that access was uneven, because:
- Family surveillance of devices for fear of the problems of electronic
  blackmail
- Not to post their photos on social media and use just nickname.
- The difficulty of get modern devices, for economic reasons or they
  do not have private devices.

Either to employment opportunities are equal, the answers (35.5%)
yes, jobs are available in the private sector more than in the governmental
sectors, except in certain occupations that require special skills because of
the difference in physical composition, the long distance to the workplace,
or some occupations that require staying at night outside the home, such
as nursing or field locations of the oil and communications sector, many
families refuse this type of work. (64.5%) shows that women have unequal
employment opportunities for the reasons:

- Government does not provide equal employment opportunities, increasing unemployment.
- Support is for men only, and not all professions are available to women.
- Sexual harassment in the workplace, especially in shops, restaurants, etc.
- The private sector gives women little fees.

Table 7 - Answers to questions 9 and 10

Is a woman able to have a successful career?		Are women allowed to participate in public and political life?	
Yes	58.7%	Yes	57.7%
No	41.3%	No	42.6%

Table (7) shows that women have access to a successful career (58.7%) need to have (3) basics:
- Education: (81.1%) answers to the importance of education for a successful career, for education gives a chance to get a good job opportunity.
- Personal skills: (77.4%) indicated the importance of personal skills, and there are no differences between men and women in cognitive skills, skills such as: leadership capacity, self-confidence and dealing with work stress and bosses.
- Other: 16.1%, include mastering computer and Internet.

(41.3%) answers no, for same opinions, causes and evidence in pervious questions.

Other question, women allowed to participate in public and political life, the answers were (58.7%) answered yes, after obtaining family and community support and women were able to participate in social activities, political life and elections.

Answer no (41.3%) because of her limited participation in society and jobs, and her role only in the home and raising children, Women participate in politics only in the Kota system, (or belong to any political party) not to their competence and abilities.

Table (9) percentage of questions

Have you ever suffered or know someone who has been exposure to domestic violence?		In your country, is there support to create cooperation (balance) between family and work	
Yes	74.2%	Yes	31%
No	16.8%	No	69%
Better not to answer	9%		

The table shows that the support percentage is very weak according to 69% of the sample compared to the yes answer rate (31%), meaning that 3/4 the sample almost does not find support from the family, spouses and society, despite the social roles and responsibilities that add additional psychological stress to it.

74.2% were exposed to domestic violence, which is a very large percentage compared to the percentage that was not exposed 16.8%, while 9% preferred not to answer, perhaps the reason is that the woman was exposed to violence and does not want an answer, or she does not know other types of violence.

As for the participation of women in the research, 93.5% of the sample (155), therefore, the opinions and evidence were from life in all its dimensions, so the answer were close, identical and expected, as analyzed above, while the participation of men (6.5%) was very weak for the reasons mentioned in this paper.

In conclusion, the importance of being a woman in Iraq is because women are more generous and powerful than men, they are half of society, and they represent life, the future, and the source of love and peace.

Women seek to develop herself, family and society because she has the abilities and capabilities for this and can work to change the reality of women for the better.

4.3 A study of marginalized groups in Pakistan: analysis of survey about importance of Pakistani women (Muhammad Iqbal Chawla[35])

In a patriarchal society like Pakistan, women are struggling for their due share in society. Cultivation theory suggests that frequent viewing of media messages makes an individual prone to accept and believe these messages as real and true. Through the hegemonic position of men and irresponsible media, the women would learn that a devoted housewife is a culturally acceptable way for them. So, they may learn to quash their aspirations of establishing their career of interest and exchange them with the "ideal" representation of women that they get through the everyday media. Media usually depicts the desire rather than the reality. The main aim of the present research is to explore how women perceive themselves as part of society in its various forms.

A survey was conducted about "The Importance of Being Woman Today" in Pakistan. The questionnaire contained twenty questions and there were 198 respondents.

Age-wise 81% of respondents were young of ages 18-30 years whereas the remaining 19% were of ages 31-56 years. Gender wise 91% were females while the rest were either male or preferred not to reveal their gender. Profession-wise, 76% were students at different levels, 35% belonged to the workforce while 22% were involved with the family.

Regarding the chances of finding a job, 64% felt that men had better chances while the remaining 36% disagreed. About having equal access to technology such as the internet, 67% felt that women were disadvantaged while the remaining 37% disagreed. Whether women had as good opportunities as men to participate in public life, particularly politics, 68% disagreed while the rest agreed. Whether the women enjoyed support to balance job and family life, 51.5% agreed while the rest disagreed. Whether women had as successful careers as men, 77% replied in affirmative while the others disagreed. As to what contributed to the development of careers of women, educational attainment topped with a score of 86% followed by personal skills at 43%. Whether the respondent ever experienced domestic violence or knew someone who suffered such violence, 43% replied in affirmative, 36% in negative while over 20% preferred not to answer this question. Whether to be a woman was different from being a man in Pakistan, 75% agreed while 25% disagreed. When the respondents

---

35   Prof(R) Dr Former Dean Arts & Humanities, University of the Punjab, Lahore, Pakistan.

were asked to elaborate in what ways were women different from men, some admitted that men and women were just different, some felt women were physically weaker than men while a large proportion of respondents stated that in addition to socio-cultural hindrances, Pakistan was a male-dominated and conservative society that discriminated against women by denying them social equality and empowerment.

When asked whether being a woman was important in Pakistan, most agreed. When asked to describe in what ways was it important, the respondents stated that women were creators, influencers, the foundation of family, and the epitome of love, sacrifice, and courage without whom life would be colourless, however, many respondents could not understand the meaning of word "importance" and talked about social inequality and discrimination against women in the society at large.

Most respondents agreed that it was difficult to be a woman in today's Pakistan and cited several reasons in this regard. The respondents admitted that Pakistan being an Islamic country, religion bestowed several rights upon women, and therefore, respect for women was more in Pakistan than in any other country of the world. However, still, most respondents stated that Pakistan was also a conservative society dominated by males, and therefore, women suffered from social inequality, discrimination, lack of security inside the house in the form of domestic violence, and lack of safety outside the house in the forms of harassment, rape, honour killings, etc.

When the respondents were asked about the policies of the Pakistani state towards women, 37% thought these were fair, 28% felt these were not up to the expectations of women, 20% said that they were not aware of policies about women while the rest said that either the policies were wrong or did not exist at all. In comparative terms, when the respondents were asked whether the conditions of women had changed during the last ten years, most respondents replied in affirmative.

In conclusion, this study aims to understand the perception of Pakistani women regarding their social, economic, cultural, and political roles in society. Instead of identifying the stereotyped portrayal of women in Pakistan, this study aimed at inquiring and investigating the extent to which women in Pakistan have been successful in creating their space in society. The survey clearly shows that women in Pakistan are acquiring important places and positions in the main body politics of the state machinery. This has been possible only due to their outstanding performance in various professions; therefore, they are getting their place on merit, not on a gender basis. Pakistani women have improved their standard of living and are aspiring towards even more significant places in society. Despite social taboos, their progress and current position is a healthy sign for their prospects but to achieve parity with the Western society Pakistani women will have to focus on their duties as well as demanding rights based merely on gender.

4.4 *The importance of being woman today - Pakistan chapter (Raana Malik)*

Background: Pakistan is the world's 5th most populous country with a population of 220.1 million (2020). The ration of male to female is 106 to 100. Pakistan has ratified and signed several international commitments to achieve gender equality and provide safe and secure public places to gain equal opportunities for education, health, work etc. These include Convention on the Elimination of All Forms of Discrimination against Women 1979 (CEDAW), Beijing Declaration and Platform for Action 1995, Sustainable Development Goals etc. Furthermore, in the past two decades, a lot of pro-women legislation has been passed to protect women's rights in the country. The Constitution of the country also does not discriminate based on sex in any walk of life. In the survey conducted in Pakistan, total 198 respondents participated, among which mostly were females.

Findings: Q.1: Is it difficult being women today in your country?

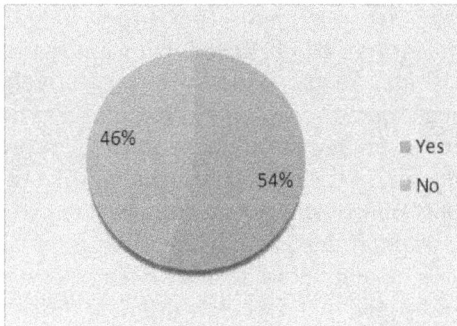

Almost half of the participants (54%) believed that for a woman, it is difficult to live in Pakistan whilst the remaining 46% thought otherwise. The qualitative data reveal different themes on this thinking pattern.

Q.2. Can you explain the reasons for your answer to Question No. 1?

Participants reporting 'Yes' to the statement that 'being women is difficult to live in Pakistan' gave multiple reasons in support of their claim including patriarchal society, overall low female literacy, lack of safety and security, women's vulnerable position at public places, limited freedom of free choice or decision making on any matter of life i.e. work, education, life-partner, preference given to males in a household, gender discrimination, no support of husbands at home, poverty, and unemployment. The major reasons mentioned by majority (78%) of these participants were women facing harassment at the public places, discrimination against women at the workplace and male domination. A participant mentioned that "males of every age harass, and they don't even spare disabled girls and transgender." Another respondent said, "If no male family member is available at home, I take a small boy either or an elderly lady to accompany me to the bus stop. Otherwise, I have to take an off from my work". The limited job opportunities and lack of economic sustainability had overall worsened the living standards in the country. Around 60% participants were of the view that women trying to take their own life decisions must face criticism from the family and society. Thus, mostly women comply with the decisions taken by their parents and family.

Contrary to the above viewpoint, 46% participants thought that it is not difficult being a woman to live in Pakistan. Of these, 74% participants argued that our religion (Islam) has given all the rights to the women of Pakistan, so it's not difficult to women live in Pakistan. Most of the participants (64%) believed that women are enjoying equal status as given to men in the society; they can freely work outside their homes, equal opportunities for education are available, freely participate in sports, and are strong enough to take care of them. One of the respondents said, "It's only 20% women who are making outcry over the plight of 80% women in Pakistan. Majority of the women are living peacefully as per rights given by their religion (Islam)". Another participant said, "The amount of respect Pakistani women gets is not given to any other women in the whole world". Some of the participants were of the view that in our Pakistani society, parents are the biggest supporters of their daughters, so it is not difficult to be a woman while living in Pakistan.

Thus, the survey shows a divided opinion of the participants, however, little more participants favour the option that it's difficult for women to live in Pakistan.

Q.3.What is your age?
Majority (80%) of respondents fall in the age bracket of 18-30 years which means a major cluster of the respondents consists of young people. The rest about 20% participants are in the age range 31-56 years. There is no participant in the later age groups.

■ 18-30 ■ 31-56 ■ Over 56

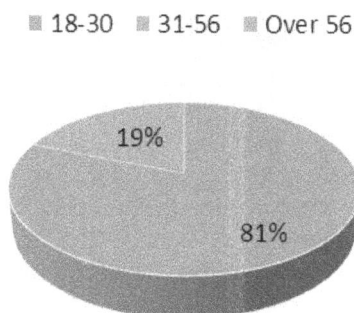

4) Which is your main activity? You can answer one or more of the following options
198 responses

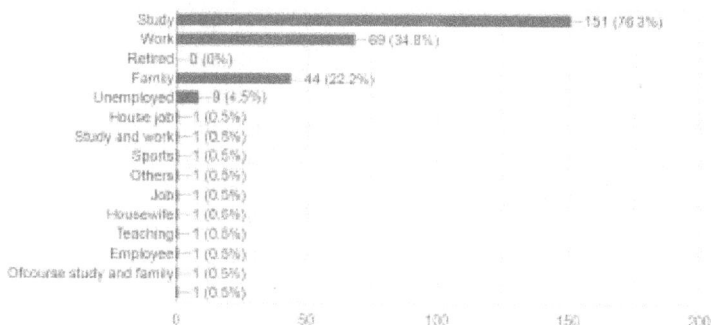

The survey found that 76% respondents are students and are presently enrolled at different levels of education in educational institutions. It surely corresponds with the age bracket of 80% respondents as in local context, the average age of the College/University students/graduate fall in this cohort. The second biggest group (34%) is working people.

Q.5. Being woman in your country is different from being man?

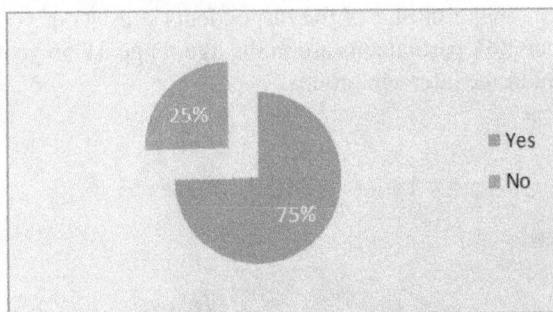

The survey indicates that three-fourth of the participants agreed that men and women are enjoying different status in the Pakistani society, whilst one-third disagreed and believed that men and women have equal status in Pakistan.

Q.6. Please can you explain the reasons for your answer to Question No. 5?

As majority of the participants thought that men and women have different status in the Pakistani society, the major reasons given by them includes social and cultural hindrances faced by women as compared to men in taking independent decisions and growing in life; a deep rooted patriarchal perception of 'good woman', the one who stays at home and takes care of her family and children; women are dependent on men for living and needs; women are weak in nature, hence, they are dependent on men for their protection; honour of the family is associated with women's virginity; women bears dual burden of work; less job opportunities and glass ceiling for women; and limited mobility of women. A participant mentioned that "all the gender equality is in the papers; the reality is far different". Another set of responses mention that women and men are different because they have different duties to perform.

The rest of the 25% participants argued that being women in our country is no different from being men. They based their arguments mainly on religion (Islam) arguing that our religion has given equal rights to men and women and there is no discrimination. A participant said, *"Women are given equal rights to men in Islam and so does our Constitution"*. Women are free to join any profession of their choice. Another participant pointed out, *"media have given women a voice, and awareness"*.

Q. 7. According to you, how are the policies of your country about women?

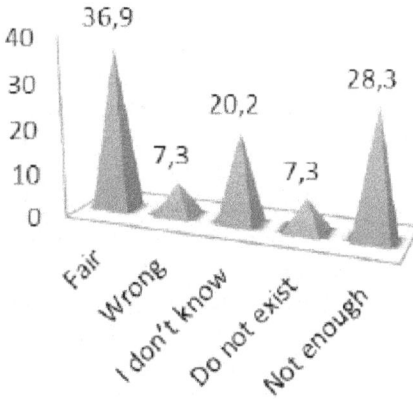

The survey found a split response of participants. Around 40% participants believed that pro-women policies are fair enough for bringing gender equality in the country and providing equal opportunities to women to use their potentials. Whereas, around 30% participants thought that the existing policies are not enough and more needs to be done to achieve gender equality in the country. Another about 20% participants took no side and said, 'don't know'. Interestingly, about 7% participants were not aware of the pro-women policies and legislation in the country.

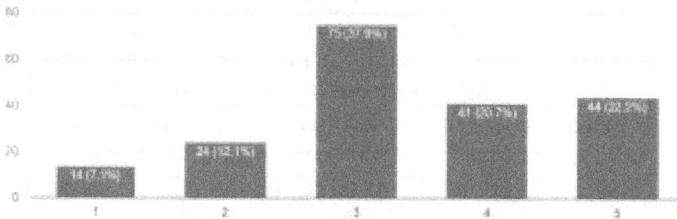

8) From 1=nothing to 5=a lot, according to you, compared to 10 years ago, women's conditions in your country have changed, not only within the worforce?
198 responses

The participants were asked to rate the changes in the conditions of women in the last 10 years. In total, more percentage of participants agreed that conditions of women have changed in the last decade, specifically, work conditions. A participant told, "Situation at the workplace has improved since the 'Protection against Harassment of women at the Workplace Act, passed in 2010". However, 37% participated rated the change at the margin, meaning that more positive steps need to be taken.

Q.9 Please can you explain the reasons for your answer to Question No. 8?

Participants were also asked to give reasons for the choices made in the previous question. The participants gave arguments mentioning sectors. In Education, there has been a lot of change in women's conditions. A participant said, "Education has changed the mindsets of people and now they have become more liberal as compared to the last 10 years". Majority of the participants emphasized the importance of education as the game-changer for the improved condition of women in Pakistan in the last 10 years. Pro-Women Legislation in the last decade has given awareness about the rights of women. The participants mentioned that pro-women had given women confidence to come out of their homes to work and study. A participant said, "Women stand for their rights and raise their voices, this is the reason for their changed status in today's society". Another reason indicated was Employment. The work opportunities are better available to women now. Employment and work have made them stronger than ever. One of the participants believed, "A little improvement made during last 10 years is due to the global impact. The women status is improving globally". Women have become free to choose between activities. Time has changed and it provides more opportunities and facilities to women now.

On the other hand, participants not believing that women's condition has not been changed in the last decade gave the arguments that: There is no improvement in the fate of women in the last 10 years. They remain the same for centuries in our country mainly due to a conservative mindset. Though education is improving but it is not creating a change in society. Women remain dependent and living like slaves. Though laws are being made, but little is found for their implementation on the ground. Many NGOs and organizations are working but the mindset of society is not letting them bring any solid change, so the conditions of women are not improving in any way. Women's safety remains the biggest issue and it has not been changed in the last decade. In many underdeveloped rural areas, the condition of women even worsens in the last 10 years. So, the societal mindset about women has not changed despite changes in the social fabric and technological advancement.

Q.10. Do you think men and women have the same access to technology-such as Internet-and the same opportunities thanks to technologies in your country, also in the labour force?

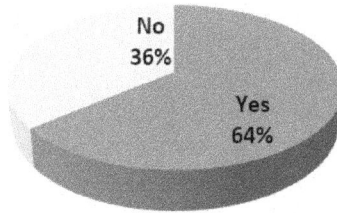

The survey found that 66.7% of the respondents thought that men and women have equal access to technology such as internet also in the labour force. However, 33.3% reported gender imbalance in access to technological facilities and labour force participation in Pakistan. In reality, according to the GSMA's "Mobile Gender Gap Report 2019", only 50% of Pakistani women owned a mobile phone as compared to 81% of men in the country. And the labor participation rate for women is 19% as compared to 81% for males.

Q. 11. Do you think women find a job in your country as men do?

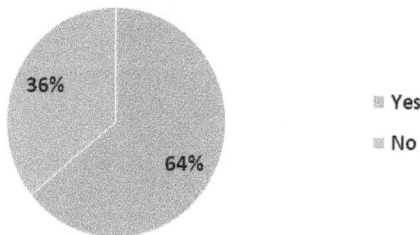

The data shows that 64.1% of participants agreed that a woman can find a job as a man can do in our country whereas 35.9% of participants disagree with the statement.

Q.12 Can you explain the reasons for your answers at Questions No. 10 and No. 11?

The participants who believed that there are equal opportunities for women and men to use technology viewed the role of technology as a major contributor to finding jobs for them. They also thought of education as a qualification for different job opportunities and the use of technology to enhance their chances of being selected. Some of the participants also expect the government to play its role in providing equal job opportunities to both the genders.

However, respondents who see inequality in the access to technology and the internet amongst both genders in Pakistan argued that it is because of the conservative mindset of the society. Parents/families do not allow their daughters to use the internet and distrust them. Moreover, for rural women, the opportunities for technological access and formal employment are very limited. A participant mentioned, "For rural women with low technical skills and vocational training, there are no jobs for all". "Culturally, jobs are gender-specific in our country like construction work for men and household chores work for women only".

13) Do you think women are able to have a successfull career in your country as men do?
198 responses

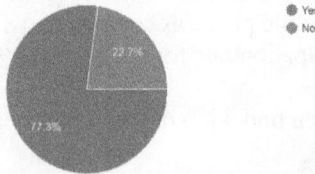

● Yes
● No

22.7%

77.3%

The survey indicates that majority (77.3%) of participants reported that they thought women have a successful career as men do in Pakistan. But 22.7% participants held the opposite viewpoint.

14) Do you think women are allowed to participate in public life, especially politics, in your country as men do?
198 responses

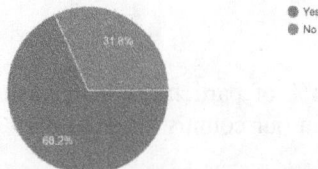

● Yes
● No

31.8%

68.2%

The data shows most (68.2%) of the participants reported that women can equally participate in public life and can have political participation as men do in our country. However, 31.8% participants reported that women are not allowed to participate equally as men in the public and political places.

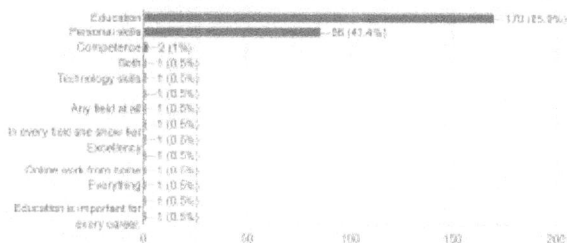

15) According to you, which are the conditions for a woman for a career development ? Please choose one or more of the following answers
190 responses

Majority (85.9%) of the participants mentioned Education as the most important factor for the career development of women in Pakistan. Furthermore, 43.4% participants stressed on the need of personal skills as an important condition for career development. Other factors include competence, technology skills, interest in the field, etc., for career advancement of women.

Q.16 Can you explain the reasons for your answers at Questions No. 13, 14, and No. 15?

The most obvious reasons given by the participants for their choices are as follows:

Most of the participants mentioned that women can manage multiple tasks and are strong headed to deal with numerous challenges. That is why they are participating in public and political spheres equally as men do. Education also helps women for public participation and educated women can work in a better work environment which is also safe for them. Due to education and skills, they got more opportunities now. Equal rights are given in the Constitution of Pakistan, so there is no sex discrimination. Gender does not specify ability; therefore, opportunities are same for both men and women, though women suffer more as compared to men.

On the contrary to the above viewpoint, participants also mentioned that male domination, public pressure, no liberty in a public place, no support of family are the major reasons for lack of public and political participation of women in the Pakistani society. Finding a job for a woman is difficult due to familial pressures. Women even need permission from the parents/ family to get education. Furthermore, Harassment at the workplace, and the conservative mindset of the people propagating that the ideal place for women is at home not in public are also hindrances faced by women. A participant mentioned, "People cannot tolerate an independent woman". Political space in Pakistan is tabooed for women to participate so equal opportunities are not available for women politicians. One of the participants said, "Politics is a dirty game and women are not supposed to be part of it".

17) In your country, is there support for women to balance family and job?
198 responses

About half (51.5%) of the participants held the view that women have support to balance family and work in Pakistan. Whist almost another half (48.5%) of participants thought that women got no support to balance work-life situation.

18) What is your gender
198 responses

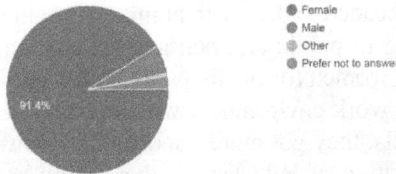

The gender division of data is females (91.4%), whist males and others constitute 9.6%.

19) Have you ever suffered or know someone who suffered for domestic violence?
198 responses

- ● Yes
- ● No
- ◉ Prefer not to answer

A reasonable number (43.4%) of the participants reported that they knew someone or had experience themselves domestic violence. Some of the participants (20.2%) did not prefer to answer the questions and (36.4%) participants total negate that they have experienced or heard of any case of domestic violence.

Q.20 Is it important to be a woman today? Why?

As most of the participants consist of females, thus, majority of them liked their gender. They argued that it is very important to be women as they are born free, and blessed by GOD; without women, the world cannot exist; they are the mothers, sisters, daughter's and wives. One of the participants said, "A woman is the one who gives birth to mankind". Women have a major role in the upbringing of human race, and she ensures stability, and progress in life. It is not an option but a blessing of GOD. A nation cannot be built without women, men need them. One of the participants mentioned that "Women are the pillars of the society, but men do not accept this and treat them as servants".

In conclusion, the survey showed a mixed response of the participants. It's worth mentioning here that majority of the participants were young female students. They openly had given their opinion about the status of women in today's Pakistani society. Women can be better judge of the situation as they themselves are facing the issues on daily basis. Mostly women participants have acknowledged the role of education, capacity building and use of modern technology as keys to improve status of women in the society. The government's role in passing pro-women legislations in the last decades is also appreciated. The deep-rooted conservative mindset of the society is identified as the major reason faced by women in growing upward in the society. A massive awareness campaign is needed through media, specifically, social media to change the patriarchal attitudes and norms in the Pakistani society.

4.5 *Men Vs Women: analysis of survey about importance of Indian women in society (Muhammad Iqbal Chawla)*

Much has been written about the high politics in India but very few unearthed the commoners and therefore historians started a new branch of knowledge which is called subaltern studies. Though the concept was not new as Antonio Gramsci already had done such studies, however, the people's history or history from below has become an interesting study and new branch of knowledge where the researcher focuses on the marginalized groups of the society including peasants, laborers, women, students, etc. In India Subaltern studies gained currency when they investigated the peasant movements in India, but later women were also explored with the same approach of knowing history from the below. Similarly, this study, employing the subaltern approach and method, aims at exploring, investing, and analysing how Indian women felt about their gender. Being a woman in today's India was the main question that was answered by the Indian women. The state and society in India are most liberal in South Asia where women's rights and empowerment are much better than its neighbouring countries. However, women still are struggling for their due share in society. Women are playing an equally important role along with the men in building state and society and as result, India is an emerging fast-moving economy in the world. No wonder if we can ascertain their position and satisfaction in society. In this regard a survey was conducted and here is a brief of the survey.

A survey was conducted about "The Importance of Being Woman Today" in India. The questionnaire contained twenty questions and there were 190 respondents.

Age-wise, 69% of the respondents were young people of ages 18-30 years, 28% were of 31-56 years while 3% were old of ages above 56 years. Gender wise over 81% were females while over 18% were males. Profession-wise, over 62% were students at different levels while over 37% were members of the workforce.

Over 64% of the respondents thought that the chances of getting employment for women in India were as good as that of men while over 36% disagreed. Whether both the genders had equal access to technology such as the internet, 74% agreed while 26% disagreed. Whether women had as good opportunities as men to participate in public life, particularly politics, 71% agreed while 29% disagreed. Whether the women enjoyed support to balance job and family life, 63% responded in affirmative while 37% in negative. Whether women had as successful careers as men, 80% responded in affirmative while 20% responded in negative. As to what contributed to the development of careers of women, educational attainment topped with a score of 88% followed by personal skills at 62%. Whether the respondent ever experienced domestic violence or knew someone who suffered such violence, 51% replied in affirmative, 31% in negative while 18% preferred not to answer this question.

Whether to be a woman was different from being a man in India, 82% agreed while 18% disagreed. When the respondents were asked to explain in what ways were women different from men, a few cited biological reasons, some stated that women were physically weaker than men but most of the respondents revealed that it was the social norms of the society rooted in religion, culture, patriarchy, male chauvinism, etc that discriminated against women by depriving them of social equality, making them dependent upon men, denying them freedom of action and assigning them stereotyped roles such as house-minders.

When asked whether being a woman was important in India, most agreed. When asked to describe in what ways it was important, the respondents stated that women were creators, influencers, the foundation of family, and the epitome of love, sacrifice, and courage, however, many respondents could not understand the meaning of the word "importance" and talked about social inequality and discrimination against women in the society at large.

Most respondents agreed that it was difficult to be a woman in today's India and cited several reasons in this regard. Although apparently the society is considerate and respectful towards women, however, life was difficult because of male dominance, gender inequality, social inequality, lack of freedom, sexual abuse, diminishing safety in view of the rising crimes against women. Life was more a problem for the women of northern India whereas the women of urban south India, particularly Kerala felt that being a woman was not much of a problem.

When the respondents were asked about the policies of the Indian state towards women, 47% thought these were not up to the expectations of women, 25% thought these were fair, 20% said that they were not aware of policies about women and a very small percentage of respondents said that either the policies were wrong, or these just did not exist. In comparative terms, when the respondents were asked whether the conditions of women had changed during the last ten years, most respondents replied in affirmative.

In conclusion, no doubt, India has given enormous importance to the rights of women and empowered them so that they can contribute to every field particularly in the social, economic, and religious domains. As modernity made inroads, contemporary women in India have got more importance in the state machinery, family, and society because they are playing important role in every important arena of productivity. Therefore, the state and society have emerged as one of the fastest-growing economies and liberal countries in the world. As compared to other South Asian counties women in India are more vibrant. The women still feel that they are different from men for multiple reasons such as biological, social norms, religion, culture, male chauvinism. They held these ongoing factors rooted in the social cause of discrimination against women by depriving them of social equality, making them dependent upon men, denying them freedom of action, and assigning them stereotyped roles such as house-minders which causing social inequality and discrimination against women in the society at large. However, the other side of the picture is that most women in India, besides contributing to the state machinery, feel happy because they still are creators, influencers, the foundation of family, and the epitome of love, sacrifice, and courage.

CONCLUSIONS

When the writing of the pages of this book ends, the world is celebrating March 8, Women's Day, with its gaze turned to the barbarism perpetrated by Putin's war in Ukraine. Once again, the women and children, even the babies of that country, pay the price. Once more, the weight of cruelty and atrocities rests on women's shoulders. How long, still?

"I applaud the House of Representatives for introducing today the Violence Against Women Reauthorization Act (VAWA), and I urge Congress to come together in a bipartisan manner to ensure swift passage of VAWA legislation in both the House and the Senate. Strengthening and renewing VAWA is long past due. Delay is not an option, especially when the pandemic and economic crisis have only further increased the risks of abuse and the barriers to safety for women in the United States". Statement by President Biden on the Introduction of the Violence Against Women Reauthorization Act of 2021, on March 08, 2022 focus on an emergency of the last two years: "Domestic violence is being called a pandemic within the COVID-19 pandemic, with growing evidence showing that the conditions of the pandemic have resulted in escalated rates of intimate partner violence, and in some cases more severe injuries" [1].

It's indeed a result, a significant goal that domestic violence isn't considered anymore a "family issue" that should be left to families to

---

1   In 2019, a bipartisan coalition in the House of Representatives passed the Violence Against Women Reauthorization Act of 2019, which included significant improvements and increased pathways to safety that were proposed by advocates, survivors, lawyers, experts, prosecutors, and law enforcement who are in the trenches protecting and supporting survivors. Every single Senate Democrat signed on to the Senate version of the House-passed bill, but Republican Senate leadership refused to bring VAWA to the floor for a vote. "This should not be a Democratic or Republican issue – President Biden said in his Statement on March 08, 2022 - it's a matter of justice and compassion. I am grateful to see the House of Representatives champion ending gender-based violence, and I urge Congress to follow past precedent and bring a strong bipartisan coalition together for swift passage of VAWA".

address in private. Studies demonstrated that in the first two decades following VAWA's implementation the rates of domestic violence declined significantly. While there has been significant progress in efforts to prevent and improve the response to domestic violence, sexual assault, dating violence, and stalking, there is still much work to do.

In the previous chapters we tried to find out what women have in common today in the various countries of the world. One aspect first clearly emerges, namely that women are still more or less discriminated against than men. Research on gender inequality uses limited and sectoral areas as a reference. The comparison between more different geographical, political, and cultural areas, as broad as possible, delimits the field of research to recurring themes and common problems. The speed with which information moves in internet determines the possibility of comparing different situations in various social contexts. This is what we have done with a group of scholars, academics and researchers from fourteen different countries - Cuba, Haiti, India, Iraq, Iran, Italy, Ivory Coast, Mexico, Pakistan, Peru, Poland, Tunisia, United States and Venezuela - to bring out as much as possible in a synchronous and transversal way the gender discrimination for women's experiences at work, in family, for education, as it has been described and analysed in the previous chapters. In a comparative study starting from a socio-political perspective, we used surveys of about 2.500 people, men and women, aged 18 and over, belonging to different social classes, interviewed in the fourteen countries, between February and June 2021. Many different languages spoken: Italian, English, French, Spanish, Urdu, Polish, Persian, Arabic, Haitian Creole and Malayalam. This provided us with a unique, natural experimental setting to investigate gender's inequality, and lack of institutional policies in a comparative perspective.

From the research emerges that women have increased their earnings, education and fields of occupation, and continue to have longer average life spans than men. Results show, anyway, that in the varied landscape of countries considered on average to be over one in two people believe, in general, it is still difficult to be a woman in their own country today. Only one third of respondents believe women's policies in their country are right and less than the majority believe there's a possibility of having support in one's own country to balance and reconcile family and work. Only in possibility to access the internet there's no gender discrimination. But if we stand at the labour market, economy and job opportunity, not to speak for the tragedy of domestic violence, there's still a lot to do. Just to stay at the drama of gender violence, results show on average of circa six out of ten of respondents that they have suffered or know someone who has suffered from domestic violence.

Altogether, results show surely the conditions of women changed nowadays compared to ten years earlier but what we expected is confirmed: in general women are still discriminated against men in different countries, no matter where they are, with greater or lesser intensity. Much has changed compared to the past, but much remains to be done. Why?

Evidence from across the globe shows that the role of woman in contemporary society is still under evaluated and misestimate (Bigio et al. 2019; Rose 2021; Selwaness 2019; Friedrich, Engelhardt, Schulz 2020; Netto, Noon, Hudson, Kamenou-Aigbekaen, Sosenko 2020; Besamusca 2020). There are concerns that a different distinction between women and men role can be made, for example in men's movement into 'women's work', (Moskos 2019) or about family policies' interaction with national levels of earnings inequality (Hook and Paeka 2020). The study of women's understanding of their lives is common in literature; we showed it in a comparative key of lecture to enforce the conclusion of a social habit and conflict as a constitutive reality for women. Consequently, with respect to the perspectives through which women are invited to make sense of their lives, the metaphor of conflict enforces a worldview based on traditional gender roles (Grünberg and Matei 2019). Women, especially young ones, are disproportionately impacted by the sharp rise in unemployment and economic downturns compared with men (Costa Dias, Joyce, and Keiller 2020).

Our research placed the social, economic and political role of women in terms of culture, economy, politics and geography at the centre of the investigation. The qualitative study of the research produced a large data set. Using thematic analysis, the responses are associated with the themes of rights, justice, bias, opportunities and effects. The difficulty of being a woman today is ever and everywhere. Previous and most recent studies show situations of social or personal difficulties for women referring to defined geographical areas or specific historical periods. From an historical point of view, it's relevant, for instance, the "rear-guard of the vanguard" about the role of women, in Chile, in the period 1930–73 (Salgado 2020) or the analysis of evolution toward revolution and the development of street protests in the Islamic Republic of Iran (Ghasseminejad et al. 2020). Referring to the contemporary aspects in the United States, analysis is focused on female body aspects or women's processes of finding jobs, forming families or more over gender differences in adolescents' work and family orientations (Ezioni 2019; Lippert and Damaske 2019; Hayforda and Halliday Hardie 2021).

Difficulties reconciling work and family formation have been also identified as an important but under-researched factor in low female employment rates in North Africa (Selwaness and Krafft 2021). In Australia, inequalities in professional norms are considered by comparing the responses of screen composers on barriers to women's advancement (Cannizzo and Strong, 2020) and national family policies playing a role in shaping mothers' employment; interaction with national levels of earnings inequality to differentially affect mothers' employment outcomes by educational attainment (Hook and Paek, 2020). Researchers indicate that social position moderates the relation between motherhood and self-employment status (Besamusca, 2020) These findings imply also that the context in which motherhood premiums are studied matters.

On one hand, eastern European countries' capitalist growth models have been important determinants of female labour force participation since the early 1990 (Avlijas, 2020). While supply-side policies, which stimulate female entry into the labour force, such as family reconciliation and childcare, may be important drivers of female work (Avlijas, 2020). On the others, scholars further argue that the paradigm of work–family conflict is challenged by the fluid realities of the actual world for which the social imaginary of work–family conflict assumes that vulnerability is a constitutive reality for women. With respect to the perspectives through which women are invited to make sense of their lives, the metaphor of conflict enforces a worldview based on traditional gender roles (Grünberg and Matei, 2019). Last studies also identify how women are excluded from screen industry work through being labelled as 'risky', 'difficult', 'killjoy' and other stereotypes about women (Eikhof et al., 2019; Wing-Fai et al., 2015). Other scholars demonstrate how cultural myths specific to professional practice may help to reproduce gender inequality regimes (Cannizzo and Strong, 2020).

Naturally, sexual violence against women is fully considered in the former scientific literature. It's increasingly well-known even if those suffered by immigrant women are less known (Pannettier et al. 2020). But the grand challenge to stop family violence has included many social scholars with expertise in child maltreatment and gender-based violence (GBV) who have been actively seeking common ground and shared purpose (Kulkarni et al. 2021). Intimate partner violence (IPV) is another significant public health issue and studies indicate important differences in predictors, dynamics, and outcomes of different types of IPV (Hardesty and Ogolsky, 2020). According to data collected since 2015 though the Femicide Watch initiative, and data available from the UN Office on Drugs and Crime (UNODC), among the victims of all intentional killings involving intimate partners, more than 80% of victims are women. On the other hand, so many cases of femicide have been reported during COVID-19 that it is overshadowing a pandemic of femicide and related gender-based violence against women worldwide. The highly contagious nature of the disease and its fast spread throughout the globe have led States to impose different restrictive measures on the movement of people to promote physical distancing among the population and therefore reduce opportunities for contagion. Such measures also included the redirection of resources towards fighting the COVID-19 outbreak by scaling down all services considered non-essential - retail shops, restaurants, and other hospitality sectors shut during this period -, rightly including services and/ or protection mechanisms for women against gender-based violence, such as shelters, helplines, protection orders and reproductive health services, many of which have been reduced or suspended (Šimonović, 2020). The rise in femicides and violence was taking the lives of women and girls everywhere around the world, as the coronavirus continues to rage out of control.

Compared to the studies and research carried out so far, the research we have conducted it reproduces a novelty in the understanding of the role of women in contemporary society comparing such different living conditions in such many countries. Our findings echo the trends of the "Report of the Special Rapporteur on violence against women, its causes and consequences" by the UN the Special Rapporteur on violence against women, its causes and consequences. The result that is achieved is paradoxical: there is a remarkable continuity in social trends concerning women, so much so that, as it has seen, they occur identical in all countries. It has been well established that it's still difficult being a woman today worldwide. It emerges it is difficult to be a woman in own country today, whatever it is, even harder during the pandemic (Šimonović, 2020), but not only a cause of it: it is hard to work, live in family or find a job, because mainly of the lack of freedom, the man mentality, *machismo* and more. It is impressive to read directly from the words of the interviewees the protest and the condemnation of the obligation to wear *Hijab*, the veil that Iranian women are forced to wear, as well as the denunciation of Haitians of suffering continuous and persistent harassment in the workplace, so much so to be an unsurpassable fact. Gender discrimination still passes today, 2022, for "La falta de Libertad y la imposición machista" (i.e. the lack of freedom and the macho imposition, Cuba) or because "Women are denied of basic human rights" (India); or more "ىباختنا قح چیه ارىز نىدارىم ومهو زیچ ىجارباریی اسـت" (i.e., because we have no rights, everything is compulsory, Iran); or again for "feminicidios, maltrato, exclusión, patriarcado, injusticia social y política" (i.e. femicides, mistreatment, exclusion, patriarchy, social and political injustice Mexico).

There are still gender norms and stereotypes that make it more difficult for women to be successful in the workplace, and puts pressure of them to take parental/family roles that are not equitable. The common tragedy of domestic violence emerges clearly from the IWT research: it's impressive the general average in the fourteen countries considered, almost six out of ten respondents, exactly 57.1 percent, declaring that they have suffered or know someone who has suffered from domestic violence. One gravy aspect is for sure the evidence brought from our research concerning the intersection between the COVID-19 pandemic and the pandemic of gender-based violence against women, with the focus on domestic violence.

How to recover this difference then and what is the judgment on the policies adopted by the respective governments for women? There is little trust in institutions if only about a third of respondents believe women's policies in their country are right. Mainly national policies are considered wrong, insufficient or not enough from the great majority of respondents - 61.1 percent - expressing a negative opinion on the policies of their respective governments for women. This result mirrors the evidence found in other research pinpointing interpersonal inequality and adding that in the absence of organizational justice this failure would render a negative effect on women personal happiness, job satisfaction, motivation and performance, moreover gender discrimination in organizations (Güven, 2020). Research shows that gender diversity in leadership correlates with better governance (Bigio and Vogelstein, 2020) and the importance of different factors, to better target policy interventions to open opportunities for women (Selwaness and Krafft, 2020). It is worth noting that during prepandemic times, specific economic, educational, and welfare restructuring reforms, and their interactions, have impacted female economic opportunities, and have led to substantial female exit from the labour market in some countries, while not in others (Avlijas, 2020).

If, as we have seen above, the orientations have been different in the various countries considered in the research, regarding the aspects highlighted so far, a profile that has instead been common has been that relating to the possibility for women to access technology in their own country and to the internet specifically. Our data show, on average, that the respondents believe women have the same possibility of accessing technology, and internet, to an extent equal to 74.65 per cent: three out of four respondents believe that in their country there is no difference between women and men in the ability to access the internet. In addition, the composition of gender inequality at the intersection of technology, meritocracy and internet access opportunities reveals the attempt to resolve inequalities (Cannizzo and Strong 2020). Why and how do we explain this difference? From our point of view, it is a simple and banal observation: when the gender's role is confused with the customer's role, it becomes self-evident that the market and political decision-makers work to break down all barriers of inequality. There is no interest in discriminating between men and women when it comes to making profits. Conversely, where rights follow the individual as such, the delay in breaking down discriminating barriers derives from the lack of interest in doing so.

In sum, our data show that women still suffer a condition of inequality across the world indifferently. They are still waiting for a more equitable distribution of rights. Based on this, what do we expect to happen in terms of gender equality in the future? First, we expect that there will be a surge of interest and demand for more equitable conditions for women. For example, over three-quarters of all interviewees in our survey responded that they would like to receive equal conditions of treatment at labour market, education system, family, or simply going outside the evening without having the fear of being raped or just disrespect. In line with low female employment, namely women's care work, previous research has identified challenges in reconciling marriage and market work as an important driver of low rates of female employment (Selwaness and Krafft, 2020). There are also signs of change in the struggles against patriarchy and neoliberal expectations and regimes that influence women's autonomy (Özkazanç-Pan and Pullen 2020). While recent research has revealed gendered disadvantages faced by women in both work and education (Cannizzo and Strong 2020), we discuss not only work but life disadvantageous conditions to women by comparing the responses of men and women on barriers to women's advancement in their daily life and profession.

The expansion of more opportunities for all women would be a very welcome step in the right direction in tackling some of the gender inequalities caused by the sexist culture and by enabling more women to enter or stay in a family and labour contest more equal and right. The complex mechanisms through which the interaction of patriarchy with other dimensions of identity in domestic and workplace intersects with the way in which it interacts with other dimensions of identity within the home focus also on the gender dynamics (Netto et al, 2020). Changes in the perception of women role in contemporary society may also help men fight the "femininity stigma" of considering woman such as a less important human being. This can then lead to a more equal consideration of belongings and identities, as it has been seen lately during the pandemic, which can further help reduce gender inequality in many countries, in US for instance, where the current working culture is that of a masculine ideal worker norm (Acker 1990; Berdahl et al. 2018).

The awareness of inequality does not sufficiently disrupt the gender-normative views of who is responsible for discrimination and who is responsible for carrying on it in family, work and education condition. In some cultures, more than others, women and girls not only in certain disadvantaged and marginalized groups have been particularly affected by compounded and intersectional forms of discrimination. We talk about those from minorities, indigenous, Afro descendant, migrant and rural communities, older women, women and girls with disabilities, homeless women, and women deprived of liberty and victims of trafficking (Šimonović, 2020). But what really impresses in our research is the frequency and diffusion of the responses of those who complain of lack of respect, *machismo*, violence, attempts at abuse. That's why we decided to report them literally, without filters, to make evident that they are so many and so frequent in almost all the countries considered in our investigation. So much, that reading the answers and not looking at the country of origin of the interviewees, it is difficult to understand which geographical area they come from.

This may especially be the reason of the rise of insecurity we are seeing and likely to see soon because of the spread of the increase in cases of domestic violence and femicide in the world, possibly amplified in countries where culture, education and stereotype roles and behaviours to the detriment of women, privileging men. In such scenarios, women may be left more vulnerable given their limited capacity to expand their existing demands, for example, of working conditions compared with those of men (Chung and van der Horst 2018; Lott and Chung 2016), and their weak bargaining positions, both at the workplace and at home (Acker 1990; Hochschild and Machung 1989). To tackle this issue, we need first changes in our laws on equal opportunities between women and men to better protect women not only when work–family boundaries no longer become clear, but so that the rise in security and safety conditions of life does not lead to further exploitation of, or unhealthy levels of discrimination and violence against women. We also need to be able to provide policies in consideration of the fact that the COVID-19 pandemic represents an opportunity to bring about meaningful and lasting change at the national, regional and international levels, as it has placed the issue of gender-based violence against women, and domestic violence against women in the spotlight (Šimonović, 2020). There is therefore a need to intensify controls and preventive actions not only in the family, as well as in the workplace, in public activities, making the reactions to violations certain, immediate and proportionally severe. Certainty, immediacy and adequacy of actions must be the three pillars that must inspire the action of the legislator in eliminating the conditions that favor the spread of a discriminatory gender culture. At the same time, it is necessary to guarantee victims, such agreements in a broad sense, every form of relief and reparation with equal immediacy and effectiveness.

This is especially true if we are serious about undoing some of the harm caused by the pandemic (Kurtz 2021; Šimonović 2020) and, lately, the ongoing war in Ukraine to gender inequality. We should treasure at least of this period for reflection on what we value as individuals, as families, and society not by going back at the starting point once the pandemic and the war is over. Achieving awareness of the value of women and at the same time of their vulnerability is the key to implementing national protection, incentive and protection policies, which are still too often inadequate.

Women are aware of their importance: "las mujeres tienen sabiduría, destreza, paciencia, criterio propio, autodeterminación, saben lo que quieren (i.e., women have wisdom, dexterity, patience, their own criteria, self-determination, they know what they want, Cuba); "La femme est celle qui peut concilier, travail, famille et études et s'en sorte avec brio. Elles sont des héroines nos femmes. La femme est l'essence même de la société (i.e., the woman is the one who can reconcile work, family and studies and succeeds brilliantly. Our women are heroines. Women are the very essence of society, Haiti); "There is no society without women (India)"; مهم چ نوز نز، و درم وردو انسان هسته انسن فارغ زا جنسیتشون و اگه هم اب اینا دید هب نز نگاه (i.e., It دوش بسیار پیشرفت تخواهد کرد و برای جامعه مفید خواهد بود) is important because men and women are both human beings, regardless of their gender, and if we look at women in this way, they will make a lot of progress and will be useful for society, Iran).

The highlighting of the practices to be eliminated and those to be promoted in many areas could be preparatory to the implementation of training interventions about discrimination against women. There is an emphasis in being a "democracy" or a "democratic country" in some of the respondents, so much that gender equality seems to be a consequence of democracy - "è una paese democratico con parità di sesso" – and the belief in the legal and political system emerges in many responses with a desire to see further protection, as if things look okay in the abstract, and not so okay in practice.

The cognitive elements arise from this study we think will be able to guide the construction and promotion also of new models to be adopted in the training of young and very young generations, in order to foster a change in cultural orientations with respect to gender equality in accordance with those promoted on the subject by the conventions of the Council of Europe and the United Nations. This final phase of the project, of dissemination and restitution of the results, aims to define formats indicators that can provide useful tools for the recognition and construction of incorrect forms of representation of behaviour against women and help in the definition and adoption of standards and practices that are perfectly respectful of the dignity of women. The potential application of the project can all be traced back to the social impact it wants to determine. The question is defining socio-cultural intervention strategies through the planned action-research activities that can contribute to the development in the social fabric of cultural antibodies capable of resisting and countering the gender inequality and even more the virus of male violence against women.

Ten years ago, the Istanbul Convention defined an international and shared regulatory framework perfectly capable of functioning as a guiding tool in the fight and contrast to violence against women. National legislations, albeit with some delay, have formally aligned themselves with the Istanbul Convention, have transposed its address, accepted its definitions, tried to translate its principles into legal provisions aimed at combating violence against women and offering its victims an increasingly full legal protection. Certainly, therefore, the Convention has traced a virtuous path, normative and juridical, to be able to resolve the social problem of violence against women. But not enough, if we still assist at a deep lack of gender equality.

If the norm can certainly have a decisive role of direction, it is also by intervening in depth in the social fabric, in its daily practices and in its routines, that it will be possible to definitively dismantle the cultural structures on which gender inequality takes root, starting from its symbolic dimension made up of prejudices, stereotypes and discrimination, daily and often unconscious. Our investigation by entering directly into the places of construction of social reality, its schemes, its roles, and its expectations wanted to contribute to the maximum socialization of these principles. Reproducing and legitimizing stereotyped and discriminating representations *in primis* of gender relations and then, consequently, also of violence against women, the action of the legal system not only risks failing its professional mandate (for example by systematically allowing forms of secondary victimization of the injured party) but can also contribute confirming the widespread socio-cultural constructs on which violence against women takes root.

The research group, aware of the socio-cultural relevance of the results and their potential social impact, intends to strengthen the usual work of disseminating the results to extend it, not only to the academic sphere but to the socio-professional categories involved. Moreover, the world of information, and of the press in particular, in dealing with violence against women has systematically tried in recent years to equip itself with a set of rules capable of guaranteeing a correct and non-toxic narrative of the journalistic story (e.g. in Italy the so called *Manifesto of Venice*). Too often, however, these principles are disregarded in the news and in the commentary on facts relating to gender-based violence. The ability to recognize stereotypes, prejudices and discrimination in the representation of gender equality represents a goal of this research activity also in this field.

There is still a long way to go, and the goal of gender equality in the world is still far away to reach. The European Union is aware of this and among the six priorities of the Van der Leyen Commission for 2019-2024 makes direct reference, as part of the objective of "Promoting the European lifestyle" and protecting its "Rights fundamental ", to the need to eliminate gender-based violence, as well as the Organization of Restricted Nations which among its 17 Sustainable Development Goals (Agenda 2030) identifies as one of the priorities, in the context of the fifth goal (Gender equality), the contrast and reduction of violence based on gender and, in particular, domestic violence. The still too large distance that separates the Istanbul Convention from a fully inclusive, just and equitable society can only be bridged by stopping in the places that make a decisive contribution to the social construction of reality and its representations.

The aim of our research was to verify whether and to what extent pockets of inequality, or even discrimination against women, were still present in the world, from the West to the East, from the North to the South of it, over every geographical border. We believe we have shown that there is still a widespread inferiority of women towards men, a legacy of stereotypes and prejudices that are difficult to overcome. Having turned on the lights on often little-known societies or on the fringes of knowledge due to geographical position, penetration difficulties or political regimes, has allowed us to highlight situations that are often even more grievous. The expectation is that the difficulties still encountered in overcoming all these cultural, regulatory and economic barriers may diminish soon. With the communication and the knowledge of these situations we hope that we have been able to promote at least a greater awareness of them.

REFERENCES

Abbatecola, E. e Stagi, L (2017), Pink is the new black. Stereotipi di genere nella scuola dell'infanzia, Rosenberg & Sellier, Torino. Bems, N. (2004), Framing the Victim: Domestic Violence, Media, and Social Piroblem, Aldine Transaction, New York.

Acker, Joan. 1990. Hierarchies, jobs, bodies: A theory of gendered organizations. *Gender & Society* 4 (2): 139–58.

Akuamoah-Boateng, Clara. 2020. Balancing Work, Family and Personal Life: Perspectives of Female Staff at the College of Distance Education, University of Cape Coast, Ghana. *International Journal of Educational Administration and Policy Studies*, Vol. 12 N. 1 pp. 43-51 Jan-Jun.

Andrew, Alison, Sarah Cattan, Monica Costa Dias, Christine Farquharson, Lucy Kraftman, Sonya Krutikova, Angus Phimister, and Almudena Sevilla. 2020. How are mothers and fathers balancing work and family under lockdown? *Institute for Fiscal Studies*. https://doi.org/10.1920/BN.IFS.2020.BN0290.

Avlija, Sonja, 2020. Growth Models and Female Labour in Post-Socialist Eastern Europe. *Social Politics*, Volume 27, Number 3.

Azar and Vasudeva, 2006. Self-efficacy and self-esteem: A comparative study of employed and unemployed married women in Iran, *The German Journal of Psychiatry*, 9 (3) (2006), pp. 111-117.

Berdahl, Jennifer L., Marianne Cooper, Peter Glick, Robert W. Livingston, and Joan C. Williams. 2018. Work as a masculinity contest. *journal of Social Issues* 74 (3): 422–48.

Besamusca, Janna, 2020. The short or long end of the stick? Mothers' social position and self-employment status from a comparative perspective. *Gender Work Organ* 27:1285–1307 DOI: 10.1111/gwao.12483.

Bigio, Jamille, Vogelstein, Rachel. 2020. Women under Attack: The Backlash against Female Politicians. *Foreign Affairs*, Vol. 99, Num. 1.

Bilotta, Bruno Maria. 1991. *Identità femminile e identità burocratica*, Messina, Italy, Armando Siciliano Editore.

Blumberg, R. L. (2007), Gender bias in textbooks: A hidden obstacle on the road to gender equality in education, UNESCO, Paris.

Bohner, G. (2001), Writing about rape: Use of the passive voice and other distancing text features as an expression of perceived responsibility of the victim, «British Joumal of Sodai Psychology», 40.

Cannizzo, Fabian, Strong, Catherine. 2020. Put some balls on that woman': Gendered repertoires of inequality in screen composers' careers. *Gender Work Organ*. 27:1346–1360 DOI: 10.1111/gwao.12496.

Chung, Heejung. 2020b. Return of the 1950s housewife? How to stop coronavirus lockdown reinforcing sexist gender roles. *The Conversation*, 30 March. https://theconversation.com/return-of-the-1950s-housewife-how-to-stop-   coronavirus-lockdown-reinforcing-sexist-gender-roles-134851 (accessed November 23, 2021).

Chung, Heejung, and Mariska van der Horst. 2018. Women's employment patterns after childbirth and the perceived access to and use of flextime and teleworking. Human Relations 71 (1): 47–72. https://doi.org/10.1177/0018726717713828.

Cuculo F., 2012, Childhood transformation: a sociological-juridical profile, in Childhood and Society, vol. 2011.

Di Gennario G., 2014, Diritti della persona e sostegno dei servizi sociali: come conciliare l'effettività della tutela giurisdizionale e quella della protezione, in Diritto e giustizia minorile, vol. unique, p. 31-35.

Friedrich, Carmen, Engelhardt, Henriette, Schulz, Florian, 2021. Women's Agency in Egypt, Jordan, and Tunisia: The Role of Parenthood and Education. *Population Research and Policy Review* 40:1025–1059 https://doi.org/10.1007/s11113-020-09622-7.

Fuller-Thomson, Esme and Agbeyaka, Senyo, 2020. A Trio of Risk Factors for Childhood Sexual Abuse: Investigating Exposure to Parental Domestic Violence, Parental Addiction, and Parental Mental Illness as Correlates of Childhood Sexual Abuse. *Social Work,* Volume 65, Number 3, July.

Ghasseminejad, Saeed, Taleblu, Behnam Ben, Katz, Eliora. 2020. Evolution toward revolution: the development of street protests in the Islamic Republic of Iran. *Journal of International Affairs*, 73, no. 2.

Giorni, E.; Tonello, F. (2013), Moral Panie: T he Issue of Women and Crime in Italian Evening News, in "Sociologica. Italian Journal of Sociology On-Line", 3 Il Mulino

Gius, C.; Lalli, P. (2014), «I loved her so much, but I killed her»: Romantic love as a representational frame for intimate partner femicide in three italian newspapers, in "ESSACHESS.Journal for Communication Studies", n.7, voi. 2, pp. 53-75.

Grünberg, Laura, Matei, Ștefania. 2020. Why the paradigm of work–family conflict is no longer sustainable: Towards more empowering social imaginaries to understand women's identities. *Gender Work Organ.* 27:289–309. https://doi.org/10.1111/gwao.12343.

Hardesty, Jennifer L., Ogolsky, Brian G. . 2020. A Socioecological Perspective on Intimate Partner Violence Research: A Decade in Review. *Journal of Marriage and Family*, 82 (February): 454–477. DOI:10.1111/jomf.12652.Hilbrecht, Margo, Susan M. Shaw, Laura C. Johnson, and Jean Andrey. 2008. "I'm home for the kids": Contradictory implications for work–life balance of teleworking mothers. *Gender, Work & Organization* 15 (5): 454–76.

Hayforda, Sarah R. Halliday Hardieb, Jessica. 2021. Gender Differences in Adolescents' Work and Family Orientations in the United States. *The Sociological Quarterly*, Vol. 62, No. 3, 488–509 https://doi.org/10.1080/00380253.2020.1775529.

Hochschild, Arlie, and Anne Machung. 1989. The second shift: Working parents and the revolution at home. New York: Viking.

Hooka, Jennifer L. and Paeka, Eunjeong. 2020. National Family Policies and Mothers' Employment: How Earnings Inequality Shapes Policy Effects across and within Countries. *American Sociological Review*, Vol. 85(3) 381–416.

Islam, 2019 Science, technology, engineering and mathematics (STEM): Liberating women in the Middle East, *World Journal of Education*, 9 (3) (2019), p. 94.

Killick, Elizabeth, Griffiths, Mark. 2021. Why do individuals engage in in-play sports betting? A qualitative interview study. *Journal of Gambling Studies*. Mar, Vol. 37 Issue 1, pp. 221-240.

Knight, Carly R., and Mary C. Brinton. 2017. One egalitarianism or several? Two decades of gender-role attitude change in Europe. American journal of Sociology 122 (5): 1485–532.

Kulkarni, Shanti J., Kohl, Patricia L., Edmond, Tonya. 2020. From "Stop Family Violence" to "Build Healthy Relationships to End Violence": The Journey to Reenvision a Grand Challenge. *Social Work*, Volume 65, Number 4, October.

Lauve-Moon, Katie R., Enman, Shelby and Hentz, Vanessa. 2020. Mainstreaming Gender: An Examination of Feminist Methodology in Social Work Research. *Social Work*, Volume 65, Number 4 October. https://academic.oup.com/sw/article/65/4/401/5911273 by 81695661, OUP on 20 January 2021.

Leenders, Joke, Bleijenbergh, Inge L., Van den Brink, Marieke C.L. 2020. Myriad potential for mentoring: Understanding the process of transformational change through a gender equality intervention. *Gender Work Organ*. 27:379–394. https://doi.org/10.1111/gwao.12385.

Lippert, Adam M., Damaske, Sarah Finding Jobs, Forming Families, and Stressing Out? Work, Family, and Stress among Young Adult Women in the United States. 2019. *Social Forces* 98(2) 883–912, November. https://academic.oup.com/sf/article-abstract/98/2/885/5253226

Lott, Yvonne, and Heejung Chung. 2016. Gender discrepancies in the outcomes of schedule control on overtime hours and income in Germany. *european Sociological Review* 32 (6): 752–65.

Manente, M. T. (2019), La violenza nei confronti delle donne dalla Convenzione di Istanbul al «Codice Rosso», Giappichelli, Torino. Merli, A. (2015), Violenza di genere e femminicidio, in "Diritto Penale Contemporaneo", vol.1, pp. 430-468.

Marchetti, Maria Cristina. 2016. *Uguaglianza di genere: la presenza femminile nei ruoli decisionali* in Marsocci P (edited by), *Partecipazione politica transnazionale, rappresentanza e sovranità nel progetto europeo*, Atti degli incontri del progetto EUPoliS, Vol II, Napoli, Editoriale Scientifica, 2016 pp. 191-203. ISBN 9788863428728.

Monckton-Smith, J. (2012), Murder, Gender and the Media. Narratives of Dangerous Love, Palgrave Macmillian, New York.

Moskos, Mega. 2020. Why is the gender revolution uneven and stalled? Gender essentialism and men's movement into 'women's work'. *Gender Work Organ*. 27:527–544. https://doi.org/10.1111/gwao.12406.

Netto, Gina, Noon, Mike, Hudson, Maria, Kamenou-Aigbekaen, Nicolina, Sosenko, Filip, 2020. Intersectionality, identity work and migrant progression from low-paid work: A critical realist approach. *Gender Work Organ*, 27:1020–1038. DOI: 10.1111/gwao.12437.

Niemi, J., Peroni, L., & Stoyanova, V (Eds.), (2020), International Law and Violence Against Women: Europe and the Istanbul Convention, Routledge, London.

Nworgu, Queen Chioma. 2020. A Critical Overview of the Impact of social media on Online Small Businesses Owned and Run by Women Entrepreneurs: A Case Study of London-Based Female Entrepreneurs. Bulgarian Comparative Education Society, Paper presented at the Annual International Conference of the Bulgarian Comparative Education Society (BCES) (18th, Online, Jun) https://eric.ed.gov/?id=ED608381.

Özkazanç-Pan, Banu and Pullen, Alison. 2020. Gendered labour and work, even in pandemic times. *Gender Work Organ.* 27:675–676. DOI: 10.1111/gwao.12516.

Pannetier, Julie, Ravalihasy, Andrainolo, Desgrées du Loû, Annabel, Lert, France, Lydié, Nathalie. 2020. Les violences sexuelles envers les femmes immigrées d'Afrique subsaharienne après la migration en France. *Population & Sociétés*, numéro 577, mai 2020.

Petts, Richard J., Daniel L. Carlson, and Joanna R. Pepin. 2020. A gendered pandemic: childcare, homeschooling, and parents' employment during COVID-19. *gender, Work & Organization.* https://doi.org/10.1111/gwao.12614.

Pitch, T. (2002), Le differenze di genere, in La criminalità in Italia, a cura di M. Baribagli, U. Gatti, Bologna, Il Mulino, pp. 171-83.

Prados, María, and Gema Zamarro. 2020. Gender differences in couples' division of childcare, work and mental health during COVID-19. CESR-Schaeffer Working Paper No. 003. https://papers.ssrn.com/sol3/papers.cfm?abstract_id=3667803.

Richards, T. N et al. (2011), Exploring News Coverage of Femicide: Does Reporting the News Add Insult to Injury?, in1 "Feminist Criminology", 6(3), pp. 178-202.

Rose, Rachel. 2021. The Subtle and Not-So-Subtle Impact of Bias on Women and Minorities. *Federal Lawyer.* Sep/Oct, Vol. 68 Issue 5, pp. 66-70, V.1.

Saccà, Flaminia, 2021. Stereotipo e pregiudizio. Ler adici culturali e le rappresentazioni simboliche della violenza di genere. In: Stereotipo e pregiudizio. La rappresentazione giuridica e mediatica della violenza di genere. Franco Angeli.

Saccà, F., Stereotipo e pregiudizio. La rappresentazione giuridica e mediatica della violenza di genere, Franco Angeli, Milano, 2021

Simonovic, D. (2014), Global and regional standards on violence against women: the evolution and synergy of the CEDAW and Istanbul Conventions, «Human rights quarterly», 590-606.

Saccà, Flaminia, Massidda. 2018. *Women and Politics in Populist Times. A Case Study: the 2018 Electoral Campaign.* In: (a cura di): Velikaya N. (Executive Editor), Golasaeeva A.A., Moiseeva, A.N. (Editors), *Russian Revolutions and Women's Issue. Ideological Heritage, Political Transformations and New Social Practices*, p. 85-110, Mosca, Buki Vedi, ISBN: 978-5-6040535-6-0.

Salehi-Isfhani and Egel, 2007. Youth exclusion in Iran: The state of education, employment and family formation Wolfensohn Center for Development, the Brookings Institution (2007).

Salgado, Alfonso. 2020. The Rearguard of the Vanguard: Women, Home and Communist Activism in Chile, 1930–73. *Gender & History*, Vol. 32 No. 2 July, pp. 393–410.

Schnurr, Stephanie, Zayts, Olga, Schroeder, Andreas, Le Coyte-Hopkins, Catherine. 2020. 'It's not acceptable for the husband to stay at home': Taking a discourse analytical approach to capture the gendering of work. *Gender Work Organ.* 27:414–434 https://doi.org/10.1111/gwao.12408.

Selwaness, Irene, and Krafft, Caroline. 2021. The Dynamics of Family Formation and Women's Work: What Facilitates and Hinders Female Employment in the Middle East and North Africa? *Population Research and Policy Review* https://doi.org/10.1007/s11113-020-09596-6

Shiffer-Sebba, Doron, Behrman, Julia, 2021. Gender and Wealth in Demographic Research: A Research Brief on a New Method and Application. *Population Research and Policy Review* 40:643–659 https://doi.org/10.1007/s11113-020-09603-w.

Sibel, Güven, Bülent, Güven. 2020. Organizational Justice and Being a Woman; What Female Lecturers Say. *International Journal of Progressive Education*, Vol. 16 N. 4 pp. 302-311.

Šimonović, Dubravka, 2020. Report of the Special Rapporteur on violence against women, its causes and consequences. Intersection between the coronavirus disease (COVID-19) pandemic and the pandemic of gender-based violence against women, with a focus on domestic violence and the "peace in the home" initiative. UN General Assembly, A/75/144.

Stermac, Lana, Cripps, Jenna, Amiri, Touraj, Badali, Veronica. 2020. Sexual Violence and Women's Education: Examining Academic Performance and Persistence. *Canadian Journal of Higher Education*, Vol. 50 N. 1 pp. 28-39.

Taylor, R. (2009), Slain and slandered: A content analysis of the portrayal of femicide in the news, in "Homicide Studies", n. 13, pp. 21-49.

Tazzyman, Abigail. 2020. Women's self☐presentation and the transition from classroom to workplace. *Gender Work Organ*; 27:327–346. https://doi.org/10.1111/gwao.12375.

United Nations. 2020. The impact of COVID-19 on women. Policy brief. Geneva: United Nations. https://www.unwomen.org/-/media/headquarters/ attachments/sections/library/publications/2020/policy-brief-the-impact-of- covid-19-on-women-en.pdf?la=en&vs=1406.

Williams, Joan C., Mary Blair-Loy, and Jennifer L. Berdahl. 2013. Cultural schemas, social class, and the flexibility stigma. *Journal of Social Issues* 69 (2): 209–34.

MIMESIS GROUP
www.mimesis-group.com

MIMESIS INTERNATIONAL
www.mimesisinternational.com
info@mimesisinternational.com

MIMESIS EDIZIONI
www.mimesisedizioni.it
mimesis@mimesisedizioni.it

ÉDITIONS MIMÉSIS
www.editionsmimesis.fr
info@editionsmimesis.fr

MIMESIS COMMUNICATION
www.mim-c.net

MIMESIS EU
www.mim-eu.com

Printed by
Rotomail Italia S.p.A.
in May 2022

www.ingramcontent.com/pod-product-compliance
Lightning Source LLC
Chambersburg PA
CBHW020502270326
41926CB00008B/709

* 9 7 8 8 8 6 9 7 7 4 0 5 8 *